"With *The Jungians*, Tom Kirsch reveals another of his many talents. He's a storyteller, who tells about the social and political twists and turns of the Jungian movement since its first days in Zurich. Dr. Kirsch, out of his love for the rich history, has dug thoroughly into the consciousness of several Jungian schools of thought and organization – their faithful followers, factions, geographic and cultural influences. Accessible and well told".

Clarissa Pinkola Estés, Ph.D.
Author of *Women Who Run With the Wolves*,
The Gift of Story and *The Faithful Gardener*

"It is rare that an author and his subject are so perfectly matched. Only Tom Kirsch could have written this wonderful and important narrative. To grasp who 'the Jungians' are and how they arrived at their present level of cultural significance, you must read this book. This is the first and to date the only comprehensive history of the Jungian movement. It is based on original research, first-hand knowledge, and in-depth interviews with most of the major figures in the field. The vivid portraits of individual figures, many of whom are now deceased and were known by the author personally, are priceless. This book belongs in the library of every serious student of analytical psychology and psychoanalysis".

Murray Stein
President-elect of the International Association for
Analytical Psychology and author of *Jung's Map of the Soul*

"Dr. Kirsch's meticulously detailed, scrupulously researched, narrative history of analytical psychology is a book that has been urgently needed, not only by specialists but also by the general reader who wants to understand the origin and development of Jungian psychology. This book is an important ground-breaking study that will be influential 'must-reading' for many years to come".

Deirdre Bair
National Book Award winner
Biographer of Samuel Beckett, Anais Nin, Simone de Beauvoir,
and (forthcoming) C.G. Jung

The Jungians

The Jungians: A Comparative and Historical Perspective is the first book to trace the history of the profession of analytical psychology from its origins in 1913 until the present.

As someone who has been personally involved in many aspects of Jungian history, Thomas Kirsch is well equipped to take the reader through the history of the 'movement', and to document its growth throughout the world, with chapters covering individual geographical areas – the UK, USA, and Australia, to name but a few – in some depth. He also provides new information on the ever-controversial subject of Jung's relationship to Nazism, Jews, and Judaism.

A lively and well-researched key work of reference, *The Jungians* will appeal not only to those working in the field of analysis, but is also essential reading for all those interested in Jungian studies.

Thomas B. Kirsch was President of the International Association of Analytical Psychology from 1989 to 1995, and President of the Jung Institute of San Francisco from 1976 to 1978. He currently works in private practice in California, and is a Lecturer in the Department of Psychiatry at Stanford University Medical School.

The Jungians

A comparative and historical perspective

Thomas B. Kirsch

London and Philadelphia

First published 2000 by Routledge
11 New Fetter Lane, London EC4P 4EE

Simultaneously published in the USA and Canada
by Taylor & Francis Inc.,
325 Chestnut Street, Philadelphia, PA 19106

Routledge is an imprint of the Taylor & Francis Group

© 2000 Thomas B. Kirsch

Typeset in Times by Graphicraft Limited, Hong Kong
Printed and bound in Great Britain by TJ International Ltd,
Padstow, Cornwall

British Library Cataloguing in Publication Data
A catalogue record for this book is available from the
British Library

Library of Congress Cataloging in Publication Data
A catalogue record for this book is available from the
Library of Congress

ISBN 0-415-15860-5 (hbk)

To Joe Henderson, for teaching me
what it means to be "Jungian."

Contents

Preface

This is a book which spans my lifetime. In a sense, I became a part of this book without knowing it. My parents both had their major analyses with Jung in the 1930s at a time when Nazism was on the rise. They fled Germany to end up in Los Angeles, with intermediate stops in Tel Aviv and London, and were involved in the founding of Jungian groups in Berlin, Palestine, London, and Los Angeles. I grew up in Los Angeles with Jung, Hitler, the Holocaust, and World War II as central themes in my upbringing. Through my family I met many of the founders of analytical psychology from different parts of the world. They became part of my extended family, and many of them stayed in my parents' house when visiting Los Angeles.

I chose medicine as a profession because I wanted to become a psychiatrist and possibly a Jungian analyst. That was certainly the hope and expectation of my parents. My own first connection to Jungian analysis took place in Zurich. Realizing that training in Zurich was not what I sought, I went to the one place in the United States where one could study Jungian analysis while maintaining a connection to the larger world of psychotherapy and psychoanalysis, then at its pinnacle of influence. In San Francisco I had the good fortune to meet Joseph Henderson, who in turn has been my analyst, teacher, mentor, and dear friend. At the time of writing, he is approaching the young age of 97, and although slower physically, he is as intellectually and socially alive as ever.

Through my analysis I discovered that, unlike my parents and Jung, I had an equal interest in the outer world and was not as inner directed as they were. This, in part, led me to become, in time, president of the Jung Institute in San Francisco and later on vice-president and then president of the International Association for Analytical Psychology. I served in the latter two capacities for eighteen years and witnessed the rapid growth of analytical psychology all over the world. It was my good fortune to be the president when the Berlin Wall fell in 1989 and to receive the outpouring of requests for information on Jung and analytical psychology from all the former Eastern bloc countries.

Many of my colleagues have asked me to write down my experiences, because the combination of my early family background and my later experience of serving on the IAAP Executive Committee has given me a unique vantage point from which to view the growth of analytical psychology. However, as with all history, my point of view is subjective, and someone else writing this chronology would emphasize completely different aspects. Furthermore, I have concentrated on the social and political developments within the Jungian community and have not attempted to write an intellectual history. Others are much better qualified to do that. When discussing conflicts within the Jungian community, I have tried to leave out personalities as much as possible. Only when a specific event had a significant impact on the development of the professional group have I given more details. Many thorny, controversial, and complex issues are covered in this history, and I expect that not everyone will agree with the conclusions reached.

Finally, although this book is meant for those interested in the field of analytical psychology, I hope that it will enjoy a wider readership. It touches on matters of the soul, as expressed through analytical psychology, and so I trust that others outside of the field will find something of value in this history.

Thomas Kirsch

Foreword

There are many unanswered questions about the depth psychologies, and those asking these questions – as well as those answering them – do so from many different perspectives, disciplines, and professions. As one who reads and thinks about these writings, I have found myself asking three questions over and over again: *What* are these psychologies, what are the forms of thought and action which compose them? *Where* do they come from, what are their origins? *How* do they affect our culture and the lives we live within that culture?

On each of these counts, Tom Kirsch has written an important, timely, and generous book. *The Jungians* sheds new light on these three questions, which have been around now for almost one hundred years, when the depth psychologies first appeared. Strictly speaking, his book is – topically at least – more on the second, for it is a history of the internal development of Jungian psychology from its origins in the mind and life of Carl G. Jung in Zurich, Switzerland, in 1912–1913, through its growth into various kinds of groups, societies, institutes, and the like, and ending with its contemporary international organizations.

There are many ways to think about and "do" the history of the development of the depth psychologies. Thinking of this history as the history of a social movement has the advantage of emphasizing the interactive nature of the development, which otherwise tends to be overlooked, even excluded. Movements are sites upon which crucial issues about an emerging field are contested and negotiated by key figures. As such, the movement is an essential part of the history, for its activities and interactions are events which succeed the life of the creative and originative figure but also precede the present-day collective, institutional organizations which represent what was once a movement.

Movements originate in the wide social context of a society as a whole. That society is composed of a center, where elites and the power they possess are located, and a periphery, where "ordinary" citizens, who do not have power, live. Within this frame, movements are intermediate structures which begin at the periphery and drive toward the center in order to acquire recognition, status, and legitimacy. In this way, movements mediate between the creative and originative figure and the acceptance of his/her ideas by society, through the social process of institutionalization. *The Jungians* is the story of this journey or passage from a collection of ideas in the mind of one man to what is today recognized in many countries as Jungian or analytical psychology.

As Kirsch's narrative unfolds, we see men and women coming to Zurich in the 1920s from Europe, as well as from the United States, to meet Jung, to consult with him, and to learn more about his new philosophy of the unconscious, "analytical psychology." And by watching these interactions take place, we also begin to understand the effects which this new form of thinking has on those who allow it to influence them.

This was also true in the case of Freud's psychoanalytic movement. To use the metaphor of the stage: when the curtain rose, there was one spotlight and it shone on one figure in the middle of the stage; but then, as time passed, other spotlights began to shine on other parts of the stage, and other figures emerged from the darkness. I call these "shadow figures," because they were there all the time, it was just that we did not see them.[1] For example, the publication of the Freud–Fliess correspondence brought one such figure into the open, as did the publication of the Freud–Jung correspondence a bit later.[2] The disclosure of these and other shadow figures has helped Freud's followers recognize and come to terms with their enormous group idealization of Freud, which is only now breaking down, thereby releasing new creative energies. However, this idealization should not be seen as an error of judgment or as a form of psychopathology. Rather, it helps us understand the nature and power of a key leader's ideas, as well as the effect of those ideas upon the culture in which he wrote, and which continues to respond to him today. Knowledge like this becomes accessible only in the context of "the movement."

1 The term "shadow figure" is used here in its ordinary language sense, and the metaphor of the stage, with its implications for light and dark, recognizing and being unable to recognize. No reference to Jung's analytical psychology is intended.
2 See J. Masson (ed.) (1985) *The Complete Letters of Sigmund Freud to Wilhelm Fliess, 1887–1904*, translated by Jeffrey Moussaieff Masson, Cambridge: Harvard University Press, Belknap Press. See also W. McGuire (ed.) (1974) *The Freud–Jung Letters*, Princeton: Princeton University Press.

As a chronicle of the Jungian movement, *The Jungians* is not only important – it is, after all, the first history of its kind to be written – it is also timely. Its publication occurs at a strategically important moment in the history of both Freud's and Jung's depth psychologies, by making the latter relevant for a deeper understanding of both. To understand this relevance, we must remember that Jung was nineteen years Freud's junior, the Jungian movement was never as large as the Freudian, nor did it spread as rapidly, and the maturing of the two movements during the war years was also consequently different.

These circumstances have given Kirsch valuable time and the subsequent opportunity to collect and organize a great deal of new information with which to create for the first time a sweeping and cumulative sense of the Jungian movement as a whole. Kirsch notes that Jung's earliest followers were men and women who came to his home in Zurich to meet and to consult with him, or, as it was then said, "to analyze with him" during the 1920s. As a result, what can be called a cohort[3] of followers formed a cohesive group around Jung, drawn together by shared bonds of intense personal intimacy with him and with each other. This web of relationships was structured by a new and remarkable set of ideas and practices. But then, as time passed and a Jungian movement took shape, a second and then a third generation of analysts matured. They wanted to introduce innovations into both theory and practice. Most of the time, however, the first generation objected strenuously to such innovations. In many cases splits occurred, and in more than a few a second and more "classical" institute or society was formed, based on loyalty to Jung and on a shared sense of "purity" of thought and practice which ensued.

This is an interesting piece of well-documented information. It does not "prove" anything, but it does open up fresh areas of possible conjecture and investigation. One such line of thought will see in these events an impressive set of idealizations of a single figure which drew together a talented and ambitious group of followers, a group which in its structure (but not in its contents) closely resembled the early phase of Freud's psychoanalytic movement, some ten or twenty years earlier. Other readers will follow different lines of thought. But whatever the

---

3 Ordinarily, the term "cohort" refers to any group of people with a time-specific common experience. The most important elements of a cohort are shared age and shared particular historical events. For further discussion, one may consult "Cohort, Cohort Analysis," in *The Concise Oxford Dictionary of Sociology*, ed. Gordon Marshall, New York: Oxford University Press, 1994, p. 64.

new direction is, thanks to Kirsch's "hands on" documentation and his "hands off" lack of totalizing closures, we have in hand a wholly new set of "shadow figures" to help us think further about the history of this and other depth psychologies.

Kirsch has also been able to comment on two issues in particular which have been repeatedly and widely discussed for years, but without resolution. His book is not about these issues, but his studies and the course of the narrative they organize has allowed him to present new information on both. The necessary information that might advance a deeper understanding of these issues has remained contextualized in the movement, which is also to say that it could not have been found either in Jung's life and thought or in the discursive practices of any contemporary Jungian institutes.

The first issue is the psychoanalytic movement's continuous efforts to discredit Jung and his followers – that is to say, to withhold legitimation from them. This has been possible because the psychoanalytic movement has for some time now occupied the center of professional psychotherapy and has therefore been in a position to dispense legitimacy, whereas other, more recently evolved psychotherapeutic movements have continued to remain more or less on the periphery.

The second issue is Jung's anti-Semitic remark(s) in the 1930s. Much later in his book and in a very different context, Kirsch takes up the origins and development of analytical psychology in Southern California. He points out that many European Jews fleeing Nazism, along with many non-Jewish refugees, found the Los Angeles area especially attractive. Among these were European Freudian psychoanalysts, and, in the late 1930s and early 1940s, qualified Jungian analysts began to arrive. Many were from the cohort which had analyzed with Jung in the 1920s. Although not as numerous as the Freudians, all of these Jungian "founders" were of German-Jewish extraction. None of them experienced anti-Semitic gestures of any sort on Jung's part, for if they had, they would have withdrawn. For obvious reasons, these analysts were placed under enormous stress by the post-war Freudian accusation of Jung's anti-Semitism. Later in his history, in an entirely different context, Kirsch describes in detail the social background of Jung's anti-Semitic remark(s). Still later, and in yet another context, he notes that, currently, one-third of all Jungian analysts continue to come from Jewish backgrounds.

Just as in the first case above, new information can lead to new and different conjectures. For example, it is a well-known observation that a great many of the members of the early psychoanalytic movement were Jewish.[4] However, it is not as well known that many of the early Jungian analysts were also Jewish. As in the first case, these new data do not "prove" anything, they do not "take sides." But we are invited to explore in fresh ways this aspect of the history of the Jungian movement.

Kirsch's book is not only "timely" in the senses just indicated, it is also "generous." It takes a special kind of generosity – one could call it "professional" generosity – to maintain the necessary distance from one's data, when one is writing as an "insider" and these data admit to alternative conclusions. However, Kirsch is also generous personally. A respected senior Jungian analyst, he was for eighteen years an officer of the International Association for Analytical Psychology, and has personally travelled to most of the Jungian societies about which he writes. His father and mother were first-generation Jungian analysts who fled the Holocaust, emigrating to the United States in the 1930s. This story is also his story. At moments, it is almost a *Bildungsroman*.

In conclusion, each of the three questions with which these remarks began has a surface and a depth dimension. Studying the history of analytical psychology as Kirsch does in this book illumines its origins, from Jung up to the present, and this is the right place to begin. But, such histories are only foregrounds in a much wider frame. One must also speak of their backgrounds, of their remote or "deep past." To say the same thing in a more current idiom, we have yet to address "the history–memory problem" directly. The "histories" we presently have of the depth psychologies – including this one – are still rich in living memory, but they are poor in history, in "deep memory." Current discussions of Freud's "Jewish identity" are a step into this more distant or deep past. Jung was easily as deeply implicated in his own deep past. In this sense, the history of the depth psychologies is still just beginning. Many shadow figures remain.

Peter Homans Ph.D.
Professor Emeritus and Visiting Professor,
Department of Religious Studies,
and Department of Psychology,
University of Chicago

---

4 See, for example, D.B. Klein, *Jewish Origins of the Psychoanalytic Movement*, New York: Praeger Publishers, 1981.

Acknowledgements

A book of this nature could not be written without the input and cooperation of many people and organizations.

First, I am most grateful to the Ann and Erlo van Waveren Foundation for its generous support which allowed me to take the time necessary to undertake this project. I would also like to express my gratitude to the Grants Committee of the International Association for Analytical Psychology which aided me in bringing it to completion.

I want to thank the editors at Routledge, Edwina Welham and Kate Hawes, for their help in bringing it out.

The following analysts have assisted most generously in multiple ways: in Australia, Craig San Roque and André de Koning; in Austria, Eva Pattis-Zoja and Andreas von Heydwolff; in Belgium, Jef Dehing and Alex Luyckx; in Brazil, Roberto Gambini and Walter and Paula Boechat; in Germany, Hannes Dieckmann, Hans Joachim Wilke, Kurt Höhfeld, Theo Seifert, Barnim Nitsch, Fred Plaut, Brigitte McLeod, and Raymund Schaeffer; in Denmark, Lisbet Myers, Ole Vedfelt, and Pia Skogemann; in England, Ann Casement, David Howell, Moira Duckworth, Baroness Vera von der Heydt, Marianne Jacoby, Renos Papadopoulos, Andrew Samuels, Martin Stone, and Jan Wiener; in France, Christian Gaillard; in Israel, Dvorah Kutzinski, Gustav Dreifuss, Geula Gat, and Eli Weisstub; in Italy, Paolo and Lydia Aite, Priscilla Artom, Aldo Carotenuto, Bianca Garufi, Concetto Gullotta, Mario Realfonzo, and Luigi Zoja; in Japan, Hayao Kawai; in the Netherlands, Christopher Mead; in New Zealand, Wilson Daniels; in Switzerland, Robert Hinshaw, Adolf Guggenbühl-Craig, Toni Frei-Wehrlin, Mario Jacoby, Gotthilf Isler, Theo Abt, and Immanuel Kennedy; in the United States, John Beebe, Joseph Henderson, David Tresan, Joe Cambray, Gilda Frantz, Charles Taylor, Murray Stein, Alma Paulsen-Hoyer, Edward Edinger, Christopher Whitmont, Clarissa

Pinkola Estés, June Singer, Alexander McCurdy III, Thayer Greene, and Beverley Zabriskie.

Other individuals have been very helpful with information and moral support: Deirdre Bair, Geoffrey Cocks, Marta Fülop, Inga Holle, Peter Homans, Magnus Ljunggren, Regine Lockot, Michelle McGee, David Orlinsky, Sonu Shamdasani, Myrtha Gruber-Humbert, Rali Neumann, Ilse Westmann, Irving Yalom, Jacques Rutzky, and Lore Zeller. Responsibility for the opinions expressed in this book (and for any errors it may contain) is, of course, my own.

There are certain individuals who deserve special mention:

First, I would like to thank Greg Brombach and Frank Smith who kept my computer in working order.

Andreas von Heydwolff from Salzburg helped locate and translate archival documents relating to Jung and Jungian activities during the Nazi regime, which were crucial to some of my conclusions.

Ursula Egli has untiringly helped me with translations from German, Italian, and French, and has made sure that I never lost track of the task at hand. Without her intelligence, sensitivity, good humor, and attention to detail, this book would have been nearly impossible to finish.

Tom Singer read every chapter as it was written and provided a supportive, but gently critical hand throughout. I had not known before of his remarkable editorial capacities, in addition to all his other magnificent qualities.

Andrew Samuels has been a wonderful friend and ally. His vast knowledge of analytical psychology, the world of publishing, and his general good humor have helped to bring the book to fruition.

Jean Kirsch has been at my side throughout, reading and editing every chapter as it came from my printer. I hope she realizes my deep debt of gratitude towards her for this and many other things.

Permission to use photographs from the following sources is acknowledged: Michelle McKee from the Analytical Psychology Club in New York for the photographs of Esther Harding, Eleanor Bertine, and Kristine Mann, and from the Bailey Island Conference, held on Bailey Island, Maine, in 1936. Lore Zeller for pictures from the first IAAP Congress in Zurich and for early photos of Los Angeles members. Mario Realfonzo for a photograph of Ernst Bernhard. Dvorah Kutzinski for a photograph of Erich Neumann. Robert Hinshaw for photographs of the early Jungian Community in Zurich.

Abbreviations

AGAP	Association of Graduate Analytical Psychologists of the C.G. Jung Institute Zurich
AIPA	Associazione Italiana per lo Studio della Psicologia Analitica
AJA	Association of Jungian Analysts, London
AJB	Associaçao Junguiana do Brasil, São Paulo
ANZSJA	Australian and New Zealand Society of Jungian Analysts
APC	Analytical Psychology Club
ARAS	Archive for Research in Archetypal Symbolism
BAP	The British Association of Psychotherapists – Jungian Section
B.C.P.	British Confederation of Psychotherapists
BSJP	Belgian School of Jungian Psychoanalysis
CASJA	Council of American Societies of Jungian Analysts
CIPA	Centro Italiano di Psicologia Analitica
DGAP	Deutsche Gesellschaft für Analytische Psychologie
DGPT	Deutsche Gesellschaft für Psychotherapie und Tiefenpsychologie
DPG	Deutsche Psychoanalytische Gesellschaft
DPV	Deutsche Psychoanalytische Vereinigung
DSAP	Danish Society for Analytical Psychology
ETH	Eidgenössische Technische Hochschule
GAP	Group for the Advancement for Psychiatry
IAAP	International Association for Analytical Psychology
IAPA	Irish Analytical Psychology Association
IGAP	The Independent Group of Analytical Psychologists (London)
IPA	International Psychoanalytic Association
IRS	Inter-Regional Society of Jungian Analysts
ISST	International Society for Sandplay Therapists

JANP	Jungian Analysts – North Pacific
MSAP	Medical Society for Analytical Psychology (San Francisco)
NESJA	New England Society of Jungian Analysts
NYAAP	New York Association for Analytical Psychology
OAJA	Ontario Association of Jungian Analysts
OEGAP	Oesterreichische Gesellschaft für Analytische Psychologie
PNSJA	Pacific Northwest Society of Jungian Analysts
SAAJA	Southern African Association of Jungian Analysts
SAP	Society of Analytical Psychology London
SBePA	Société Belge de Psychologie Analytique
SBrPA	Sociedade Brasileira de Psicologia Analitica
SEPA	Sociedad Española de Psicologia Analitica
SFPA	Société Française de Psychologie Analytique
SGfAP	Schweizerische Gesellschaft für Analytische Psychologie
SJA	Society of Jungian Analysts (of Northern California)
U.K.C.P.	UK Council for Psychotherapy
VSJA	Venezuelan Society for Jungian Analysts

Introduction

This book is the first attempt to trace the history of analytical psychology from its origins in 1912 with C.G. Jung in Zurich until the present time. It is neither another biography of Jung nor is it a historical development of theories in analytical psychology; rather, it is an account of the growth of analytical psychology as a profession, with its institutions, regulations, processes, and splits. It is also, within limits, an internationally oriented book in which the facts of the development of analytical psychology are connected to the cultural specifics within each country.

"Analytical psychology" is the term C.G. Jung used to differentiate his own psychology from Freud's. It has its origin as a separate school of psychology during the 1920s, when many people from many countries sought out Jung for personal reasons and later decided to become analysts.

First, to orient the reader, a brief synopsis of the history of the Freud–Jung relationship will be given. Jung was introduced to Freud's psychoanalysis in December, 1900, when his chief at the Burghölzli Clinic, Professor Eugen Bleuler, asked him to review Freud's *The Interpretation of Dreams*. Subsequently, Jung utilized Freud's theories to explain his work on the word-association tests and complex theory. In 1906 he sent his monograph *Psychology of Dementia Praecox* to Freud, which led to their meeting in Vienna in 1907. They had an immediate rapport with one another, as evidenced by the fact that they talked for thirteen hours non-stop at that first meeting. Perhaps Jung being Swiss, his intelligence and charisma, plus the fact that he was the first non-Jew to express a serious interest in psychoanalysis, led Freud to anoint him his "crown prince." At the first official meeting of the International Psychoanalytic Association in 1910, Jung was elected president, and was made editor of the *Jahrbuch*. Jung was reelected as president three times until his removal at Freud's behest in 1913. They had no further contact. For many years thereafter hostility existed between Freudians and Jungians. This has changed markedly in recent times as psychoanalysts and analytical psychologists have found many areas in common which they can discuss. The specifics of these areas of commonality are addressed in the individual historical chapters as well as in the concluding chapter.

World War I (1914–1918) was an important time for Jung. His professional and personal relationship with Freud had just ended, leaving him in isolation, as most members of the International Psychoanalytic Association (IPA) sided with Freud. Jung entered a period of deep introversion and disorientation which he described in his autobiography, *Memories, Dreams, Reflections*. He emerged in 1918 feeling himself to be a changed person. Jung was ready to present his ideas to the world, his hypotheses on the nature of the human psyche. In *Memories, Dreams, Reflections* he states that everything which followed was an outgrowth of the inner experiences which occurred during this critical phase of his life.

The term "analytical psychology" has never gained wide acceptance in either the professional psychotherapy world or with the lay public. "Jungian Analyst" and "Jungian Analysis" are common terms, but there is great variability worldwide in how these terms are used. In my opinion analytical psychologists have not yet been able to integrate fully the work of Jung, and until Jungian analysts do that, his name retains its value as an important symbol. Many theorists and practitioners have made significant contributions to the field, so it is no longer the product of one man's work. Freudian psychoanalysts seem to have undergone a similar metamorphosis. Thirty or forty years ago the term "Freudian analysis" was much more common than today, when so many different branches of psychoanalysis exist. In analytical psychology one senses a shift, as those who were personally connected to Jung die, and the field undergoes many changes in theory and practice.

Analytical psychology began naturally with Jung in Zurich, but it quickly spread to England, the United States, and Germany. Analytical psychology has had a continual presence in these four countries from the beginning to the present. As a result their histories will be presented in greater detail. Israel and other European countries have had a lesser presence of analytical psychology for many decades, interrupted by World War II, and their histories will be outlined as well.

There are three nodal points which, combined, bring an end to the initial phase of analytical psychology. First, the founding of an Institute in Zurich in 1947, reluctantly approved by Jung, brought academic and educational aspects into the training, and the personal analysis was no longer the only requirement to be an analyst. Second, in 1955, the International Association for Analytical Psychology was founded in Zurich, which began a worldwide professional organization. Third was the death of Jung in 1961, following which differences surfaced that had previously remained unexpressed. In a very short time an un-official division between the "developmental school" of London, and the "classical school" of Zurich emerged. The nature of this contro-versy and its implications for the future of analytical psychology will be thoroughly reviewed in this book.

After the death of Jung in 1961, the history and development of analytical psychology subtly shifted. Established professional societies grew, and their status within their respective countries began to change. Jungians received some respect. By the mid-1960s changes in the outer world produced a counter-culture against modern technological think-ing and a gradual turning towards non-rational and feeling values. Jung's psychology was taken up by some of its leading spokespersons, and his popularity soared. Many people sought Jungian analysis, and some wished to become Jungian analysts. Professional groups began to spring up throughout all of Western Europe and the United States. In the 1970s professional groups formed in Latin America, Brazil and Venezuela, Australia and New Zealand, and there was interest in South Africa, Japan, and Korea. The next major development came in 1989 with the breakdown of the barriers in Eastern Europe and the former Soviet Union. Currently, there is an emerging interest in analytical psychology in China, which is still in its early phases. So, today analyt-ical psychology truly has an international character, and how this has happened will be delineated in this book.

The first two-thirds of the book trace the development and history of analytical psychology in each country where it has become estab-lished; the largest and most developed Jungian centers are discussed first, and the locations where later developments have occurred follow.

A separate chapter will be devoted to the history of Analytical Psy-chology Clubs, a phenomenon unique to analytical psychology, which has no parallel in psychoanalysis. The first Club began in Zurich in 1913 or 1914. Others developed in Basle, Paris, Rome, London, Berlin, New York, San Francisco, and Los Angeles. Membership required some hours (25–100) of Jungian analysis and a letter of recommenda-tion from the analyst. In cities where a Club developed it was often the forerunner of a professional group. Regular lectures, a large library, and social functions were common to all the Clubs. How they differ from more recently formed "Friends of Jung" in various parts of the world will be discussed.

Another chapter focuses on the formation and history of the International Association for Analytical Psychology which has provided an umbrella organization for all national and regional groups. As the professional organization to which all analytical psychologists belong, its minimum standards of practice are respected worldwide.

C.G. Jung was an immensely complex person, with wide-ranging interests. His influence on culture and spiritual matters was enormous. It is beyond the scope of this book to examine just how influential he was in these areas. That would require an expertise which I do not have. However, I shall examine his role as president of the General Medical Association for Psychotherapy from 1933 until 1940; his activities in that arena, in that period, made a major impact on his stature in the world of psychotherapy and psychoanalysis up to the present.

The results of the research into the history are discussed in Chapter 20. A summary and interpretation of many of the themes of this book are included there, and some implications for the future of analytical psychology are considered.

Analytical psychology begins with Jung in Zurich, and that is where the book begins.

1 Analytical psychology in Zurich

ORIGINS

Analytical psychology had its origins in Zurich, Switzerland, and consequently this city holds center stage in the history of the Jungians. C.G. Jung was born on the Swiss side of the Lake of Constance on 26 July 1875, studied medicine in Basle, and moved to Zurich in 1900. From 1909 until his death on 6 June 1961 he lived and worked in the same house in Küsnacht on the Lake of Zurich. The tower he built at Bollingen, a small village on the Obersee, the continuation of the Lake of Zurich, was his refuge where he spent extended periods of introverted time. It is not the purpose of this book to give a detailed description of Jung's life, as numerous biographies are available by authors such as Barbara Hannah, Sir Laurens van der Post, Vincent Brome, Gerhard Wehr, Paul Stern, Frank McLynn, Ronald Hayman, Deirdre Bair (in press), as well as Jung's own autobiography, *Memories, Dreams, Reflections*. Instead, the beginnings of analytical psychology in Zurich will be described in the first part, and events subsequent to Jung's death will make up the second part of this chapter.

Jung's theory did not arise in a vacuum, and so it is important to locate Switzerland both geographically and culturally to understand the nature of this fertile soil on which his ideas developed. Switzerland's history began over seven hundred years ago, when it consisted of rural and urban communities which desired to be independent from larger dynasties, such as the Habsburgs or the Italian dukes. No central authority existed until 1848 when a modern federal constitution was accepted, with German, French, and Italian recognized as the official languages. This constitution made Switzerland a democracy at a time when the rest of Europe was still more or less feudalistic. Switzerland was one of the spiritual centers of the Reformation, and since the sixteenth century its population has been fairly equally divided between

Protestantism and Catholicism. Jung came from a long line of Protestant ministers, and his family traced its ancestry to Germany several centuries earlier. Switzerland, because of its location in the heart of Europe, its long history of neutrality, and its magnificent Alps, has always been an important commercial, industrial, tourist, and cultural center. Although sometimes seen as "conservative" and "quaint," the Swiss have a long history of egalitarian tendencies, being among the first to free mental patients, and to admit women into medicine. Over the centuries the Swiss have been open to new ideas, and the country has been hospitable to "revolutionary" thinkers who found a temporary or permanent home there.

It is not surprising, therefore, that in the first decade of the twentieth century Zurich became the second most important center for the new science of psychoanalysis after Vienna. A collegial and personal friendship between Freud and Jung existed from 1907 to 1913. C.G. Jung was a principal figure in the institutional developments of psychoanalysis, and he became a prime architect of the international psychoanalytic movement. He was instrumental in organizing congresses, became the first president of the International Psychoanalytic Association (IPA), as well as editor of the first psychoanalytic journal, *Das Jahrbuch.* Jung introduced the rite of a training analysis, stipulating that any would-be analyst must first submit to his own analysis. This requirement has become a standard feature of all depth psychology schools. For many individuals from many countries, who later became well-known first-generation psychoanalysts, the path led through Zurich and the Burghölzli, where Jung was the *Oberarzt,* the chief physician under Eugen Bleuler.

Nineteen hundred thirteen was a decisive year: the Freud–Jung collaboration finally and irrevocably came to an end. Both men were profoundly wounded by the schism. Freud never developed another deep male friendship, as he had with Jung, while Jung was forced into a period of withdrawal, introversion, and self-analysis which lasted at least five years. In the same year Jung used the term "analytical psychology" for the first time to differentiate his psychology from psychoanalysis.

Early groups in analytical psychology

In recent years the founding of the first organizational structures relating to analytical psychology has been the subject of much discussion (Noll 1994, 1997; Shamdasani 1998a). The painstaking research of Sonu Shamdasani has reconstructed the history of analytical psychological groups in Zurich. The city was an early center for psychoanalysis, and by 1912 a well-functioning Psychoanalytical Association connected to the Burghölzli and the University of Zurich was in place. However, in 1912 the Zurich Psychoanalytical Association separated from the Burghölzli and became an independent organization, apart from any academic affiliation, which led psychoanalysis and analytical psychology to develop their own independent institutions.

A further separation took place on 10 July 1914 when Alphonse Maeder proposed that the group resign en masse, and the Zurich Psychoanalytic Association made an almost unanimous decision to separate from the IPA. This happened after Freud's denunciation of Jung and the Zurich school in his "On the History of the Psychoanalytic Movement," where Freud had established an orthodoxy which did not allow for free and unimpeded research (Freud 1914: 7).

On 30 October of the same year it was decided to rename the society the Association for Analytical Psychology on the suggestion of Professor Messmer (Muser 1984). This group, consisting mainly of medical doctors, met on a regular basis every other week until 1918, when it became absorbed into the newly formed Analytical Psychology Club. During the period between 1912 and 1918 Jung reformulated his major theories of the psyche, the collective unconscious, archetypes, individuation, and psychological types, and the meetings at the Club must have been significant.

Shamdasani's recent research has shown that between 1916 and 1918 there were two separate Jungian groups: a professional one, the *Verein*, and a second one which was a lay group, the Analytical Psychology Club. The Analytical Psychology Club in Zurich became a model for similar clubs in other cities and countries. When the two groups merged in 1918, the Analytical Psychology Club was the place to meet for individuals interested in analytical psychology.

The early training of analysts

Following World War I Jung emerged from his "confrontation with the unconscious" (Jung 1963) and his fame spread, especially in the English-speaking countries and Europe. Individuals would write to Jung, asking to see him in analysis, and if accepted they would come to Zurich for varying lengths of time. In those days analyses were usually much shorter, for many reasons – not the least of which were financial considerations which prevented protracted stays.

In 1925 Jung began to give seminars in English in Zurich (Jung 1990), and from 1928 to 1939 he gave a seminar in English each academic semester. Originally the transcripts of these seminars were distributed only selectively; however, in recent years many of them have been edited and published. Individuals who were in analysis with Jung as well as Zurich analysts were invited to attend seminars. In his role as professor at the Eidgenössische Technische Hochschule (ETH), Jung gave a weekly lecture on basic aspects of analytical psychology to the general student body, and analysands who could understand German were invited to attend. These lectures were quickly translated into English by these analysands.

The Analytical Psychology Club meetings were taking place on a regular basis, and the lectures were always in German which excluded most of Jung's American and British analysands.

The combination of analysis and seminars provided the training for the first generation of Jungian analysts. The analysis was usually done with Jung and Toni Wolff. The analysand would see Jung one day and Toni Wolff either later the same day or the following day. This type of analysis of seeing more than one analyst at a time has been called "multiple analyses" (Kirsch 1976) and has become an accepted and usual pattern in Zurich and in other countries following the Zurich model. It was sharply criticized by Michael Fordham in London (Fordham 1976), because he claimed that the transference/countertransference implications were not being analyzed and interpreted. This "multiple analyses" model allowed for too much acting out by both the patient and the analysts. When negative feelings between patient and analyst developed, the issues could be shunted to the other analyst. However, the input of two analysts of different psychological type and gender could be helpful to the patient. Jo Wheelwright, one of those who experienced multiple analyses in Zurich, stated that Jung was excellent for archetypal interpretations, while Toni Wolff was more experienced at working on personal issues, and overall he found her to be a better practical analyst than Jung (Wheelwright 1974). This pattern of multiple analyses has continued into subsequent generations of analysts in Zurich. Although still used today in Zurich and other places, the increasing importance of the transference has lessened its practice.

The relationship between Toni Wolff and C.G. and Emma Jung was controversial and remains so today. Toni Wolff came to see Jung as a patient in 1910, and he brought her to the Psychoanalytic Congress in Weimar in 1911, along with Emma Jung and Fräulein Moltzer. As the Jung–Freud relationship broke up, and Jung entered his "dark night of the soul" journey, he turned more and more to Toni Wolff. Around 1912–1913 they formed an erotic bond which lasted until the time of her death in 1953. His relationship with Toni Wolff was completely in the open, and Emma, the family, and Jung's patients were aware of it.

The two women worked together in the Analytical Psychology Club, attended Jung's seminars together, and Toni Wolff often came to the family for Sunday lunch. Over the years they established a *modus vivendi* which worked for all three of them. Because of their relative comfort with the situation, others were not asked to unconsciously carry the burden. In many personal conversations with people who were in analysis with both Jung and Wolff during the 1930s, they all said how comfortable the situation was. As a result, no one had to speak about the triangle outside the analytical circle, and the complicated relationships only became public knowledge many years after they had all died. However, this left a legacy for future analysts. Some attempted to imitate Jung, and even though several instances are known, none of them appeared to have succeeded. Analysts involved in a powerful countertransference have invoked Jung's behavior to justify their own. It is an inheritance that Jungian analysts have had to look at deeply. What seemed to work for Jung, Emma, and Toni, has not been possible for others. Today's analysts are much more cognizant of the destructive aspects of acting out the transference/countertransference relationship.

In the early days the path to becoming a Jungian analyst was fluid. Jung would write a letter stating that the person had studied his methods and was ready to practice as a Jungian. However, seeing Jung was no guarantee that an individual would receive a letter of accreditation. Many people who expected such a letter never received one, whereas others who did not plan to become analysts received Jung's blessing. In some instances Jung recommended further academic training to an analysand (e.g., Jo Wheelwright), while others were accepted with very little academic training (for instance Hilde Kirsch).

During the 1930s Jung did not seem very interested in forming his own school of psychology and psychotherapy. As president of the International General Medical Society for Psychotherapy, he was more interested in finding points of commonality among the different schools of psychotherapy. In 1938 he signed a statement produced by the International General Medical Society for Psychotherapy, which outlined points of agreement among the various psychotherapeutic schools. In Switzerland he became president of the Swiss Society for Practical Psychology, where he was again attempting to form a common, non-sectarian basis for psychotherapy. However, some of his closest associates during that period recognized the need to form an institute in Zurich where Jung's psychology could be studied. However, because of World War II, the plan had to be put on hold until 1947.

Eranos

In 1933 the first yearly Eranos conference was held in Ascona, Switzerland, on the shores of Lago Maggiore, at the home of Mrs Olga Froebe-Kapteyn, a Dutch woman with a strong interest in symbolism, art, and Jung's psychology. The initial inspiration for the Eranos conference was the encounter between Eastern and Western religions, philosophies, and psychology. Over the years Eranos developed far beyond its original boundaries and became a meeting place where ideas were exchanged on science, the humanities, mythology, and psychology. Jung attended Eranos conferences as one of the participants, but he was clearly the mediating link among all the speakers. Leading scholars from all over the world would come to this quiet, out-of-the-way place for a week of lectures, good discussions, and pleasant companionship. Jung spoke fourteen times at this conference, and the last paper he presented was "On Synchronicity" in 1951. The Eranos *Tagung*, as it was called, did not directly influence the practice of analytical psychology but reinforced the strong academic and cultural aspects of Jung's personality and psychology. Many of Jung's analysands who later became analysts attended the yearly conference. Some of the great minds of this century lectured at Eranos, including Martin Buber, Joseph Campbell, Gershom Sholem, D.T. Suzuki, Paul Tillich, among others. In recent years the conferences have continued, but the focus has changed to a more detailed study of the I-Ching. Erich Neumann, a disciple and friend of Jung, summed up the Eranos experience as follows: "Eranos, landscape on the lake, garden, and house. Modest and out of the way, and yet a navel to the world, a small link in the golden chain. As speakers and listeners, we always have to give thanks" (Jaffé 1997).

Two very practical links to the development of analytical psychology emerged from these annual gatherings. First, Olga Froebe-Kapteyn was encouraged by Jung to develop an archive of pictures portraying different archetypal symbols. She amassed a great number of pictures which eventually became the foundation for the Archive for Research in Archetypal Symbolism (ARAS), which is now housed in several American Jung Institutes, as well as in Zurich and at the Warburg Institute at the University of London. The pictures and the commentary are valuable resources for analysts and academicians interested in art history, culture, and symbolism.

A second practical outcome of the Eranos meetings was the fact that Paul and Mary Mellon attended them from 1937 through 1939. Paul Mellon was the son of Andrew Mellon, a prominent Pittsburgh banker and Secretary of the Treasury under President Coolidge. Paul's wife, Mary, developed a strong transference to Jung and devoted the rest of her short life to the furthering of Jung's work. She died in 1946, shortly before she was to return to Zurich for the first time after the war. The Mellons were captivated by the atmosphere of the conference and the collection of pictures Mrs Froebe-Kapteyn had assembled. They attended their first Eranos conference with the intention of meeting Jung, and they hoped that he would accept them for analysis. The Mellons did indeed meet Jung at Eranos, and both began analysis shortly thereafter. Later the Mellons formed the Bollingen Foundation, named after Jung's tower in Bollingen, and they supported the translation and publication of Jung's *Collected Works* in English, among other projects. For many years the publication of the volumes of the *Collected Works* was subsidized by the Bollingen Foundation so that the expense would not deter the ordinary person from reading Jung.

FIRST-GENERATION INDIVIDUALS AROUND JUNG

Emma Rauschenbach Jung (1882–1955)

Any discussion of important persons around Jung must begin with his wife of over fifty-two years, Emma. Emma Rauschenbach was born in the city of Schaffhausen near the German border. She came from a wealthy industrialist family who owned the International Watch Company (IWC), a famous name among Swiss watches. Emma and C.G. Jung were married on 14 February 1903 and moved into an apartment at the Burghölzli, where Jung was working at the time. With money from her family they were able to build a large house in Küsnacht on the Lake of Zurich, where both Emma and C.G. Jung lived for the rest of their lives. The Jungs had five children, four girls and one boy.

In 1910 Jung analyzed Emma for some months, with Freud's approval and warning of the dangers to the personal relationship. When the conflicts between Freud and Jung arose in 1911, Emma personally and on her own wrote to Freud asking him to be forgiving of Jung, because he was going through difficult times. Her attempt to mediate between the two was not successful.

The next hurdle Emma had to face was the erotic relationship between Jung and Toni Wolff, which probably began in 1913; the exact date is not known. What kinds of discussions took place among the three of them is not known, but the result was that Jung stayed with Emma, and she accepted the relationship between Jung and Toni. Toni became a part of the extended family, and the three of them would be together at various professional and social functions. For approximately forty years, until the death of Toni Wolff in 1953, this triangular arrangement was to remain in place.

It is difficult to ascertain at what point Emma began to practice as an analyst. When the Analytical Psychology Club was formed in 1916, she was named the first president. She relinquished that position after one year, and later Toni was to be president for many years. Over the years many of Jung's analysands also saw Emma. However, most of the foreign students who were in analysis with Jung up till the end of the 1930s saw Toni as the second analyst. Emma wrote a monograph on *Anima and Animus*, which was published in 1941. It became a classic within the early Jungian literature. Meanwhile she worked on her *magnum opus*, *The Grail Legend*, which she never finished, but which Marie-Louise von Franz completed after Emma's death.

Emma Jung died on 27 November 1955 from stomach cancer, only weeks after it had first been diagnosed. In a discussion with Franz Jung, the only son, he stated that his mother held the family together, and it was only because of her that Jung was able to accomplish his life's work. She took care of all aspects of family life and so many things, tangible and intangible, that Jung was free to do his creative work. Jung was absolutely devastated when Emma died, and many of his close intimates thought that he would never recover from her death. Fortunately, he did.

Toni Wolff (1888–1953)

Toni Wolff's importance to Jung has long been recognized; her influence on him was profound. Toni Anna Wolff was born in Zurich on 18 September 1888 and was the oldest of three daughters born to Konrad Arnold Wolff and Anna Elisebetha Sutz. The Wolff family resided in Zurich since the 1300s and was one of its most distinguished. The father was a merchant and a businessman in Japan prior to his marriage. Although the marriage was arranged, it was described as a happy one. Toni was her father's favorite. When he died in 1910, her mother sent her to Jung for treatment of what today would be diagnosed as depression. Jung immediately sensed her aptitude for analysis, because in 1911 he invited her along with his wife and Fräulein Moltzer to the Weimar Psychoanalytic Congress.

When Jung began his *nekyia* into the unconscious, Toni Wolff was the one he turned to. He shared his dreams and active imaginations with her, which he recorded in his Red Book. She became his soul mate for psychological matters in a way that Emma could not provide. She maintained this function for most of the rest of his life. It has been said that Jung, as he got older, turned to her less frequently.

She became a founding member of the Analytical Psychology Club in 1916 and was its president from 1928 to 1945. It was under her presidency that the 10 percent quota on Jews was passed. From 1948 to 1952 she was honorary president of the Club which was her domain.

From the 1920s on she worked as a professional assistant to Jung. Most people who entered analysis with Jung also saw her. She was considered to be more practical and worked in the personal aspects with the analysand, whereas Jung dealt mainly with the archetypal issues. She favored the term "Complex Psychology" over any other name for Jung's psychology, and when the Jung Institute was founded she wanted to name it the Institute for Complex Psychology. Her major paper was, "Structural Forms of the Feminine Psyche," published in German in 1951 and translated into English by Paul Watziliwak. Her other papers are now being prepared for publication in English by Robert Hinshaw.

On a personal level she was always described as super-elegant, dramatic in her dress, a chain smoker, who liked her cocktails but was never drunk. She never married, as Jung was the man in her life. There were rumors of other flirtations, but nothing has been verified. She suffered from severe rheumatoid arthritis, which hampered her mobility towards the end of her life. She worked until the day she died. Gerhard Adler described having an excellent analytic hour with her the day before she suffered her fatal heart attack on 21 March 1953.

Carl Alfred Meier (1905–1995)

Professor C.A. Meier's role in analytical psychology cannot be underestimated as for many years he was the "crown prince" to Jung. Carl Alfred Meier was born on 19 April 1905 in Schaffhausen, the same town where Emma Jung was born. As a young boy, Fredy, as he was known, met Jung. He received his medical degree from the University of Zurich and his psychiatric training at the Burghölzli. In the late 1920s he had an analysis with Jung. He began his private practice as a Jungian analyst around 1930 and continued to see patients until his death in 1995.

Shortly after Jung became president of the International Medical Society for Psychotherapy (IMSP), he appointed Meier as his honorary secretary for the last six years of his term. Thus, Meier shared with

Jung the experience of working with the Nazis in Berlin, as his signature was on all the correspondence. As far as is known, Meier never disclosed what happened during those years. In a personal conversation with the author, Meier stoutly defended Jung's position, saying that they were both trying to save psychotherapy in Germany. Meier thought that Goering and his colleagues were complete fools, and expected that they would be thrown out of power at any moment (personal communication). However, these personal discussions with Meier took place in the 1980s, and one can only wonder what the atmosphere was like in the 1930s. If anyone knew what Jung was thinking and feeling during that period, Meier certainly would have had that insight. One can only speculate why he did not want to speak in more detail about that period in both of their lives.

Meier was the most important man around Jung, who was surrounded by many women disciples. He was the first president of the Jung Institute, took over Jung's professorship at the Eidgenössische Technische Hochschule (ETH) in 1948, and was president of the Analytical Psychology Club from 1948–1952. He was instrumental in encouraging Jung to form an international professional association, which became the International Association for Analytical Psychology (IAAP) in 1955. When Jung retired from practice, Meier took over many of Jung's former patients.

Meier's scientific writings began with a paper in 1935 on the relationship between quantum physics and analytical psychology. This subject interested him for the remainder of his life. He wrote his first book *Antique Incubation and Modern Psychotherapy*, which was published by the Jung Institute. In the 1960s he wrote four clear and authoritative textbooks on the major aspects of Jung's theory, which have all been translated into English. In addition, there are numerous articles on diverse aspects of Jung's theory. Meier's last work was the publication of the correspondence between Wolfgang Pauli, the Nobel prize-winning physicist, and Jung in 1994. Meier was a close friend of Pauli's.

Fredy Meier was an extremely welcoming host, who liked his Scotch, Campari, and good French wines. Gatherings at his apartment were always memorable. He loved to read Homer in Greek and was a gifted classical musician. Before attending an opera he would always go through the score first. Until a year before his death he would spend at least a month a year on an island off the Italian coast diving and swimming. Even though Meier was Jung's right-hand man for almost three decades, they had a personal rift late in Jung's life. In turn Meier had very difficult relationships with his own male students. After his resignation from the Institute in 1957 Meier withdrew from most Jungian activities, so that today his name is not as well known as that of others. He died on 16 November 1995.

Marie-Louise von Franz (1915–1998)

The person most often associated with carrying on the legacy of C.G. Jung is Marie-Louise von Franz. Marlus, as she was referred to by her close intimates, was born in Munich on 4 January 1915, where her father was a colonel in the military of the Austro-Hungarian Empire. After the war the family moved to Switzerland, where the parents retained their Austrian citizenship, but in 1938 Marie-Louise and her sister were granted Swiss citizenship.

When she was eighteen (1933) and was on class trip from school, she met Jung. She wanted to go into analysis with him, but could not afford it. In exchange for analysis she did translations of Latin and Greek texts which he needed for his research into alchemy. On the basis of this work she wrote an exposition of the visions of the early mystic St Perpetua. She finished her Ph.D. in classical philology in 1943 and wrote a large and comprehensive work on fairy tales.

When the Jung Institute in Zurich opened, she was an ardent supporter and soon became one of the most popular seminar leaders with her work on fairy tales, the *puer aeternus*, synchronicity, dreams, and psychotherapy. The specific titles of her books from these seminars are too numerous to list. Because of the brilliance of her mind, her deep and passionate attention to the unconscious, her clarity in putting forth her ideas, and her devotion to the writings of Jung, she attracted a large group of students who increasingly became drawn to her work. Her prodigious writing continued on such diverse subjects as synchronicity, number symbolism, projection, dreams and death, C.G. Jung, and most centrally on alchemy.

On a personal level Jung was the man in her life. She took Jung's advice to share her life and home with Barbara Hannah. This close relationship, deeply meaningful to both women, lasted until Barbara Hannah died in 1986. Von Franz also bought a piece of property in Bollingen and had her own tower built. Like Jung's tower, it was extremely primitive without electricity and a flushing cistern.

Marie-Louise von Franz became world renowned among followers of Jung and after his death was an eloquent spokesperson for his ideas. One could compare her position to Jung with that of Anna Freud's to her father. Von Franz's interpretation of Jung's work was quite specific, and she was not afraid to criticize others who interpreted Jung in a different manner. For example, in the 1950s she was not in favor of Fordham's interpretation of Jung and did not mince words (personal communication). When many non-Jungian influences entered the Jung Institute in Zurich in the 1980s, she protested and withdrew from teaching. Eventually she founded the new "Centre for the Research into the Psychology of C.G. Jung," and became the main force behind it. Several analysts and students from the Jung Institute followed her, which led to bitter feelings between the old Jung Institute and the new research and training centre.

In the early 1980s von Franz tragically developed Parkinson's disease, which gradually began to incapacitate her. She refused to take medication to lessen the symptoms, because it would have interfered with the unconscious. The symptoms gradually became more physically exhausting, but she continued her work on a Shiite alchemical mystic. This work is still waiting to be published. She died on 17 February 1998.

Aniela Jaffé (1903–1991)

Another person closely associated with Jung's work is Aniela Jaffé, the co-author of *Memories, Dreams, Reflections*, and Jung's long-time private secretary. Born in 1903 in Berlin of Jewish parents, she was about to receive her doctorate in psychology from the University of Hamburg when she was forced to flee from the Nazis. She married a Swiss, Jean Dreyfuss, and they moved to Geneva. However, the marriage did not work out as they both had strong and independent personalities, which worked in friendship but not in marriage. They remained life-long friends. In the late 1930s she moved to Zurich where she worked as a secretary. These years were filled with many difficulties, both spiritual and physical, but eventually she had an analysis with Liliane Frey. Through her analytical work with Frey, she was introduced to Jung and subsequently had a long analysis with him.

When the Jung Institute opened in 1948, Aniela Jaffé was a natural choice to become the first secretary. With her quiet introversion and administrative experience, she did an excellent job of shaping the early programs at the Institute. In 1955 Jung needed a private secretary and tried hiring someone through the usual employment channels in Zurich, but he found himself frustrated by the lack of psychological understanding evident in the applicants. In desperation he hired Aniela Jaffé to be his personal secretary, a position she held until his death in 1961. She was able to accept his occasional outbursts of anger without taking it personally.

It was as Jung's private secretary that Jaffé suggested that they work on his biography together. At first Jung was most reluctant to do this, but over time he agreed, and that is how the book, *Memories, Dreams, Reflections* came into being. The first three chapters on Jung's childhood are Jung's own writing, but the rest of the book is Jaffé's writing, based upon the notes she took in conversation with Jung. The book is truly a co-authorship. The material contained in *Memories, Dreams, Reflections* is only about half of the manuscript, but legal battles have kept the remaining material from being published.

Although Jaffé had no formal training as an analyst, she became a highly respected and sought after analyst. She belonged to no particular faction in Zurich, and in her quiet, introverted way, she helped many people who came to analysis in a spiritual crisis. She was a highly creative individual who wrote many books. Besides *Memories, Dreams, Reflections*, she wrote a chapter on modern art in *Man and His Symbols* (1964), edited three volumes of Jung's letters in German, and was co-editor of two volumes in English with Gerhard Adler. Her own most important book is *The Myth of Meaning* (1970), where she amplified Jung's idea that man cannot live a "meaningless life." In this work she discussed "meaning" and "meaningless," and how they are interwoven in our lives. Another important work was her last major one, *C.G. Jung, Word and Image* (1979), a large-format, richly illustrated volume with many never before seen pictures of Jung and illustrations from his private Red Book.

Jaffé's apartment was filled with books, papers, and manuscripts, and in conversation she was interested in a surprisingly wide range of subjects. She was a loyal friend and beloved analyst. She died in 1991 after a short illness.

Jolande Jacobi (1890–1973)

In Jung's most intimate circle of students in Zurich, Jolande Jacobi was unique as she was the only extravert among them. She was born in Budapest on 25 March 1890 into a highly placed, assimilated Jewish family. After finishing her schooling, she married a lawyer, Dr Andor Jacobi, in 1909. As a result of the political situation after World War I they moved to Vienna. They separated when he returned to Budapest in 1922, she remaining in Vienna with their two sons. Jolande became deeply involved in the cultural activities of Vienna, and her apartment became a meeting place for famous artists, musicians, and writers. One of those visitors was C.G. Jung. She became the vice-president of the Austrian *Kulturbund*.

In 1934 she enrolled at the University of Vienna and studied psychology with Charlotte and Karl Bühler. At the same time she began an analysis with Jung and traveled back and forth between Zurich and Vienna. When the Nazis annexed Austria in 1938, she fled to Zurich where she had a small apartment. However, since she had not yet defended her Ph.D. in Vienna, Jung insisted that she obtain her degree before allowing her to practice as an analyst in Zurich. Under great duress and danger she was able to take and pass her examinations in Vienna, which then allowed her to practice in Zurich. By that time she had converted to Catholicism.

Jolande Jacobi became active in many psychological organizations in Switzerland, including the Volkshochschule, the University of Zurich, the Institute for Practical Psychology, and primarily at the Jung Institute in Zurich. Already prior to World War II she had been urging Jung to form an Institute, and after the war she pressed forward in her desire to establish a training center. It is largely due to her energy and enthusiasm that the Institute came into being. Jacobi was a founding member of the Curatorium and remained on it for nineteen years. She did a great deal of teaching and was much sought after as a lecturer worldwide. Her particular interest was in picture interpretation, and she formed a research foundation in Zurich which collected the paintings of many analysands from around the world.

Jolande Jacobi published about ninety articles and several volumes on different aspects of analytical psychology. Her most important book, *The Psychology of C.G. Jung* (1943), which was one of the earliest books to outline Jung's theories, was reprinted five times and translated into nine languages. Another important work of hers was *Complex/Archetype/Symbol* (1959). She was one of the co-authors of *Man and His Symbols*, edited by Jung, and her writings on the psychology of the feminine, individuation, and Paracelsus, were pioneering works at the time.

Her apartment in Zurich, just as the one in Vienna, became a popular meeting place for eminent artists. The decor of her Swiss apartment had a distinct Viennese atmosphere and made one forget that one was in Zurich (Jacoby 1974). After World War II she renewed her connections to Austria and received many honors from the Austrian government. In 1957 she was made an honorary citizen of Austria. At any Jungian social function in Zurich Jolande would be the life of the party, enjoying dancing and speaking with everyone. She had lived through difficult times, which are aptly described by Mario Jacoby (no relation), "that she fought much and suffered much" (Jacoby 1974).

In her later years her eyesight failed her, but she continued to work until the time of her death on 1 April 1973.

Franz Riklin (1909–1969)

Franz Riklin's relationship with Jung was almost preordained. His mother was a cousin of Jung and his father, who was a psychiatrist, worked with Jung during the early phases of analytical psychology (Baumann 1970). Riklin Sr. and Jung published *Studies in Word Association* in 1904, where the experimental data on complexes appeared for the first time.

Riklin grew up in Küsnacht and the family could trace its origins in Switzerland for many centuries, and, not surprisingly, besides analytical psychology, his other passion was his love of his native land, Switzerland. He studied medicine in Zurich and was on the path to a career in internal medicine. As a student, in the days before antibiotics, he predicted – on the basis of a dream – that a patient would recover from pneumonia. His supervising physician dismissed him from his post, and Riklin became aware of his interest in psychiatry and analytical psychology. He had analysis with Jung, psychiatric training at the Burghölzli and opened a practice of analytical psychology. When the Jung Institute opened, he began to teach there, and was elected a member of the Curatorium in 1952. From 1957 until his death in 1969 he served as president of the Curatorium.

These facts do not begin to tell the story of the impact of Franz Riklin on analytical psychology. In 1955 he was responsible for the *Festschrift* for Jung's eightieth birthday, *Studien zur analytischen Psychologie* (Riklin 1955). He was one of the leading figures in the founding of the International Association for Analytical Psychology (IAAP). When Robert Moody of London died in office, he finished the term and was reelected president of the IAAP. When he ran for reelection in 1965, he lost to Gerhard Adler and Jo Wheelwright in the only truly contested election for the presidency in the history of the IAAP. Furthermore, he was instrumental in the founding of the Swiss professional society. Thus, he was deeply involved in all the early organizational matters of analytical psychology, the Jung Institute, the IAAP, and the Swiss Society.

In his commitment to his other passion, Switzerland, he was very proud of his position as a colonel in the Swiss Army. By the end of his military career he was the commanding officer of a large military hospital. He spent much of his free time at the family farm where he enjoyed being close to the soil. He died of a massive heart attack in 1969 at the age of sixty.

The Fierz family

Several members of two generations of the Fierz family were influenced by Jung, and they in turn influenced analytical psychology. The family members who knew Jung were Markus Fierz and Linda Fierz-David. Markus Fierz met Jung at the ETH, where he was a professor of chemistry, and he wrote a history of chemistry which included much material on alchemy. His wife, Linda Fierz-David, was one of the first Jungian analysts in Zurich; she wrote two books, *The Dream of Poliphilo* (1950), and *Villa of Mysteries* (1957), a study of the frescos at Pompeii. She was active in the Analytical Psychology Club, serving in numerous important capacities.

The son, Heinrich Fierz, was an active member in the early days of the Jung Institute and became the first medical director of the Klinik am Zürichberg. He studied medicine and received his psychiatric training at the Burghölzli. He had his analysis with Jung and, surprisingly, his doctoral dissertation was on the subject of electric shock treatment.

In 1949 Ludwig Binswanger, the co-founder of *Daseinanalyse*, appointed Heinrich Fierz as director of the clinical department at the Sanatorium Bellevue in Kreuzlingen. There he introduced the Jungian point of view to other professionals. In addition, he became active in the International Society for Medical Psychotherapy, the group which Jung had presided over before World War II. In the 1950s and 1960s many students from the Jung Institute in Zurich, who wanted more clinical experience, spent time at Bellevue.

When C.A. Meier founded the Klinik am Zürichberg in 1964, he appointed Heinrich Fierz to be the medical director. Fierz maintained his interest in organic psychiatry along with his deep analytical attitude, which was an ideal combination for someone in his position. His influence was widely felt by students and staff who worked there. Many students from the Jung Institute received clinical experience working in that in-patient setting.

Fierz suffered from emphysema and eventually had to resign the directorship because of ill health. The Klinik am Zürichberg was never able to find another person who could balance the opposites of organic psychiatry and analytical psychology. After his departure, the Jungian presence at the Klinik began to decline. Fierz died in 1984 from complications of emphysema.

C.G. JUNG INSTITUTE, ZURICH

As the world began to recover after World War II, a small institute for the study of Jung's psychology was founded at Gemeindestrasse 27 in Zurich, the same building where the Analytical Psychology Club was housed. There was much discussion about the choice of its name. Toni Wolff favored "Institute for Complex Psychology," while Jung's chief concern was the omission of his name in the title. Jung's followers won out, and it became the C.G. Jung Institute. Jung gave the inaugural speech on 24 April 1948 on the subject of the history of "Complex Psychology," and he suggested areas for further research, such as: further experiments with the word-association test and family structure, more fully elaborated clinical case histories, research on dreams in relationship to physical illness, death, catastrophes, research on the normal family in terms of psychic structure, compensatory nature of marriage, and finally, much more work on symbolism – triadic and tetradic, and their historical development in relationship to philosophy, religion, and the new field of microphysics. At the end of the speech he recognized that much of the list was "mere desideratum" and "not all of it will be fulfilled" (Jung *CW* 18:475–476). It would be interesting to investigate where analytical psychology has gone and compare it with Jung's hopes for the field.

The establishment of the Jung Institute changed the way one became a Jungian analyst. It was no longer strictly a personal matter between the individual and Jung. At the Institute Jungian analytical training became part of a larger educational experience, where the individual's analysis was still paramount but where academic criteria had to be fulfilled, and formal structures began to play a significant role. However, the Jung Institute was not an international accrediting body, so that individuals could still become analysts by having personal analysis with Jung and receiving a letter of recommendation from him. It was only with the founding of the International Association for Analytical Psychology (IAAP) in 1955 that the authority for accreditation was definitively transferred from Jung personally to a professional association.

The Institute was set up along the lines of a European university, with many classes and non-compulsory attendance, the only requirement being that students pass a test in a given subject at the end of the year. Admission requirements included the minimum of a master's degree in any field, along with a personal biography and interviews. The lack of specificity in a clinical discipline went along with Jung's idea that a non-clinical background could be an appropriate foundation for becoming an analyst. The profession of a Jungian analyst was seen as a separate discipline, and one could become an analyst via theology, economics, and philosophy, just as readily as through the traditional disciplines of medicine, psychology, and social work. Such liberal admission requirements have allowed individuals, for instance, to make a midlife change and become an analyst by studying in Zurich. In the meantime, clinical requirements to practice any kind of therapy have tightened worldwide, but the Zurich Institute has remained a training center where non-clinically trained people can still become analysts. The basic tracks included the following subjects: Fundamentals of Analytical Psychology, Psychology of Dreams, Association Experiments, General History of Religion, Fairy Tales, Mythology, General Psychopathology. After taking the required courses, students have to pass a test, the propaedeuticum, in each of the given subjects. After passing the test they attend case colloquia, where patient material is discussed, and further courses to deepen their knowledge of analytical psychology. In the early days of the Institute students had to see two patients and have control supervision of their work, either individually or in a group. For the English-speaking students finding suitable patients was not always easy, and so these graduates often lacked sufficient clinical experience. In the early years symbolic understanding was emphasized over clinical training. In order to graduate from the Institute students then had to pass another set of examinations, write and defend a thesis, as well as write up patient cases using Jungian methods. The Institute was created to be international in character and offered tracks in German, English, French, and Italian. The vast majority of the early students were either American, British, or Swiss. For many years the number of students hovered around thirty at any given time, and the atmosphere was lively, intimate, and the discussions intense. Jung would visit the Institute from time to time to meet with the students, and he often attended the yearly students' party. Although the Institute in Zurich was not the first Jungian training center in the world (London and San Francisco having started in 1946), it was by far the most organized and the largest. With the presence of Jung in the background and many of the first generation of analysts providing the bulk of the teaching and analysis, Zurich was the Mecca for analytical psychology.

The structure of the Institute has some unusual and unique features. The Institute is governed by a seven-member Curatorium, chosen by the board itself, and each member can hold the position indefinitely. The president of the Curatorium is elected by the members of the board, carries out its wishes, and is not supposed to make independent decisions. Up to two members at any one time have been members of the Jung family. In actual practice members of the Curatorium have been rotating off periodically, and there has been a continued renewal and change over the years. However, on occasion a Curatorium member has stayed on for a long time and has not seen the wisdom of stepping aside. The independence of the Curatorium from outside influences was Jung's idea; he wanted the Curatorium to be free to make unpopular decisions (personal communication, A. Guggenbühl-Craig).

The Institute has an international advisory board, whose members are called patrons, and who represent major Jungian centers. For example, Jo Wheelwright, Joe Henderson, James Kirsch, Esther Harding, and Gerhard Adler were early patrons of the Institute and acted as advisors to the Institute at times of crises. In the early days, since Zurich was the most important training center for Jungian analysts, what transpired there was followed with much interest by many Jungians. The Institute in turn was equally interested in maintaining an international profile and having collegial relations with the other Institutes.

The "halcyon days" of the Zurich Institute lasted from the opening until the mid-1960s. Analytical psychology had not yet divided into different strands, Jung was still relatively unrecognized in the world, and the students who came to Zurich sensed that they were witnessing the birth of something new and special. Professor C.A. Meier was the first president of the Jung Institute serving from 1947 until 1957, at which time he resigned from the Curatorium, and had very little contact with the Institute thereafter. Aniela Jaffé was the first secretary, while Marie-Louise von Franz, Barabara Hannah, Rivkah Schaerf, and Heinrich Fierz were the principal seminar leaders. Von Franz's seminars were especially popular, and many of them were later published in book form, such as *The Problem of the Puer Aeternus* (1970), *Alchemy – an Introduction into the Symbolism and the Psychology* (1980), and *The Feminine in Fairy Tales* (1993). The American students matriculated at the Institute, such as James Hillman, Marvin Spiegelman, and Robert Stein, complainingly and teasingly declared themselves "puers," which was evidence of immaturity, of not having grown up. It was a paradoxical situation, because on the one hand, living in Zurich was "provisional" and therefore *puer*, but on the other it was leading to meaningful work as an analyst. Many of Jung's students were publishing books, and Zurich was the center of creativity in the Jungian world, so it was certainly the place to be if one wanted an immersion in analytical psychology. Even after Jung's death in 1961 there continued to be a very special feeling about studying analytical psychology in Zurich, and the Institute attracted many highly creative people who would become prominent analytical psychologists in the future.

In 1959 James Hillman, a young, brilliant, American student, who had received his Ph.D. at the University of Zurich and graduated from the Jung Institute, became the new Director of Studies. His doctoral thesis *Emotion: A Comprehensive Phenomenology of Theories and Their Meanings for Therapy* was highly regarded and was immediately published, which happened rarely in the publishing world of those days. Hillman's wide-ranging intellect brought new ideas and lecturers from different fields to the Institute.

Franz Riklin replaced C.A. Meier as president of the Institute, which continued to grow and thrive. However, the emphasis on archetypal studies and a certain informality around clinical boundaries began to cause problems for the Zurich analysts. Inappropriate professional and personal relationships were formed by some analysts with students, and in 1967 Hillman was at the center of an allegation of sexual misconduct, and the case became public knowledge. Inside the Jungian community opinions were heated and divided. However, the matter could not be confined to professional circles as the case was brought before the District Court of Zurich. This ensured that the matter was fully discussed by the Curatorium of the Institute, and also amongst the Patrons, who represented the international Jungian community. The Curatorium attempted to discuss the matter in ideological terms. Granted that Hillman had "sinned," what was the appropriate decision to take in the matter? Had this been the first time that an event of this nature had occurred? Of course not! Jung himself had been involved with a patient, Toni Wolff, and this was a clearly known occupational hazard of any analytic work. Others had succumbed to the temptation, and Hillman was most certainly not alone or the first. One question was whether Hillman showed appropriate contrition or not. This led to bitter disputes within the Curatorium, with Jolande Jacobi wanting Hillman out and others, like Riklin, wanting Hillman to stay on. The issue was not too dissimilar to what has happened recently with President Clinton in the United States. These moral questions continue to plague us, and they have no easy solutions. The deeper issues become quickly translated into practical decisions. With Hillman the decision became whether to get rid of him or let him stay as Director of Studies. Eventually, he resigned, but remained in Zurich as editor of Spring Publications.

This event was a harbinger of change in the Jungian world, as the question of boundary violations was at issue in many other Jungian training programs at the time. Clinical boundaries were to assume greater importance in the future of all training programs, including Zurich. Perhaps change happened more slowly in Zurich, because the influence of Jung's own interest in archetypal symbolism and mythological amplifications of dreams held sway longer over clinical traditions than in other training centers. It is not implied that an interest in clinical issues leads to a neglect of archetypal interpretations; clinical parameters have to be maintained while a deeper understanding of the unconscious is explored. After 1967 a complete immersion in archetypal interpretations was no longer possible. The events around Hillman's resignation galvanized changes in attitude towards training that took many years to implement. The consequences of this episode in the Institute's history were not immediately apparent to the international Jungian community, but over time changes became noticeable at the Institute. On the one hand, the Institute slowly began to lose its uniqueness, but on the other hand many students still wanted to study in Zurich and be close to the source.

Subsequently, there was a subtle change in the profile of the students who were attracted to the Institute, and there were several reasons for that: (1) the faculty at the Institute was changing, with first-generation analysts who had direct contact with Jung, and carried some of his spirit, aging and retiring; (2) the incident with Hillman had accentuated the rivalries and tensions among Zurich analysts; (3) Switzerland had become more expensive to live in relation to the rest of the world, and this acted as a deterrent. Increasingly, students came to Zurich not only because it offered excellent training but because it was one of the few remaining training centers in the world where people without degrees in medicine, psychology, or social work could obtain Jungian training. The Zurich Institute continues to offer a high level of comprehensive training in analytical psychology and gives students a depth of study not found in many other training centers.

Adolf Guggenbühl-Craig and James Hillman have had enormous influence on analytical psychology in Zurich and elsewhere. They came a generation later and were technically not part of the first generation of analysts around Jung. They were both significant figures in the early days of the Jung Institute and have remained prominent in the field. Mentioning the two together does not imply that their views are identical; they are both highly individual men who have been colleagues and friends for over forty years and share many values. They come from very different backgrounds, and their respective professional careers have taken vastly different paths.

Adolf Guggenbühl-Craig (1923–)

Adolf Guggenbühl-Craig, like his mentor, Franz Riklin before him, comes from a family with deep roots in Switzerland, going back several centuries. He was born in the Canton of Zurich in 1923 and has lived and worked in Zurich, except for a short stay in the United States where he did his psychiatric training. Since 1962 Adolf has been a dominant figure in analytical psychology in Zurich. He edited the Proceedings of the Second International Congress in 1962 (*Der Archetyp*), and in 1969 upon Franz Riklin's death took over as president of the Curatorium at the Jung Institute, a position he held for over a decade. He was also vice-president of the Swiss Society, and then in 1977 he was elected president of the IAAP, a position he held for two terms. Through these positions he came in contact with, and influenced, numerous students of analytical psychology. He is known for his outstanding ability to mediate and is held in high esteem by the worldwide Jungian community.

Guggenbühl-Craig is known for taking controversial stands on many matters, and it is often difficult to predict his points of view. Whatever position he takes, it is always direct, practical, and one that must be reckoned with. For example, in his first book, *Power in the Helping Professions* (1971), he outlines in simple terms the power shadow of being a therapist. He demonstrates the not so positive aspect of many a therapist's supposedly helpful intervention. At the present time he has retired from all positions of influence, and is seen as the *éminence grise* of the Zurich Jungian community.

James Hillman (1926–)

James Hillman, an American from New Jersey, came to Zurich in 1953 to study at the Jung Institute and obtained a Ph.D. from the University of Zurich. He went into private practice in Zurich and in 1959 became the first Director of Studies at the Institute. In this position he influenced a whole generation of students at the Institute. He resigned in 1969 when he became the focus of an international incident at the Institute. He remained in Zurich until 1978 as the editor of Spring Publications. Many of the future Jungian publishers, such as Daryl Sharp, Murray Stein, and Robert Hinshaw, got their start in the publishing world working as assistant editors at Spring Publications.

Over time Hillman moved away from individual analysis and became more focused on broader disorders of the collective. He has since called this a "therapy of ideas" rather than of persons and has named it "archetypal psychology." Although "archetypal psychology" is considered by many to be a separate strand within analytical psychology, the fact that it is seen as a "disorder of the collective" has prevented it from developing an institutional base like the other trainings in analytical psychology.

Hillman returned to the United States in 1978, first to the Dallas Institute of Humanities, and later to Thompson, Connecticut. For the past decade he has no longer practiced analysis but has been writing and lecturing. His books have gained a wide readership among lay audiences. However, through his earlier association with the Jung Institute in Zurich, and the popularity of his writings worldwide, his ideas have emerged from his work in analytical psychology and he continues to be a significant Jungian figure.

Schweizerische Gesellschaft für Analytische Psychologie (SGfAP)

The Jung Institute was the central cohesive structure for analytical psychology in Zurich, as it provided the training and the exchange of intellectual ideas. However, Riklin and others realized that there was a need for a professional organization in Switzerland which could deal with the political, administrative, and professional issues which faced the growing number of graduates working in Switzerland. The most immediate concern in those early days was that the Swiss analysts had agreed to host an international Congress of Jungian analysts in Zurich in 1962, and a structure to organize it had to be in place. Thus, a professional society, the SGfAP was founded. Riklin proposed Adolf Guggenbühl-Craig as president of the new group, because of his previous experience in organizing conferences. The vote went to Kurt Binswanger, an elderly analyst who was a member of the famous Binswanger family in Switzerland. Already hard of hearing, he did not preside for a long time. Mario Jacoby became the next president, followed by Verena Kast. Both Jacoby and Kast served for many years each, as the Society continued to grow. Outside of a yearly weekend conference each spring, there was little activity. Today there are approximately two hundred and fifty members in the Swiss society.

The SGfAP remained very much in the background, as the Jung Institute was the active organization with its teaching and research functions. However, this has changed slowly as long-term psychotherapy and analysis have come under attack from both public and governmental sources. In the past ten years the Swiss government and its federal health insurance have demanded scientific evidence to demonstrate that psychotherapy, especially analysis, works. Reimbursement for psychotherapy services is dependent upon such research. This includes analytical psychology, which must show with objective data that patients improve with Jungian analysis. A Swiss analyst, Guido Matanzas, has begun a large research project involving as many Jungian analysts as will participate, to show that Jungian analysis benefits patients in a number of parameters. This project has received general approval from the SGfAP but has also evoked protest from some analysts who think that the project is un-Jungian. It has received funding from a number of private foundations as well as the IAAP.

The SGfAP has become an important forum in the collective where psychotherapy and analysis can be discussed. In addition to its role in the collective world of Switzerland, the SGfAP has also been involved in controversies at the Institute. The Society took a stand at the time of the Hillman incident, and again in 1998 when a deep division within the Curatorium occurred. The current president of the Curatorium, Brigitte Spillmann, got a petition signed by over one hundred members of the SGfAP in her support. In other words, the role of the SGfAP is changing as political and organizational activities intrude into the process of analysis.

Klinik am Zürichberg

When C.A. Meier resigned from the presidency of the Jung Institute in 1957 he was concerned about the direction the Institute was taking because the approach to the unconscious was becoming too disconnected from modern science. As a medical doctor and psychiatrist he wanted to return to the scientific basis for the study of dreams and the unconscious. The connection between rapid eye movement and dreams had recently been discovered (Aserinsky and Kleitman 1953). Meier wanted to set up a research laboratory where dreams could be studied from a Jungian point of view, as analytical psychology had moved away from Jung's initial interest in psychotic patients. There was no in-patient facility where patients could be treated in a Jungian fashion. In 1964 the Klinik am Zürichberg for hospitalized patients was founded with private funds, and Meier realized his aim to establish a research laboratory for the study of dreams. Meier was the director of the Klinik, Heinrich Fierz the medical director, and Toni Frei the chief psychologist. At this clinic, as an elective, students from the Jung Institute could receive valuable clinical training. For a decade the Klinik am Zürichberg had a very active in-patient unit, and the research progressed. However, Fierz had to retire due to ill health, and tensions began to surface among the staff, as newer staff members had different orientations toward the psyche, and so the spirit of the Klinik changed. The bitterness between rival factions became so great that some of the major issues had to be settled by the Zurich court. This divisive battle left the Klinik without a Jungian presence, and it became a general psychiatric facility.

Establishment of the Jung Institute in Küsnacht

In the 1960s and early 1970s Jung's ideas became more popular, and the Jung Institute at Gemeindestrasse could no longer accommodate all the students. In 1973 an old mansion, which was owned by the community, in Küsnacht on the Lake of Zurich became available, and Adolf Guggenbühl-Craig, as the president of the Institute, was able to arrange a favorable lease agreement. Located close to Jung's home, the building seemed ideal to house the growing Institute. Student enrollment increased steadily, and by the end of the 1980s over one hundred of the total of 400 students were American. At the same time the Institute has widened its international character with the addition of students from Asia, Africa, and the smaller European countries. Many Japanese students have begun to attend the Institute, and there has even been a student from Mainland China. Two students from Moscow have received scholarships from German foundations to do their studies at the Institute. Faculty from the Institute have regularly taught in Hungary, Lithuania, Czechoslovakia, Poland, and the former Soviet Union. Each summer the Institute offers an intensive program where students from all over the world attend seminars and do supervision for two weeks. Some of these students later return as full-time candidates at the Institute.

As geographical boundaries expanded, so did the curriculum. Clinical issues had greater emphasis, and the number of required clinical colloquia, as well as individual supervisory hours for students, increased. Mario Jacoby (no relation to first-generation analyst Jolande Jacobi), in his role as a training analyst, first introduced Fordham's work as an essential analytic theory, and later he integrated Heinz Kohut's self-psychology into Jung's theory. For over thirty years Jacoby has been a very popular analyst and teacher at the Institute. Other analysts began to teach the theory of the British object-relations theorists, especially Winnicott. This broadening of analytic theory was anathema to some of the first-generation analysts, especially Marie-Louise von Franz, who felt that Jung's contributions were being diluted by the addition of new psychoanalytic theory.

During this period of change one particular proposal caused a deep crisis within the Institute. During his presidency Adolf Guggenbühl-Craig tried to introduce Jungian group therapy for candidates. Under the leadership of Marie-Louise von Franz, most of the lecturers and analysts went on strike and refused to have anything to do with the Institute as long as group therapy was being practiced. It was felt that group therapy was against the spirit of Jung, and Guggenbühl-Craig, as president of the Curatorium, was labeled a traitor. Endless meetings were held, and in the end a compromise was reached: group therapy is not practiced, but lectures on the subject are allowed.

These changes within the Institute curriculum demonstrated to Marie-Louise von Franz that not enough attention was being paid to the individuation process going on in the unconscious. Honoring her strong beliefs about the nature of Jung's work, she withdrew from teaching at the Institute in the early 1980s. Other analysts and candidates joined her, and they began to meet informally on a regular basis. At the time Helmut Barz was the president of the Institute, and no effort was spared to keep von Franz and her group within the overall structure of the Institute. However, by the end of the 1980s it was evident that the group around von Franz would eventually leave the Institute and form its own center.

Another crisis had been brewing for a long time and it bubbled to the surface in 1998. Brigitte Spillmann, a fairly recent graduate of the Institute, was elected president of the Curatorium. She came from a business background, and it was thought that this would be helpful in the operation of the Institute. Spillmann has initiated more policy changes within the Institute structure than the Curatorium is used to. For example, she wants term limits for Curatorium members, so that one person cannot influence policy for decades. She has made decisions without necessarily discussing them with the board, which angered some board members. The members have become polarized, and as a result it has become difficult to reach any decisions because the votes tend to split. In November 1998 four long-time members of the Curatorium, including two former presidents, Helmut Barz and Paul Brutsche, tendered their resignations. This is the most heated conflict in twenty years. At the time of writing the outcome of this struggle is not known.

Research and Training Centre in Depth Psychology

The Research and Training Centre in Depth Psychology came into being on 8 May 1994 and was incorporated as a foundation the following day. Although the actual founding of the Centre only happened in 1994, the seeds of the new foundation have been nurtured for many years.

When the original Jung Institute was formed, Jung was still active, and the seminars and colloquia were completely in tune with his basic theory. The classes were small, emphasis was on archetypal symbol-ism, active imagination, amplification, and the study of comparative dream material. Over the years the Jung Institute has grown tremend-ously, and new influences from the wider world of psychotherapy, psychoanalysis, and the basic sciences have been incorporated into the training program for students. Through experiences of broken profes-sional boundaries, conflicts with the collective, and the need to admin-ister the Institute, the value of structure has grown compared to earlier years. The increasing number of students made it necessary to have more structure. Some of the older analysts who had been with the Institute from the very beginning, like Marie-Louise von Franz, did not like the direction of the Institute. By the early 1980s she, along with some others, felt that the original spirit of the Institute was being lost; they began to withdraw and meet privately.

What happened next is hard to ascertain, but von Franz and her professional colleagues felt that their students were being discriminated against in examinations, and they were having a great deal of difficulty finishing the program. A tension was developing between the followers of von Franz and the rest of the Institute. Many discussions were held to try and work out specific issues which were dividing the Institute into two camps. The original Institute Curatorium did not want the von Franz supporters to split and form another center. The von Franz contingent was doubtful that this was possible and, after many emo-tional exchanges, decided to found its own Research and Training Centre in Depth Psychology.

The Centre's brochure reads as follows: "The aims of the Centre are, on the one hand, to further research on the unconscious psyche as well as on the relationship between psyche and matter, and on the other hand, to provide a training programme for qualified analysts." Further on the brochure states: "The Centre was founded in order to create a place where the autonomous psyche can be considered with total commitment." The entrance requirements, the importance of the personal analysis, and the structure of the actual program closely follow the model of the Jung Institute. One significant difference is that the Centre's training program is intended to attract individuals who are interested in Jungian psychology but are unable to spend prolonged periods of time in Switzerland. As at the Jung Institute, the diploma track program is open to students with a master's degree, or its equivalent, in any field. In granting the student a diploma, it does not guarantee that individual graduates will have the legal right to practice in their home country. The course lasts eight semesters, so that it takes a minimum of four years to complete. The subjects taught,

the number of hours of personal analysis and supervision, the requirement of a thesis, are all similar to those of the Jung Institute. The new
Centre has a publication named *Jungiana*, where contributions to the
psychology of C.G. Jung and Marie-Louise von Franz are included.
Books on the study of individual archetypal motifs have been published by faculty of the Centre.

On the surface the programs of the Jung Institute and the Centre seem
very similar. However, as one probes more deeply into the heart and
soul of this new center, meaningful differences emerge. In the Centre
the collective unconscious, or objective psyche, becomes the most central guide for each individual, and the value of the outer collective is
minimized. There is a subtle way in which the objective psyche, through
dreams, active imagination, amplification, is given too much weight,
if that is possible. As the world of the collective is less important,
membership in organizations such as the International Association for
Analytical Psychology or any other professional organization becomes
non-essential. Therefore, former members of the Jung Institute whose
allegiance moved to the new Centre have given up their membership in
both the IAAP and the SGfAP. Candidates graduating from the new
Centre will not be eligible to become members in the IAAP, as their
training will not be with IAAP members. The first group of students at
the Centre has consisted of twenty German-speaking and ten English-
speaking candidates.

A second and more serious problem is that many of the students at
the Centre come from other countries. The seminars are held twice a
year, each for a two-week period. During the two-week period the
students receive an intensive and full course of seminars by members
of the Centre faculty. However, during the rest of the year, the students have their analysis and supervision with analysts in their home
countries. The analysis and supervision may be with an analyst of a
different Jungian persuasion, since the Centre can only exert limited
influence.

The Centre has a subtitle to its name, "according to Carl Gustav
Jung and Marie-Louise von Franz." Students study primarily the texts
of Jung and von Franz. Thus, new developments in clinical theory and
practice are not included, because it is said that one can find all the
material one needs in Jung and von Franz; that is, one can uncover the
current solution to most problems by locating the appropriate myth,
fairy tale, or alchemical text.

Until her death in 1998 Marie-Louise von Franz was the honorary
president, and two members of the board, Gotthilf Isler and Theo
Abt, were former training analysts of the Jung Institute. At one time

Abt was also a member of the Curatorium. Although not many of the Swiss analysts have formally joined the new center, many of them have varying degrees of sympathy towards it. At this time the tensions between the Jung Institute and the Centre are still strong.

The Centre has much of the feeling of the old Institute during the 1950s and 1960s, when the number of students was small, and the courses were similar in nature to the curriculum at the Centre. In the early days of the Jung Institute students worked on their inner growth, and there were few concerns about collective issues. In those days to be Jungian was marginal, and to go to the Jung Institute fitted in with that marginal image. Since the program is relatively new, it is too early to predict the Centre's progress. At the moment there is much enthusiasm at the Centre.

Relationship to psychoanalysis

During the lifetimes of Freud and Jung relations between the respective analytic groups were often difficult, if not impossible, in many countries. Zurich became a city where every variety of psychotherapeutic or psychoanalytic group existed. After the Jung–Freud break in 1913, there was relatively little contact between Jung and the Freudians. However, in the 1930s Jung began to meet on a regular basis with several psychiatrists and psychoanalysts, including Medard Boss (the co-founder of *Daseinanalyse*), C.A. Meier, and two or three psychoanalysts. These clinical discussions went on for many years.

When James Hillman became the Director of Training in 1959, his philosophical interests reconnected the Jungians with *Daseinanalyse*. In fact, some Jungians had a second *Dasein* analysis, and some members of the *Dasein* group had analysis with Jungians. However, there was never a formal connection between the Jung Institute and any other psychoanalytic institute in Zurich. The international character of the Institute, its size, and the stature of some of its members, has led the Jung Institute to be a well established and recognized academic institution within Switzerland.

SUMMARY

Zurich is where the whole movement of analytical psychology began. Jung came into his own at the conclusion of World War I. From 1919 to 1939 he had a steady stream of visitors, students, and analysands, many of whom later became analysts. Jung wrote letters of certification for those he deemed suitable to become analysts. In 1947 the Jung Institute was formed, and becoming a Jungian analyst was based on getting an academic diploma from the Jung Institute in addition to having a personal analysis with a first-generation Jungian. The early Institute was very informal, and there were few students. The intellectual fervor and the sense of being part of a new venture made for powerful experiences. As Jung became more popular and the Institute grew, the intimate atmosphere of the Institute changed, and events and crises within the Institute necessitated greater structure. The Institute then moved to Küsnacht into an old, community-owned building. Some of the early analysts, like Marie-Louise von Franz who was a major lecturer in the early days, became disillusioned by the changes within the Institute, which they experienced as a dilution of Jung. In time they formed their own training center called the Research and Training Centre in Depth Psychology, where the teachings of Jung and von Franz are emphasized. At the same time the Jung Institute is undergoing fundamental structural changes, so that shifts in authority can be made more readily without the same people remaining in power too long.

The climate in Zurich has changed markedly since the death of Jung. To the Zurich outsider the Jung Institute often had a monolithic appearance as if nothing had changed since Jung's death. The Institute has widened its view of the psychological world to include other psychological theorists and practices, such as Winnicott, Kohut, Bion, and others, still maintaining a close tie to the original numinosity of Jung. There are the students of von Franz who remain close to the original teachings of Jung and von Franz. The Jung Institute in Zurich remains a dynamic training institution and the program evolves continually.

2 The role of Analytical Psychology Clubs

The function of Analytical Psychology Clubs in the development of the profession of Jungian analysis has not received attention beyond a historical paper by Andrew Samuels (1994) on their role in the early days of the movement. Today some Jungian analysts are not even aware that such institutions exist, or that they constituted the foundation for many contemporary institutes.

The first Club formed around Jung in Zurich in 1916 and became the prototype for other clubs. The London Club was established in 1922, New York's in 1936, and by 1939 there were Clubs in Basle, Rome, Paris, Berlin, Munich, and San Francisco. At an Eranos meeting in Ascona, Switzerland in the summer of 1939, club representatives met to weigh the merits of confederation, considering their need to communicate and coordinate efforts to further common goals and objectives. Representatives corresponded until the spring of 1940 at which time the outbreak of war halted their endeavor. By the end of the war Clubs in Berlin, Munich, Paris, and Rome had disappeared, and the initiative for confederation never reemerged, as the goal to found a training institute in Zurich gained momentum. Nevertheless, the Clubs in Zurich, London, New York, San Francisco, and Los Angeles were the first organized structures in their respective locations to represent analytical psychology. As the Analytical Psychology Club in Zurich was the prototype, and Jung was instrumental in its founding, it will be described in greatest detail.

When Jung initiated the founding of the Analytical Psychology Club in Zurich he envisioned it serving social as well as educational functions. It might give people in analysis an opportunity to meet others of like mind; analysis is a lonely venture at any time, but eighty years ago stigma against such endeavor, which is not entirely gone today, was especially strong. Jung was interested in providing a social context for his largely introverted, internationally diverse group of analysands; he saw the Club as a setting for them to experiment with their newly found psychological understanding (Shamdasani 1998a). Analysands and analysts all mingled in a single setting.

The Club became a venue for formal discussions between Jung, his students and analysands, and invited speakers. Jung presented his latest writings for discussion, and both the famed and the relative neophyte were invited to speak about their special area of interest as it pertained to analytical psychology. Professor C.A. Meier (personal communication, 1995) reported that in the 1930s the Zurich Analytical Psychology Club was *the* place for intellectual discussion, with Jung as an active participant. In fact, Meier remembered it as the high point of his seventy-year involvement in the Jungian world. Guest speakers included the Nobel prize-winning physicist and founder of quantum physics, Wolfgang Pauli; the novelist, Herman Hesse; the Kundalini expert, Professor J.W. Hauer; the Sinologist, Richard Wilhelm; and the Indologist, Heinrich Zimmer.

One special Club function pertained to Jung's method of amplifying images from dreams and active imagination, a technique he himself used during his "confrontation with the unconscious." Analytical Psychology Clubs developed excellent libraries to enable research for theological, mythological, and anthropological comparisons of symbols. Analysands spent many hours in the library of the Club searching out various meanings of a particular dream image, as Zurich became a kind of "magic mountain" for many an analytic pilgrim.

Club membership was difficult to obtain, though, and only those considered sufficiently well analyzed were elected on a case-by-case basis. German was its official language, excluding all British and Americans who were not fluent in German.

The roots of the Analytical Psychology Club in Zurich go back to 1913 with the foundation of the Zurich Psychoanalytic Association, comprising members of the so-called "Zurich School," as distinct from the "Vienna School." Most were medical doctors. The group itself was part of the International Psychoanalytic Association, of which Jung was president. Its first recorded meeting took place at the Seidenhof Restaurant on 17 January 1913, at which two papers were presented. Two weeks later, at the same location, Jung gave his paper on libido theory, contrasting Freud's "wish-fulfillment theory" with his own theory that "dreams fulfill the meanings inherent in the self" (Muser 1984).

The first official meeting of the Zurich Analytical Psychology Club took place on 26 February 1916 when a constitution and by-laws were drawn up. Financial backing came from Edith Rockefeller McCormick, wife of the Chicago industrialist, Harold McCormick, and the daughter of John D. Rockefeller. Mrs McCormick was in analysis with Jung at the time (Noll 1997). She generously gave $200,000 towards the purchase of a building, where the Club could meet and members could stay overnight and have meals. The first premises of the Club were quite luxurious, but less ostentatious and more practical quarters were obtained in 1919 with the purchase of a house at Gemeindestrasse 27 in the English quarter of Zurich, which is still the home of the Club. It also became the home of the first Jung Institute from 1948 to 1973, until it moved to its present quarters in Küsnacht.

A significant early member of the Club was Emilii Medtner, a Russian émigré, who had begun analysis with Jung in 1914, eventually befriending him and his family and included in many family events. Medtner, a Russian symbolist, had his own ideas about intuition, the nature of the symbol, and other philosophical subjects. It is clear that he influenced the development of Jung's thought. Medtner was the Club's first librarian, a member of its board, and he presented a lecture series on intuition (Ljunggren 1994). Medtner also translated three volumes of Jung's writings into Russian and was in the process of making a French translation when funding from Edith Rockefeller McCormick ran out.

The social function of the Club was especially important. There was an annual Christmas dinner, where Jung introduced what came to be called the "Alleluia Game" (Hannah 1976:191–197). Members formed a circle and one went into the middle; a rolled-up napkin was tossed across the circle, which the "piggy-in-the-middle" had to intercept; when caught, the one who threw it would became the new "piggy." The game is similar to a ceremonial "ball-dance" of the medieval church but was eventually banned because of its pagan connotations. It was a big success at the Analytical Psychology Club, where it eased a rigidly formal, social hierarchy. As might be expected, intimate friendships as well as intense rivalries developed between Club members.

A review of Club documents reveals the following facts about membership demographics in the 1930s. Xenophobia, the fear of an influx of "strangers" which would alter the "Swiss character" of the Club, was evident. This problem was discussed at the annual membership meeting in May 1936, when a posture of resistance against "too many Jews" manifested itself. The secretary reported the following comment by Jung: "He stressed that Jews are an important cultural factor in Europe, even though their racial difference cannot be denied. If they produce a bad effect, then the person who is being affected must seek for reasons within himself or herself. The Club should expose itself to such effects and consciously deal with them, instead of holding others responsible for an unpleasant influence."(Mattoon 1996:714)

Thenceforth, the executive committee of the Club decided on the admission of foreign and Jewish applicants. This came up again in 1940, and in late 1944 the executive committee wrote an internal eight-page commentary on the Club's new statutes. This commentary was distributed only to members of the executive committee and was regarded as secret. It contained the following sentence: "The number of Jewish members may under no circumstances exceed ten per cent of the total membership, and the number of Jewish statutory guests should not exceed twenty-five per cent." Three weeks later the commentary was revised, eliminating the phrase "under no circumstances," and advising that "if possible" the number of Jewish members should not exceed 10 percent. At the meeting of 25 January 1945 the clause was discussed again, and its necessity to maintain the "Swiss" character of the Club was reaffirmed. This clause remained in effect until 1950 when Sigmund Hurwitz, a Kabbalah scholar and Jung's dentist, raised the question in response to Jung's suggestion that he join the Club. Hurwitz said that he would only consider membership when the clause stipulating a quota of Jews was removed. Within six weeks it was eliminated and Hurwitz joined the Club (personal communication).

In spite of the quota, many of Jung's Jewish students were members of the Club during that entire period. Lectures on Jewish subjects were part of its program; for instance, in 1930 James Kirsch gave a lecture entitled "A Contribution to the Problem of the Present-Day Jew in the Light of Modern Psychology." At the time Kirsch was living in Berlin, and he described the difficulty of the modern Jew, recently emancipated from the ghetto, to assimilate the European attitude. The lecture has historical significance, especially in light of the events in Germany and Europe that soon followed.

As one chronicles this segment of history, one sees that twice Jung intervened, each time in favor of Jewish people. Significantly, Jung never sat on the executive committee of the Club and had no administrative authority. Toni Wolff was president at the time of these events, and C.A. Meier and Linda Fierz-David were members of the executive committee. When the quota on Jews was first uncovered by Aryeh Maidenbaum in 1988, it produced a shock within the Jungian community (Maidenbaum and Martin 1991). From today's perspective such quotas are unconscionable, yet in that era they were the rule rather than the exception. Quotas, particularly against Jewish people, were operative in schools, colleges, universities, the workplace, and social clubs, and lasted well into the 1950s in both America and Europe.

Jung's relationship to Nazism and anti-Semitism has surfaced in many different contexts in this book. During the 1980s internal and external pressures led the professional Jungian community to face this issue. At the 1989 International Congress in Paris there were two panels on Jung and anti-Semitism (Mattoon 1990:461–499). The result was a decision by the analysts who attended to ask for an apology from the Analytical Psychology Club of Zurich. Initial efforts by Jerome Bernstein to contact present-day members of the Club failed. The following congress in Chicago in 1992 was attended by Jane Reid who was vice-president of the Club. Ms Reid lived in Zurich in 1944 when her mother was a member of the Club. Through the combined efforts of Ms Reid and John Beebe, they obtained from current members of the Club a letter of apology, dated 28 May 1993 and addressed to the president of the IAAP. The last paragraph of the letter reads as follows: "There is no question that today we regret the events of that time. In other respects we sincerely hope – and, unfortunately, it is only a hope – that all discrimination against anybody, especially against Jews, is a matter of the past" (Mattoon 1996:714).

Formation of the Jung Institute in 1948 shifted the intellectual center of analytical psychology from the Club to that body, where new ideas were then presented. Influence of the Analytical Psychology Club in Zurich has gradually waned, yet despite a lesser role it still functions in a lively fashion with an extensive library and frequent lectures.

3 Analytical psychology in the United Kingdom

INTRODUCTION

Jung was a frequent visitor to the United Kingdom, and England and Switzerland enjoyed close contact on many levels during Jung's lifetime. Although the connections between the two countries were strong, the presentation of Jung's ideas in England took on a definite British flavor. For over five hundred years the British and the Continent had a history of differences in philosophical outlook. British philosophy, from Francis Bacon, John Locke and David Hume in the seventeenth and eighteenth centuries, extending forward to John Stuart Mill in the nineteenth century, and Logical Positivism in the twentieth century, was grounded in an empiricism which did not place an emphasis on inborn human structures. The notion of the *tabula rasa*, or blank screen, was strong in British empiricism. During the lifetimes of David Hume and Immanuel Kant, a fierce battle raged on the nature of reality. Was there an intrinsic, a priori predetermined reality, or was reality only a probability which could be reaffirmed by observation? The argument raged over whether one knew if the sun was going to rise the next day. Was this known for certain (Kant), or was it only highly probable, based upon previous observation (Hume)? The argument was never settled in either of their lifetimes, and it is a question which still concerns modern philosophy. One can transfer the issue to Jung's theories, which have undergone similar changes when utilized by British analytical psychologists. Jung was steeped in Kant's philosophy, and his hypothesis of the collective unconscious and archetypes drew heavily on Kant's notion of the *synthetic a priori* and the *Ding an sich*, the thing in itself. Thus, it was inevitable that Jung's ideas would have to undergo some changes on British soil.

Psychoanalysis was brought to England by Ernest Jones in 1913. The Welshman, who earlier had emigrated to Canada, returned to

London and established the London Psycho-Analytical Society. After Jung he was the most important non-Jewish medical doctor in the psychoanalytic movement. At the time of the Freud–Jung split Jones completely backed Freud in his efforts to rid psychoanalysis of Jung.

Jung's first professional visit to the United Kingdom occurred in July 1914, when he was invited to address the Annual General Meeting of the British Medical Association in Aberdeen, Scotland. His lecture on "The Importance of the Unconscious in Psychopathology," elaborated his theory of psychic compensation. The Great War broke out while Jung was in Scotland, and he and Emma had a difficult time getting home to Switzerland. At the end of the war he returned to give another paper "On the Psychogenesis of Mental Illness" to the Section of Psychiatry of the Royal Society of Medicine. In 1920 he experimented with a seminar format which he was to use for the remainder of his life. His first seminar was on the manuscript of *Psychological Types*. A series of visits followed over a period of twenty years until the onset of World War II. Jung returned to Cornwall in 1923, where he discussed "Primitive Psychology," and to Swanage in 1925 to talk about "Dream Psychology." All three seminars were given to analysands and students of analytical psychology. Probably his most famous visit to England occurred in 1935 when he gave the "Tavistock Lectures" to a group of skeptical doctors, psychologists, psychoanalysts, and psychiatrists at the Tavistock Clinic. The attendees were highly critical at the start, but by the end of the fifth and final lecture, most were deeply touched by Jung's wit, charm, and intelligence. At the last lecture the audience asked Jung to change his topic from archetypal amplification to transference, which Jung reluctantly agreed to do. As part of his irritation with the change in subject, he stated: "Transference or no transference, that has nothing to do with the cure . . . If there is no transference, so much the better" (Jung *CW* 18:151–152). Baynes asked in the discussion, "if transference had no practical value, perhaps it had teleological value?" (Jung *CW* 18:168). Jung reiterated his point that "transference [acts] as a function of compensation for a lack of rapport between the analyst and the patient" (Jung *CW* 18:168). Given the importance that transference/countertransference has come to play in analytical psychology in England today, Jung's comments in 1935 have particular relevance.

Jung had a special fondness for England and the British people. An event of far-reaching consequence was an interview which Jung gave for a BBC television series called *Face to Face* in 1958. The combination of an exposition of his psychology and his views of the world situation, plus the magnetism of his personality, led to an outpouring of interest in his work. In the exchange, the interviewer, John Freeman, asked if Jung believed in God while growing up. Jung replied, "of course!" Then Jung was asked if he believed in God now, and he responded that he no longer "believes," but that now he "knows" in the gnostic sense. This brought out such a flood of questions from the British public that Jung finally issued a two-page explanation of what he meant by the word "know."

An informal group interested in Jung's work began to form during World War I, but none of the people were to remain with Jung, as they either became followers of Gurdjieff or returned to Freudian psychoanalysis. An Analytical Psychology Club, modeled after the Club in Zurich, was formed and held its first meeting on 15 September 1922 at the home of Esther Harding, an English physician. She moved to New York shortly thereafter and became a leading Jungian in America. Five doctors attended the first Club meeting, including Drs Mary Bell, Helen Shaw, Adela Wharton, and H.G. "Peter" Baynes, in addition to Esther Harding. Dr Baynes became the acknowledged leader of the Club, as well as the leading spokesman for Jung in Great Britain.

H.G. "Peter" Baynes (1882–1943)

Peter Baynes was born in 1882 and trained in medicine. Shortly after the Great War he became interested in Jung's psychology and went to Zurich to have analysis. From 1922 until his untimely death in 1943 he represented Jung's ideas in a variety of settings. For example, he addressed the British Psychological Society, the Society for Psychical Research, the British Institute of Philosophical Studies, and other groups which were interested in Jung's theories. Baynes became Jung's first assistant in Zurich in the 1920s, and he organized Jung's Safari to Africa in 1925. In 1928 he spent a year's sabbatical in northern California, where he met young Joseph Henderson and encouraged him to go to Zurich to have analysis with Jung. Baynes' translations of *Psychological Types*, *Contributions to Analytical Psychology*, and in collaboration with Cary Baynes, *Two Essays on Analytical Psychology*, were for many years the main works of Jung available in English. The Baynes translations have been superseded by the *Collected Works* edition. Baynes published two books, *Mythology of the Soul* (1940) and *Germany Possessed* (1941), and the latter brought him public recognition. The former book was a huge opus of amplificatory material on two cases, written in a manner similar to Jung. One of the cases was identifiable as Michael Fordham, which became a lifelong albatross for Fordham. At the same time that he was using Fordham's material in his book, Baynes was grooming Fordham to take over the leadership of the British Jungians after his own death. When Baynes died suddenly of a heart attack in 1943, Fordham had to take on the mantle without much notice. Baynes was an extraverted feeling man, who was married four times, and his third wife, Cary Baynes, was an important figure in the early days of analytical psychology. She translated the *I-Ching* from German into English, and was the co-translator of *Modern Man in Search of a Soul*, a popular book of Jung's essays. Although she was trained in medicine, she never practiced as a Jungian analyst, feeling unprepared for the task. Those who knew her well found her to be most astute psychologically. She lived well into her nineties, alternating between the Ticino in Switzerland and Connecticut in the United States. Cary and Peter Baynes divorced in the late 1930s. He married a much younger woman, Anne, which was reportedly a happy marriage. One can only speculate how differently analytical psychology might have developed had Baynes lived longer. Baynes was deeply devoted to Jung and his way of working with the psyche and was excellent in presenting Jung to both professional and public audiences. The *rapprochement* with psychoanalysis which began in the 1940s would have taken on a different character if Baynes had lived longer. A closer alliance with Jung's views would have been more likely.

EARLY HISTORY

The Analytical Psychology Club quickly grew from the initial five in 1922 to approximately twenty-five members. In the beginning, in order to qualify for membership, all the members had to be analyzed either by Jung or Toni Wolff, but this requirement was quickly changed, and analysis and recommendation by any qualified Jungian analyst became acceptable. Regular lectures, discussion groups on a variety of subjects, and a large library became the main aspects of the Club. As with the Zurich Club, important and ongoing issues were: how to relate as a group, the relationship of the individuation process to group process, and the purpose of the Club. Should the Club focus on inner archetypal issues, or should social and political issues also be considered part of the scope of the Club? What was meant by the name "Club?" Dr Baynes was the leader of these early Club meetings, and he alone was seen as a stand-in for Jung, which he did not appreciate. Membership included doctors who were practicing analysts, and lay people in other fields who had made use of analysis. By 1935 there were five analysts practicing in London. In addition to Peter Baynes, there were Culver Barker, Michael Fordham, Helen Shaw, and a lay analyst Elsie Beckinsale. In 1936 a Medical Society of Analytical Psychology was formed within the Analytical Psychology Club. The separation of the medical analysts produced some tension. At the same time the lay analysts formed their own group within the Club. Within a short period of time they joined the medical analysts to form the Society of Practicing Analysts. In the 1930s several Jungians fleeing the Nazis, such as Gerhard and Hella Adler, James Kirsch, and Erna Rosenbaum, arrived in England, and by the end of the 1930s the group had grown to twelve analysts. No separate organization for analysts existed, but all were part of the growing Analytical Psychology Club. The Medical Society of Analysts was able to formulate standards for training, which had Jung's approval and which were presented to the medical section of the British Psychological Society in 1939 (Fordham 1944a:48–58). World War II put all developments on hold.

SOCIETY OF ANALYTICAL PSYCHOLOGY LONDON (SAP)

The next important date in the history of analytical psychology was 1944 when Michael Fordham proposed a center for analytical psychology. In 1943 the British Medical Association had begun to lay down guidelines for physical and mental health, and Fordham sensed that it was time to establish a professional organization of analytical psychologists which could relate to collective structures. Fordham saw this center as part of the Analytical Psychology Club and not separate from it. In 1944 he stated:

1   It would greatly help the training of analysts and make it possible to assess their practical capability by asking younger trainees and analysts to take patients under supervision. The medical analysts would supervise this process. Emphasizing how important it was for younger analysts and trainees to see patients under supervision, it was the next most important training after one's own personal analysis.

2   If there were a center, it would be easier to attract doctors who would like to train in the methods of analytical psychology. Furthermore, the doctors could then supervise the lay analysts in their work. Having this structure in place would attract doctors returning from the war and give them a place to train.

3   Money was promised to cover the initial costs of such a center. This meant that the center would have to be registered and incorporated, so that there existed an entity to receive the money.

The center as such did not come into being; however, in 1945 the Society of Analytical Psychology was incorporated. The founding members included Gerhard Adler, Culver Barker, Mrs Frieda Fordham, Michael Fordham, Philip Metman, Robert Moody, and Lola Paulsen. Michael Fordham was the initial chairman, as the chair of council had to be a medical person. A clinic was formed where patients could be referred for reduced fee analysis, and the training of analysts in England began. In those early years many prominent psychiatrists entered the training program, and the prestige of Jungian analysis was on the rise.

Special mention should be made of E.A. Bennet, a psychiatrist, who was a lecturer at the Maudsley, one of the most famous psychiatric and psychoanalytic institutions of the time. Bennet was able to introduce Jung's concepts to the students who came to the Maudsley from around the world. Through his influence many psychiatrists, such as Alan Edwards, Robert Hobson, David Howell, Gordon Prince, Leopold Stein, and Anthony Storr, entered training in the SAP. Bennet was special in another way. He and his wife had a close personal relationship with the Jungs. Whenever they went to Zurich, they would stay, or at least meet, with the Jungs, and whenever Jung came to England, Bennet would make all the travel arrangements for the Jungs and Toni Wolff. Bennet was clearly a personal favorite of Jung, and this produced some jealousy and envy among other Jungians. In the early 1950s conflict developed, particularly between Bennet and Fordham, which caused Bennet to withdraw from the SAP for many years. In the late 1950s Fordham reached out with an olive branch, and Bennet returned to membership in the SAP. However, he resigned permanently from the SAP in 1963.

In the decades following World War II the SAP grew rapidly in numbers. Fordham was active in every part of the society and was the head of both the adult and children's sections. In addition to all his duties within the SAP, Jung asked him to be the general editor of the *Collected Works* in English. Sir Herbert Read, the art historian, and Gerhard Adler were added as editors, the latter specifically because of his fluency in the German language. Fordham was also the founder and first editor of the *Journal of Analytical Psychology*, which was and still is sponsored by the SAP. Many of the new trainees were familiar with the theories of Klein, Winnicott, and other psychoanalysts, and their influence carried over into the SAP training.

The period between 1946 and 1953 has been described as the "halcyon days" (Casement 1995). The war was over and professional lives could develop again, and relative harmony existed within the SAP. Twice-weekly analysis for trainees was required, and the divisiveness which was to arise over frequency of sessions and transference was not yet on the horizon.

By the late 1950s the training requirements were changed to stipulate a minimum of three-times-a-week analysis, placing greater emphasis on infancy and early childhood and the analysis of the transference/countertransference. Active imagination, amplification, and other typical Jungian methods were going out of favor with many analysts in Britain. Archetypal symbolism was found in relationship to the body of the analyst rather than in impersonal symbolic images, and the instinctual pole of archetypal theory was being emphasized. Fordham described the young baby's development in terms of "deintegration and reintegration." The following quotes from Fordham illustrate how his reading of Jung carries forth the point of view of the British empirical philosophers, minimizing Jung's Kantian background. Deintegration is described as:

> the spontaneous division of the self into parts – a manifest necessity if consciousness is ever to rise . . . It is the spontaneous property of the self behind ego formation.
>
> (Fordham 1957:117)

> Like the ethologists' "innate release mechanism" the deintegrate potentiates a "readiness for experience, a readiness to perceive and act" even though there is as yet "not an actual perception or action."
>
> (Fordham 1957:127)

> A deintegrate of the self would retain characteristics of wholeness.
>
> (Fordham 1985:54)

This model of ego development became the model of individuation in childhood which Fordham and others put forth. The argument between British empiricism and continental philosophy was being played out in the theoretical discussions of analytical psychology.

The first occasion where these differences were aired was at the Second International Congress for Analytical Psychology held in Zurich in 1962. A paper by Murray Jackson, a SAP member, on the meaning of the term "symbol," was strongly criticized by Esther Harding. The tension which had been developing between the "London" attitude and the "Zurich" point of view came out into the open and caused a division between the soon to be named "London school" and the "Zurich school." The "London school" eventually became the "developmental" school, and in 1962 most analytical psychologists supported the Zurich point of view. The *Journal of Analytical Psychology*, founded in 1955, began as a clinical journal for English-speaking Jungians. In the first few years of its existence papers on a wide range of viewpoints and subjects were published. After the congress of 1962 and the beginning of the developmental school, the journal took a turn toward a more scientific and clinical approach, and papers on traditional Jungian themes were no longer welcomed. This editorial policy continued for the next fifteen years. When Fred Plaut took over the editorship of the *Journal of Analytical Psychology* in 1971, he introduced a more eclectic editorial attitude towards papers written for the journal which continues to this day. The emphasis on clinical issues remains, but a variety of attitudes and methods are now included. The developmental school made its point, and many Jungians came to see the importance of that perspective.

THE SAP/AJA SPLIT

As the developmental approach within the SAP became more firmly established, the analysts and candidates who adhered to a more classical Jungian approach were not comfortable in this setting. The tension between the two has often been described as a personal conflict between Michael Fordham and Gerhard Adler, which Fordham denied, claiming that the differences were theoretical. Adler complained that his trainees were not acceptable at the SAP, and that his seminars were poorly attended. By 1975 Adler and his colleagues were ready to form their own group, where the more traditional Jungian positions could be expressed. The conflict bore a semblance to the one in British psychoanalysis between Melanie Klein and Anna Freud. After many years of feuding, the British Psycho-Analytical Society resolved the tension by developing three groups, a Klein group, an Anna Freud group, and a third "middle group," all under the umbrella of the British Psycho-Analytic Society. In this fashion a formal split was averted.

The warring factions within the SAP hoped to resolve their conflict in a similar way to the British Psycho-Analytical Society. In 1975 and 1976 five meetings took place to see if a compromise solution could be worked out. Eventually, Adler stated that his hurt and anger towards the SAP were too great, and that it was necessary to invest his energy in the founding of a new group, which was named the Association of

Jungian Analysts (Alternative Training). The SAP gave its blessing to this new group, and it was encouraged by the IAAP executive committee. Both returning Zurich graduates and English analysts of a more classical persuasion needed their own forum. The AJA was accepted as a group member of the IAAP in 1977. The split into two groups provided a sense of relief both to the two groups in the United Kingdom as well as the international Jungian community which had been a party to the ongoing struggle.

Gerhard Adler (1904–1988)

The two protagonists in this conflict could not have been more different from each other. Gerhard Adler was born in Berlin of German-Jewish extraction. He began his analysis with James Kirsch in 1929 in Berlin and from 1931–1934 was in analysis with Jung. In 1935 he and his wife, Hella, fled to England to escape Nazi persecution. He had a doctorate in psychology and was one of the original non-medical analysts in the SAP. His book, *Studies in Analytical Psychology*, written in 1948, is still widely read as an introductory text to Jung's psychology. A second book, *The Living Symbol* (1961a), is a case study of a traditional Jungian analysis. He was the co-editor with Aniela Jaffé of the published letters of C.G. Jung, a member of the editorial committee of the *Collected Works* in English, and from 1971–1977 a two-term president of the IAAP. Gerhard Adler, along with his wife Hella, was the intellectual and spiritual leader of the AJA. When the AJA developed splits of its own later on, Adler devoted the last few years of his life attempting to resolve those tensions. He no longer published any articles or books in analytical psychology, and his role in the ensuing split within the AJA left his reputation tarnished. Although he had received wide support from the international Jungian community in his struggles with Fordham, when similar political battles occurred within the AJA, he was seen in a less favorable light.

Adler was a close associate of Jung from the early 1930s until Jung's death. Originally Adler was asked by Jung to contribute a chapter to *Man and His Symbols*. Adler withdrew his contribution over a dispute with the publisher.

Michael Fordham (1905–1995)

Michael Fordham was one of the most creative first-generation analysts after Jung, and he was the acknowledged leader of analytical psychology in England for over fifty years (1943–1995). He was born into a family of landowners, the youngest of three children. His father was in local politics and his mother, whom he adored, had trained to be an opera singer. She died as the result of an asthmatic attack when Michael was fifteen, and family life as he had known it came to an end. He went on to study medicine and physiology at Cambridge University. Through the intermediary of H.G. "Peter" Baynes, a friend of the family, Michael was introduced to Jung's writings and in 1933 began a short (seven months) analysis with Baynes. In 1934 Fordham traveled to Zurich, but when he was not allowed to work in Switzerland he could not afford to have an analysis with Jung. Instead, he did another short stint of analysis with Baynes in the years 1935–1936. Subsequently Fordham wrote to Jung about changing analysts and asked for Jung's opinion about Hilde Kirsch, whom he had met at meetings of the Analytical Psychology Club in London. At the time he approached her for analysis, she was a nursing mother and had no intention of becoming an analyst. However, Michael Fordham not only became her first analytical patient, but in this process Jung indirectly legitimized her as an analyst. Fordham's analysis with Hilde Kirsch continued until October 1940, when – during the Battle of Britain – she emigrated to the United States on short notice. Little is known about the content of Fordham's analysis with Hilde Kirsch. Fordham states in his autobiography, *The Making of an Analyst* (1993), that as he was developing an erotic transference towards his analyst, she handled it by inviting him for dinner to meet her husband. Thus, Fordham had one very public analysis, written up for posterity in a book, and the other quite personal and foreshortened by the exigencies of the war. Hilde Kirsch's departure from England in 1940 concluded Fordham's formal Jungian analysis.

Before leaving the subject of Fordham's analyses, an interpretation of what it meant for Fordham, and subsequently the future of analytical psychology in the United Kingdom, is relevant. It is my opinion that the combination of not seeing Jung, having a public analysis with Baynes, and having Hilde Kirsch terminate the analysis abruptly, left him with wounds which never healed. While most of his other first-generation colleagues and friends were in analysis with Jung, Fordham was denied this experience, and this affected his feelings towards Jung for the rest of his life. He loved and respected Jung very much, but without the direct experience of analysis with him he always felt outside the inner circle. It leaves one to wonder whether envy and jealousy colored his relationships to Gerhard Adler and E.A. Bennet, both of whom had close personal relationships to Jung following their analyses. Fordham had little money when he sought out analysis, and Baynes charged little for the sessions, but in return received permission from Fordham to publish his drawings and active imaginations. The description in Baynes' book, *Mythology of the Soul* (1940), made Fordham identifiable and labeled him a schizophrenic. Subsequent history shows that the diagnosis was wrong. Fordham must have had borderline characteristics as a young man, but his subsequent development and genius showed that he had mastered his most severe psychopathology. Furthermore, his second analyst, Hilde Kirsch, suddenly leaving England during the war, repeated the experience of the loss of his mother. There are several pieces of evidence which point toward the significance of the experience for him. James Astor's excellent book, *Michael Fordham* (1995), reports that Fordham's analysis ended in 1939, when it actually continued until September 1940. This demonstrates the extent of the deprivation which Fordham experienced when Hilde Kirsch left. In personal conversation with the author, Fordham stated that he found the analysis with Hilde Kirsch helpful in grounding him as a young adult man, but it was not analysis in his sense of the term. To illustrate the circumstances, it should be pointed out that the author was the baby being nursed at the time Fordham first made the call to Hilde Kirsch.

During the period of his analyses, 1933–1940, Fordham was in child psychiatric training, where he was in contact with the various psychoanalytic currents then available. He was influenced principally by Melanie Klein's work because her views on early unconscious fantasy were compatible in his mind to archetypal theory. He was attracted to her method of doing analysis with children. In *The Life of Childhood* (1944b), revised as *Children as Individuals* (1969), Fordham outlined a theory of child development which was as dependent upon the nature of the child as that of the parents. In a later formulation he stated that "the ego grows out of the interaction between deintegrates and the environmental mother, and her extensions" (Fordham 1985:36). Prior to that Jung theorized that the child's psychology was completely dependent upon the unconscious psyche of the parents and one only needed to analyze the parents in order to cure the child. This view had been elaborated by Frances Wickes in her *Inner World of Childhood* (1927).

Fordham introduced infant-observation into the training of child analysts. His interactions with psychoanalysts had a mutually long-lasting, beneficial result, with the inclusion in the theory of analytical psychology of many insights from psychoanalysis and psychoanalytic technique. The majority of analytical psychologists in England practice a mixture of analytical psychology and object-relations theory as a result of the pioneering efforts of Fordham. His theory of child development has permeated analytical psychology. His work on both the syntonic and illusory aspects of transference and countertransference has been generally accepted. Fordham evoked powerful reactions both positively and negatively. He often described himself as an *"enfant terrible,"* and he could be extremely provocative at meetings. His status within the worldwide Jungian community was controversial during the late 1950s and early 1960s when he championed the "developmental" over and against the "classical" point of view. A further issue was that Fordham did not acknowledge that he had changed his views from a more traditional Jungian to one which explicitly included British object-relations theory. When another training program, the Association of Jungian Analysts, was formed in 1976, and it began to have political battles of its own, general opinions swung back in favor of Fordham. By then Fordham's work had begun to be more widely accepted, and he sensed that he was no longer considered a maverick.

His position mellowed as he aged, and in his later years he expressed more appreciation towards all aspects of analytical psychology. Frequently he was asked why he had remained a Jungian, when it seemed that his theories were more consonant with object-relations theory. He always replied that he was "Jungian" and that he was extending Jung's research. Then, with a twinkle in his eye, he would say, "It wouldn't look good if the founder of analytical psychology in England defected to another school, would it?" (personal communication, November 1994). Fordham was destined to find his own individual path. He published several books on analytic technique, the self, Jungian psychotherapy, and a short autobiography, *The Making of an Analyst* (1993). By the time of his death in 1995 his status as one of the truly great pioneers in analytical psychology was ensured.

Baroness von der Heydt (1899–1996)

The Baroness was a most unusual person who had an extremely interesting and long life. She was brought up in a German-Jewish business household, but she married into non-Jewish German nobility with Kaiser Wilhelm II in attendance at the wedding. The marriage ended in divorce, and with rampaging inflation in Germany after the Great War, her financial situation changed. As a young woman, in the 1920s, she met Jung at a lecture at the School of Wisdom in Darmstadt. In a circuitous manner she ended up in England where she trained as a psychotherapist. She began analysis with John Layard during World War II, and soon after the war went to Zurich for analysis with Jung, who remembered her from the Darmstadt days. The Baroness returned to London and became an active member of the SAP. Although not particularly close to the Adlers, she was theoretically aligned with them and became a founding member of the AJA, while retaining her membership in the SAP. She converted to Catholicism as an adult and became concerned with matters of psychology and religion. Her commanding presence, her eloquence of speech, and her strong personality left a deep impression on all those who met her, and people sought out her sage advice. For most of the last decade of her life she lived in a Catholic retirement home, where she saw a steady stream of visitors. Although bedridden, her mind was absolutely clear, her opinions definite, and her passion for the psyche and spirit obvious. She died age ninety-six in 1996.

AJA AND IGAP

From 1977 through 1981 the AJA thrived. The two populations, one classically trained in London and one classically trained in Zurich, coexisted harmoniously, and the Adlers were the acknowledged leaders. However, in 1982 a serious problem developed when a long-standing member, applying to become a training analyst, was turned down by the AJA. A second long-standing member, who also wished to become a training analyst and feared the same outcome, threatened war if the first member was not made a training analyst. War broke out!

The new division within the AJA also displayed a London–Zurich split. The London-trained analysts within the AJA were more clinically based, advocating three-times-per-week analysis, emphasis on transference, and strict boundaries in the analytic setting. However, to distinguish themselves from SAP analysts they were theoretically aligned with the classical prospective approach to the unconscious over an emphasis on infancy. On the other hand, the Zurich-trained members of the AJA did not specify three-times-per-week analysis, nor was transference analysis as central to their work as it was to the London-trained AJA members. The Zurich-trained people utilized a model which Jung himself had used in the early days of analytical psychology, and one which was still prevalent in Zurich at that time. A further issue, which occurs in every country where there is a Jungian training, was the acceptance of Zurich-diploma candidates upon return to their home country. To join the AJA they had to see a case under supervision and attend monthly meetings for a year before being assessed by the professional committee. This was not easily accepted by the Zurich-trained analysts who had just undergone a most rigorous academic training and did not feel that they should be submitted to yet another examination upon their return to their own country. It appeared to be a criticism of their training.

The situation came to a head in June 1982 at the Annual General Meeting, when it was time to elect a new chairman. The membership evenly divided with twelve votes for each candidate. No amicable decision could be reached between the two factions, and the hostility among the senior members, who were also evenly divided, was intense. The AJA was completely paralyzed and turned to the IAAP for mediation in the conflict. In October 1982 Gerhard Adler presented his point of view and the complicated details of the situation to the IAAP executive committee. Although Adler was a past president of the IAAP, the committee did not find his views of the conflict to be persuasive and feared that he was just trying to hold on to power, as the AJA was unraveling before his very eyes. At the Jerusalem Congress in 1983 the IAAP executive committee took up the issue again, and AJA members of each side presented their views. In the end the IAAP executive committee recommended suspension for the AJA until a resolution between the two factions could be reached. As a vice-president of the IAAP at the time and a native English speaker, the author spoke to all sides in AJA and SAP both before and during the suspension. No resolution was in sight. The split-off group of the AJA, the "Independents" as they were called, were organizing a study program along the lines of an academic institution, offering specific courses in analytical psychology, with little emphasis on training. They did not want the responsibility of training analysts, which always evoked so many power issues. They wanted to offer analytical psychology under less stressful conditions.

No resolution of the stalemate was in sight at the beginning of the following international congress in Berlin. Finally, a private deal was made between the IAAP president and the British professional societies, whereby both the AJA and the Independents would become group members of the IAAP, and another group, the British Association of Psychotherapists (BAP), would be accepted as a fourth separate professional group from the United Kingdom. The BAP had wished to join the IAAP for many years but had not found suitable conditions to make an application. The BAP was closely aligned with the SAP, and the turmoil within the AJA was just the stimulus that the BAP needed to make its own application. The symmetry of the situation, the number four, so important in Jungian circles, and the relief to have found an agreeable solution, prompted the IAAP delegates to readily accept the plan and accredit the four professional societies. In addition to the SAP and the AJA, there was now the BAP and the split-off group from the AJA, the Independent Group of Analytical Psychologists (IGAP).

The BAP warrants further description, because it has a structure unique to Jungian training programs. It was founded in 1951 as The Association of Psychotherapists, changed to the "British Association of Psychotherapy" in 1972. After World War II training in psychoanalysis was limited, and there was a need for another training center. Initially there was only a Freudian section, but in 1965 Marianne Jacoby was asked to found a parallel training for Jungians. Marianne Jacoby, a German-Jewish refugee, had come to England in 1936, having studied psychology in Germany and Austria. She and her husband were close friends of James and Hilde Kirsch, and she entered Jungian analysis. Marianne Jacoby remained outside the official Jungian circles but worked in a Jungian orientation. She was a member of the BAP and in 1965 was asked to organize a Jungian training section within the BAP. In 1974 she was made an individual member of the IAAP in recognition for her work in organizing training at the BAP. The Freudian and Jungian tracks have been separate, and there has been a joint chairperson who was almost always a Freudian, because there were many more Freudian than Jungian members in the BAP. Only one Jungian, Hester Solomon, held the chairmanship of the joint council. Attempts have been made to integrate the two trainings, but to no avail. However, the Jungian track is parallel to the Freudian track inasmuch as both the training analysis and training cases must be three times a week. Senior SAP analysts like Rosemary Gordon, Hugh Gee, and Alison Lyons have taken an active part in the Jungian BAP training, as have senior analysts from the British Psycho-Analytical Society in the Freudian section. Thus, the Jungian training in the BAP is similar to that of the SAP. To include the BAP Jungian section as a fourth group in the IAAP seemed reasonable.

The compromise solution happened so quickly that members of the executive committee had scarcely an opportunity to appraise the longer-term implications. There was and is a structural issue with the BAP Jungian section. It does not concern the quality of the training but the fact that the BAP Jungian section is not an independent society. It is a minority section within a much larger Freudian section. Thus, it does not have the freedom to act independently, and one could theoretically have the British Psycho-Analytical Society influencing the Jungian section of the BAP through the joint BAP and, thus, the policies of the IAAP. If the structure of the BAP could have been studied in more detail before the IAAP congress, this issue could have been clarified.

Each society is an "all England" organization, but most of the members of all four societies reside and practice within greater London.

The IGAP and the AJA are approximately half the size of the SAP or the BAP, and they all seem to be functioning.

SUMMARY: BRITISH GROUPS

The reasons why these splits occur in psychoanalytical circles are unclear. Unfortunately they are rather common. Differences in ideology, clinical practice, and personalities, plus power issues, are usually at stake. Each developing society has a problem with incest. The founding fathers and mothers take on a number of roles, including analyst, supervisor, teacher, and often some important role with significant others of the candidates and new analysts. How the founders play out this role is crucial. Whether the founders can let go of the authority as the younger analysts grow and develop is a central point. In the British situation one can think of the Jung/Fordham relationship. At the First International Congress in Zurich in 1958 it was clear that Michael Fordham was interpreting Jung's theories in a new way which was not consonant with the classical Jungian point of view. Many of the classical analysts thought that Fordham was no longer "Jungian," and that some action should be taken against him. However, Jung was open to Fordham's innovations and encouraged others, like Marie-Louise von Franz and Barbara Hannah, to let him be (personal communication, Joseph Henderson). Jung realized that his students needed to find their own paths, just as he had done in relation to Freud. On the other hand, Gerhard Adler in the AJA did not give the same freedom to the younger analysts. The Adlers wanted all the candidates to have either supervision or analysis with them, and many balked at this requirement. As most of the candidates were in analysis with them in any case, both the positive and negative transferences were often acted out within the professional society. Whether this kind of splitting of societies is creative or destructive is not easy to judge. Adler thought that the split was creative for the situation in England (Casement 1995). Clearly, it depends upon the individual situation and events over time. Since the 1986 division, the four societies in England have been coexisting.

THE UMBRELLA GROUP

In 1986 when it was agreed that there would be four groups in England, then-IAAP-president Dieckmann asked Andrew Samuels to organize an umbrella group consisting of representatives from all four groups. From informal beginnings the meetings of the umbrella group are now being held on a quarterly basis, with each society rotating as the host. Lively and heated discussions on issues of mutual concern, including the Jung archives, joint conferences and workshops, the Jung Memorial Lecture, and Jungian politics are held. One of the first decisions made was the elimination of "Alternative Training" from the name of the AJA. There seems to be a growing liaison among the four professional groups and the Analytical Psychology Club, and there is a possibility for cooperation. However, given the stormy background and development of analytical psychology in Great Britain, it is no wonder that professional politics are an important element of the discussions and provoke the most passion.

Two much larger umbrella organizations have been founded in Great Britain, the United Kingdom Council for Psychotherapy (U.K.C.P.), and the British Confederation of Psychotherapists (B.C.P.). The U.K.C.P. is the true umbrella organization for all psychotherapists in England, which numbers over 3,000 psychotherapists of all persuasions. All the Jungian organizations are members of this umbrella organization. In 1992 the B.C.P. was formed to be an umbrella organization for all psychoanalytic organizations. The members of the B.C.P. were not comfortable having the broad spectrum of psychotherapists representing psychoanalytic issues. Both the SAP and the BAP have become members of the B.C.P., but the IGAP and the AJA have not been invited to join. Standards are the issue, and this is expressed in terms of the frequency of sessions per week for analytic candidates, and the frequency with which clinic patients are seen by the candidates. The procedures by which candidates are made professional members is a key requirement. What constitutes the "standards" of the B.C.P. has been divisive to the Jungian community in England. The IGAP and particularly the AJA have been extremely upset that their criteria for training have not been deemed acceptable to the B.C.P. The AJA's formal standards meet the requirements of the B.C.P. Recently, in 1998, for the first time a Jungian, Ann Casement, has been made the chair of the U.K.C.P., and perhaps her leadership can help to assuage some of the partisan conflicts.

A further problem concerns the title of "analyst" (Casement 1995). In Great Britain a distinction between psychoanalysis and psycho-analytically oriented psychotherapy is made, and only members of the British Psycho-Analytical Society may call themselves "psychoanalysts." Thus, Freudian members of the BAP may not call themselves "psycho-analysts," whereas the Jungian members, by virtue of their membership in the IAAP, may call themselves "Jungian analysts." However, within the B.C.P. the Jungian members of the BAP are called "Analytical

Psychologists – Jungian," whereas the SAP members are referred to as "Analyst – Jungian." In the U.K.C.P. the members of all four Jungian groups are called "Analytical Psychologist–Jungian Analyst."

These subtle differences in name imply a hierarchy within both the Freudian and Jungian communities. Within the Jungian community the SAP sees itself as the true carrier of analytical psychology in England so that they are entitled to claim the term "analyst." They were the original society and have the tradition of upholding analytical psychology within the United Kingdom. However, rivalries, competition, and feelings of superiority and inferiority abound among the four groups. The question of identity, "Who is a true 'Jungian'?" is ever present in England. It is expressed in these different labels and who is admitted into the more prestigious umbrella group, the B.C.P. These issues are discussed within the Jungian umbrella group, but the emotional level is such that not much progress has been made.

According to Ann Casement, the atmosphere in the Jungian umbrella group has begun to change. She notes that there are differences within each society, as well as between all the societies. The umbrella group has sponsored joint workshops and lectures, as well as two memorial lectures with speakers from abroad. As the groups work together, Casement believes that there is a growing acceptance of the differences among the groups.

CURRENT STATUS OF ANALYTICAL PSYCHOLOGY

It was in this atmosphere of *Sturm und Drang* in London that Andrew Samuels developed his classification of analytical psychologists into classical, developmental, and archetypal schools. Briefly summarized, the classical school, consciously working in Jung's tradition, focuses on self and individuation. The developmental school has a specific focus on the importance of infancy in the evolution of the adult personality, and an equally important emphasis on the analysis of the transference and countertransference. The developmental school has a close relationship to psychoanalysis, although influence in the opposite direction is not significant. The archetypal school focuses on imagery in therapy with little emphasis on developmental issues. When Samuels' book *Jung and the Post-Jungians* came out in 1985, most analysts did not like being labeled in this way, as it went against the grain of individuality and authenticity.

Since the book's publication there has been a continual evolution of the tripartite division. The classical and developmental schools still exist, but the archetypal school as a clinical discipline never gained acceptance as a separate entity in England. The archetypal school has either been integrated or eliminated, probably a bit of both. In the evolution of the classical and developmental schools extensions have developed at both ends of the spectrum, which qualify as separate schools. On the classical side, a new (ultra-classical) school has developed which emphasizes the original works of Jung and Marie-Louise von Franz (Research and Training Centre in Depth Psychology). At the other end of the spectrum are those analysts who have become primarily psychoanalytic but originally trained at Jungian Institutes. Rather than using psychoanalytic concepts in a Jungian way, those who would proffer "merging" in the Winnicottian sense, adopt the rules of abstinence and neutrality in a psychoanalytic way, value the psychoanalytic frame over the analytic relationship, and value transference/countertransference over fantasy and dream images. The enthusiasm for psychoanalysis has come about through Jungian analysts who are not satisfied with either their classical or developmental Jungian analysis. They found a more satisfying analysis within the psychoanalytic model. An idealization follows which states that psychoanalysis is in some way superior to the Jungian way, and that all Jungians should follow the psychoanalytic way. This has been a common pattern in many countries, including Great Britain, the United States, and Germany.

If the classification into four types, ultra-classical, classical, developmental, and "merging" with psychoanalysis is recognized, there are four professional societies and the Analytical Psychology Club in England where these attitudes are expressed. The Analytical Psychology Club has continued to exist all these years, and members of each professional society are both members and speakers at the Club. The main interest of the Club is in the direction of classical Jungian themes, and the focus is on philosophical and cultural issues. The IGAP members are predominantly labeled as classically oriented, but with some interest in developmental issues. The AJA membership is probably equally divided in its interest between classically and developmentally oriented analysts. The SAP and the BAP are basically developmentally oriented. The ultra-classical has the least representation. These labels are general and serve as orientation to the situation of analytical psychology in Britain.

Clearly, there is communication back and forth among the groups on an informal level as well as by means of the umbrella group. As the actual leaders involved in the splits retire and recede into the background, tension among the groups has lessened. At the time of writing there is still little crossing over in terms of teaching and supervision, but one hopes that this might change in the future. For the moment each society is functioning in an independent manner.

RELATIONSHIP OF ANALYTICAL PSYCHOLOGY TO PSYCHOANALYSIS

Analytical psychology in England has been heavily influenced by psychoanalytic thinking, but formal contact between the two has been minimal. Michael Fordham was an exception since in 1945, through his friendship with the psychoanalyst John Rickman, he began a forum between psychoanalysts and analytical psychologists in the medical section of the British Psychological Society (Astor 1995). In 1962 Fordham was elected chairman of the Royal–Medical Psychological Association, which later became the Royal College of Psychiatrists. However, in spite of these important positions, analytical psychologists have not been able to obtain formal recognition from the British psychoanalytic community. To demonstrate this problem Robert Wallerstein, in his presidential address "One Psychoanalysis or Many" to the International Psychoanalytic Association, concluded that in the future there would really have to be many psychoanalyses (Wallerstein 1988). Every kind of psychoanalytic model was included, except the Jungian, because Jungians did not believe in "the facts of transference and resistance." To make his point Wallerstein quoted a paper by Goodheart (1984) on Jung's relationship to his niece when he was twenty-one as evidence that Jungians did not believe in transference. Wallerstein, as Professor of Psychiatry at the University of California in San Francisco, has had frequent contact with Jungians. Wallerstein's statement, however, reveals the problem that analytical psychologists encounter in receiving formal recognition from psychoanalysis. In the United Kingdom there has been arguably more contact between psychoanalysis and analytical psychology than in any other country, but in spite of the contact there are no formal ties. One senses that the British Psycho-Analytical Society has the authority, and that all other analytic societies, including the Jungian ones, recognize it for their professional identity.

JUNG AND ACADEMIA

As in most other countries, Jung and analytical psychology have generally developed outside the academic setting. However, in 1993 the Centre for Psychoanalytic Studies at the University of Essex was founded. It offers a range of post-graduate degree courses, public lectures, short specialist courses, and opportunities for research (Papadopoulos 1996:94–97). Subsequently the Society of Analytical Psychology established a Chair in Analytical Psychology for that Centre. Since the fall of 1995 Renos Papadopoulos and Andrew Samuels are equally sharing the half-time position. This position has been widely discussed in the media and in professional circles, and the placement of the Centre structurally in the midst of a university has been a positive opening for analytical psychology. There is contact with other departments within the university, and the students participate in a rich and varied psychoanalytic curriculum. It is still too early to report any specific results from this program.

SUMMARY

The history of the development of analytical psychology in England has been tumultuous, with numerous conflicts and splits. The interest in analytical psychology has been consistently strong from its inception in 1913 until the present. Jung liked visiting England, speaking English, and had many British friends and colleagues, including Baynes and Bennet. The sudden death of Peter Baynes in 1943 left a vacuum in leadership within the Jungian community. Michael Fordham, the heir apparent, was only thirty-eight at the time, and his relationship to Jung was and continued to be ambivalent for the rest of his life. The transition in leadership took place during World War II, when communication between England and Switzerland was not possible. By the time the war ended, Jung had suffered a near-fatal heart attack in 1944. He always had limited energy for organizational aspects of his psychology, and after 1945 he withdrew even more.

The first split occurred within the Jungian ranks when Fordham and Bennet had grave differences about the direction of the SAP. This happened in the early 1950s, and Bennet withdrew from the SAP without resigning. This split is not so well known. In the late 1950s Bennet returned to an active status within the SAP but finally resigned in 1963 when the developmental school became predominant. By 1963 Fordham was openly espousing Klein, Winnicott, and other British psychoanalytic theorists and emphasizing their importance in the practice of analytical psychology. Meanwhile Gerhard Adler continued to theorize and practice in a more classical Jungian fashion. Adler complained about the fact that his colleagues were being marginalized within the

SAP. When the tension within the SAP developed, most of the sympathies of the Jungians outside of England resided with Adler, and Fordham was seen as the deviant from the Jungian position. In 1976 it was decided to form an alternative association for Jungian training, known as the Association of Jungian Analysts (AJA), with Gerhard Adler as the leader. There was peace for a few years, and the two societies seemed to function in a parallel fashion. However, a split developed within the AJA between the Zurich-trained, and the English-trained clinically oriented practitioners. This split was even more emotional than the one between the "developmental" or Fordham-oriented and the "classical" or Adler-oriented schools. When Adler was again at the center of an even more tumultuous storm, the attitudes towards the earlier conflict began to shift, and the international Jungian community began to realize that Adler, for all his intellectual and analytical gifts, was difficult when it came to questions of power. Jungians in general, and not just in England, were becoming much more interested in the interface between analytical psychology and psychoanalysis, symbolized by Fordham.

Most analytical psychologists in England practice some hybrid of analytical psychology and object-relations psychoanalysis at the present time. Those who practice a more classical Jungian therapy are in the minority. The political issues of an umbrella organization of all analytical psychologists in England has not been settled. It is important to emphasize that the historical developments in England have foreshadowed similar events in other countries. Because of Fordham's individual relationship to psychoanalysts and his particular relationship to Jung, these events occurred in England decades earlier than in other countries.

The four British professional societies will host the next International Congress in Cambridge in the year 2001, which will be the first international Jungian congress in England since 1974. The political influence on all psychotherapies in the United Kingdom continues to plague analytic groups, but the Jungians are on better terms with each other than they have been since before World War II. It means that each group has settled down, and the four hundred-plus Jungian analysts are doing analytic work with their patients in a peaceful atmosphere and continue to be creative in the field of analytical psychology.

4 Analytical psychology in New York

GENERAL INTRODUCTION

The history of the development of analytical psychology in the United States is a complex story, involving many people, covering vast distances, and extending over a considerable time period. In contrast to most European countries where there is a concentration of cultural activities in the capital city, one does not find the same degree of focus in the United States. At the time of Jung's first visit in 1909 the nation was still in a state of westward expansion. East coast institutions dominated intellectual life and psychological studies. Analytical psychology first took root in New York, and two decades passed before it got established in San Francisco and Los Angeles. These three centers developed relatively independent of one another and have unique histories. They developed during Jung's lifetime, and he had contact with individuals of each center. New Jungian groups did not develop in the United States until the early 1970s.

Jung visited the United States before he founded a separate school of psychology. In fact, Jung made three trips to the United States between 1909 and 1912 as an adherent of psychoanalysis and colleague of Freud. These visits were mainly to the eastern seaboard, centered around Boston and New York. Both Freud and Jung were widely acclaimed on their first visit in 1909 and were enthusiastically greeted by the medical elite and the intellectual establishment. One prominent example of this phenomenon was James Jackson Putnam of Harvard Medical School, regarded as the founder of American neurology. When Freud and Jung made their famous ocean voyage together to speak at Clark University in Worcester, Massachusetts, they spent a five-day vacation at the Putnam Camp in the Adirondacks. Putnam was a member of a group of Harvard professors, including his close friend William James, who had been holding regular discussions and seances on spiritualism for over twenty-five years. Jung, with his research in these matters, greatly appealed to this group. Thus, Jung was better known and perhaps more eagerly received than Freud in the United States during the first decade of this century (Taylor 1998). William James, the father of American psychology, who met both Freud and Jung in 1909, felt much more attuned to Jung than Freud. He thought that Freud was obsessed with sexual matters and had too narrow a view of human nature, whereas Jung's emphasis on spiritual matters appealed to his own nature. Putnam, on the other hand, remained closer to Freud. However, through his cousin Fanny Bowditch Katz, whom he sent to Jung for analysis, Putnam kept up an indirect contact with Jung until his death in 1918. Ms Bowditch sent him frequent letters describing her analysis with Jung (Noll 1997).

The conference to celebrate twenty-five years of psychology at Clark University in October 1909 was a historic event. Clark University, under Stanley Hall, had the leading psychology department in the United States. Since most of the other prominent centers of psychology were located abroad, many famous psychologists from Europe were invited to participate in this week-long celebration. Jung and Freud were invited independently to participate and both were given honorary doctorates. Jung was only thirty-four years old at the time. Freud invited Sandor Ferenczi along as his guest, and the three made the long ocean voyage together. During the week-long journey Freud and Jung analyzed each other's dreams, and this has been the subject of much speculation and continued controversy (Jones 1953). What we do know from Jung's letters to his wife is that he fell in love with the United States, and Freud did not. This was to be Freud's only visit to America whereas for Jung it was to be the first of many. He returned the following year on an emergency basis to see a patient, Joseph Medill McCormick, scion of a wealthy Chicago family, who suffered a relapse in his battle with alcoholism (McGuire 1995).

In 1912 Jung returned once more to deliver a series of lectures on psychoanalysis at the medical school of Fordham University in New York. One could make a strong case that analytical psychology, as a separate field, had its initial public expression then and there. Although we know from the Freud–Jung correspondence and Jung's publication of the "*Wandlungen und Symbole der Libido*" in the *Jahrbuch* (English translation: *Psychology of the Unconscious* [1991]) that differences in viewpoints were emerging, it was only in the Fordham lectures that Jung made these differences explicit and public. While accepting Freud's view of infantile sexuality, he relativized its importance and began to state that a neurosis develops because of a conflict in the present, and that one must analyze the *actual present* to rid the person of suffering. Furthermore, Jung expanded the concept of libido beyond Freud, who defined it primarily in terms of sexual and aggressive drives. Jung defined libido as psychic energy in general, inclusive of sex and aggression, and consisting of other primary drives as well, such as the nutritive and the spiritual. In his preface Jung stated "my criticism does not proceed from academic arguments, but from experiences which have forced themselves on me during the ten years of serious work in the field" (Jung *CW* 4). Freud could not accept Jung's direction in psychoanalysis, and this was the beginning of analytical psychology as a separate field. World War I and Jung's period of introversion only slowed down the pace of its eventual development.

Between 1912 and 1940 only a few individuals practiced analytical psychology in the United States. New York was the only city where analysts began to form a group.

EARLY HISTORY

The first Jungian in the United States was Beatrice Hinkle, a physician who made the first English translation of *Wandlungen und Symbole der Libido* as *Psychology of the Unconscious* in 1916. The translation was widely and enthusiastically reviewed in both the English and American press (Shamdasani 1998b). Beatrice Hinkle has the further distinction of having set up the first psychotherapy clinic of any kind in the United States at the Cornell Medical College in New York in 1908. She studied and analyzed with Jung in 1911 and then returned to New York, where she joined Constance Long, a British physician who had also analyzed with Jung, and two American physicians, Eleanor Bertine and Kristine Mann. The four physicians formed a small study group. Beatrice Hinkle is not as well known as some of the others, probably because she tried to alter Jung's theory of typology, adding two subtypes which she called the emotional introvert and the subjective extravert (Henderson 1982). Her book *Recreation of the Individual* failed in its purpose and did not survive its first printing. However, she was a well-respected psychiatrist and did practice as a Jungian in New York until the late 1940s. The two younger women, Eleanor Bertine and Kristine Mann, had met as medical students at Cornell Medical College, where Beatrice Hinkle held a position in the Neurology Department. In 1919 Eleanor Bertine arranged for Drs Hinkle and Long, established analysts, to speak before an International Conference of Medical Women. Dr Kristine Mann was also a participant at that conference. Following the conference Mann and Bertine went to Zurich for analysis with Jung. While there they met Esther Harding, an English physician, who was also in analysis with Jung. Esther Harding and Eleanor Bertine developed a close relationship, which was to continue for the next forty years. In 1924 they decided to relocate to New York. They returned to Zurich for analysis two months each year, and spent summers at their residence on Bailey Island, Maine, where they also saw analysands. They were both influential in the New York Jungian community, but Esther Harding was truly the first important Jungian in America.

Esther Harding (1888–1971)

Esther Harding was born in 1888 in Shropshire, England, the daughter of a dental surgeon, and the fourth of six sisters. She was taught at home by a governess until the age of eleven and was an avid reader. She wished to become a missionary doctor and attended the London School of Medicine for Women, where she was one of nine students. She graduated in 1914 and began working in a hospital for infectious diseases. There she wrote her first book, *The Circulatory Failure of Diphtheria*; she also contracted the disease. After recovering she met Constance Long, who gave her Beatrice Hinkle's translation of Jung's *Psychology of the Unconscious*, which led her to enter analysis with Jung in Zurich.

Esther Harding became an influential analyst, a prodigious writer, and frequent lecturer in the United States and Canada. Her first Jungian book *The Way of All Women*, published in 1933, was an immediate best seller. Translated into many languages, it has introduced many people to Jung's psychology. She practiced analysis in New York, and every summer Esther Harding, Eleanor Bertine, and Kristine Mann attracted analysands from all over the United States and Canada to their home on Bailey Island, Maine. The setting of Bailey Island with its quiet surroundings, far away from the distractions of daily life, was conducive to profound experiences of the unconscious. Bailey Island was also the place where Jung gave a seminar in 1936 after having lectured at the Harvard Tercentenary on "Psychological Factors in Human Behavior." Esther Harding wrote many books, including *Psychic Energy, Woman's Mysteries, The Parental Image,* and *The I and the Not I,* along with numerous papers on a variety of subjects ranging from depression to religion.

In addition to her writing, lecturing, and analyzing, Harding was also a builder of Jungian organizations. In 1936 she was a prime mover in founding the Analytical Psychology Club of New York, which is still an active group today. As more analysts settled in metropolitan New York, she became the acknowledged leader of the loosely knit professional group, which became the Medical Society for Analytical Psychology–Eastern Division in 1946. All her life she saw New York as the logical Jungian center for all of the United States, and she developed a typical New Yorker's view of the United States, in which anything west of the Hudson River did not really exist.

In 1945 another Jungian group began to form in San Francisco. Jo Wheelwright, its representative, met with Harding off the coast of Maine to discuss territorial issues relating to spheres of influence between their two groups. According to Wheelwright, a well-known Jungian raconteur, who told stories with a healthy dose of hyperbole, they agreed to divide the nation at the Mississippi River. The Los Angeles group formed shortly thereafter, and the three groups remained the only Jungian centers in the United States for the following two decades.

When Esther Harding was in her seventies, William Kennedy encouraged her to form a national foundation in the name of C.G. Jung. As a young boy Kennedy had lived in the Jung household in Küsnacht for a number of years. Now living in New York, he was extraverted, intuitive, and full of new ideas. The idea of a national foundation caught Esther Harding's attention, and she put her energy and money behind the project. In 1963 the C.G. Jung Foundation came into being and her estate, combined with the estate of the Bertine sisters, Eleanor and Estelle, eventually provided an endowment for the continuation of its activities. William Kennedy served as its Executive Director for many years.

In 1968 a conference was held at Bailey Island to commemorate Esther Harding's eightieth birthday and to honor her significant contributions to analytical psychology. On that occasion many leading Jungians from around the world delivered papers to honor the role she played in analytical psychology. In 1971 she died in her sleep at an airport hotel in London, having just visited her family in England. She had stopped there on her way home from a wonderful vacation in Greece. Esther Harding had a keen intellect and was British to the core, very proper, even austere. She was a formidable person and not one to cross lightly. A young London-trained analyst, Murray Jackson, got a dose of her critical intelligence and allegiance to Jung when she was the discussant of his paper on "The Nature of Symbols" at the second International Congress of Analytical Psychology in Zurich in 1962. She flatly stated that he did not understand what Jung meant by the term "symbol." He left analytical psychology shortly thereafter to join the Kleinian movement.

Esther Harding's influence was a major factor in how analytical psychology developed in New York and by extension in other parts of the United States. During the almost fifty years of her leadership of the New York Jungians, there was very little contact between Jungians and psychoanalysis, but there was a good relationship to theologians. Many of the early trainees in New York were former ministers. Esther Harding's career spanned the period when Jungians and Freudians rarely spoke to one another. She had a close allegiance to Jung and criticized the personalistic and narrow scope of psychoanalytic theory and practice.

In turn, the Freudians were disparaging towards the Jungians' so-called "mystical tendencies," and did not believe that Jungians were doing analysis. In many instances they did not even realize that a Jungian group existed in New York. The environment between Jungians and Freudians was particularly hostile during the formation of psychoanalytic and Jungian training institutes. The legacy of Harding's negative attitude towards non-Jungian therapists made *rapprochement* to other psychotherapy schools in New York more difficult. On the other hand, she had strong religious convictions, and her ideas spoke to the clergy. Thus, her complete devotion to Jung was both a strength and, at the same time, kept the Jungian group isolated from other professional colleagues. During the past decade the isolation of the Jungians in New York has lifted dramatically. Liaison now exists with the Sullivanian group, the William Allison White Institute, and also with the Columbia Department of Psychiatry.

Between the two world wars: 1919–1940

Beginning in the 1920s, other Jungian analysts began to practice in New York, who were not so closely aligned with Drs Mann, Bertine, and Harding. The most influential individual was Frances Wickes, a lay analyst, whose book *The Inner World of Childhood* (1927) became a best seller, followed by *The Inner World of Man* (1938), and *The Inner World of Choice* (1963). Henderson describes her work as being inspirational rather than analytical (Henderson 1982). She had a special gift of working with people in the arts, and with her intuitive wisdom she helped many individuals with their creative blocks. She had begun as a schoolteacher, and had no professional training as a psychologist. As a widow with no living children (her son had died at a young age in a drowning accident), and someone who lived well into her nineties, she amassed a considerable fortune. Students and analysands honored her by establishing and contributing to a foundation carrying her name, and the Wickes Foundation supported various Jungian causes. There was friction between Frances Wickes and the three women doctors. Wickes, as a lay person and widow, had a different perspective from the three single professional women.

Jung returned to America in 1937 and after the "Terry Lectures" on "Psychology and Religion" he gave a five-part seminar to the Analytical Psychology Club in New York on "Dream Symbolism and the Individuation Process," later to become *Psychology and Alchemy*. This was to be Jung's last visit to the United States.

An important American analyst who practiced in New York from 1938 to 1940 was Joseph Henderson. He had gone to Jung for analysis in 1929 and during that year decided to go to medical school in order to become an analyst. He was welcomed warmly by both the Jungians and the psychiatric community in New York. His practice in New York was next to the office of Professor Karl Binger and other psychoanalysts with whom he was on friendly terms. Karl Binger had earlier studied with Jung in Zurich and later became a prominent psychoanalyst in Boston. Despite their theoretical differences they became friends, which was unusual at the time. In 1940 Henderson returned to his roots in the West, where he became one of the founders of the San Francisco Jungian group.

There were several other independent analysts practicing in New York during this period. Eugene Henley, a psychologist, and his wife, Helena, had worked with Jung on a regular basis and were practicing as analysts during the 1930s until the late 1950s. Dr Margaret Nordfeldt, a rather self-effacing woman analyst who, like Frances Wickes, worked with persons suffering from creative blocks was active in the Jungian community during those early days. By the end of the 1930s there were twelve analysts in the New York area, but they did not belong to a formal group. They were known as "referral analysts" by the Analytical Psychology Club.

The influx of Jewish émigrés from Europe in the late 1930s swelled the ranks of psychoanalysis, while the Jungian enclave remained small.

Following the model of Zurich and London, New York started its own Analytical Psychology Club in 1936. The format was similar to that of other Clubs with monthly meetings, and papers presented by analysts, lay members of the Club, and guest speakers. The Club published a monthly *Bulletin* for members. A number of continuous discussion groups and many professionally led seminars were organized over the years under the Club's auspices. The membership has increased so that at the present time there are between 100–200 members. As in other early centers of analytical psychology, the Club became a center for

Jungian thought, and even today there is more collaboration between the Club and the professional society than in most other cities. In 1941 the Club started to publish an annual journal, entitled *Spring*. A founding member of the Club, Jane Pratt, was the financial backer of this project. From the very beginning it was an important publication, because it included work in progress by Jung and Neumann which was translated and published in English. In 1970 the Analytical Psychology Club sold its rights to the journal and transferred them to James Hillman who, at the time, was living in Switzerland. When Hillman moved back to the States, he brought the publication with him and continues as its editor. Under his editorship, the content of *Spring* has shifted its focus from classical Jungian articles to those reflective of Hillman's own "archetypal psychology."

One more enduring achievement of the Analytical Psychological Club was the establishment of the Kristine Mann Library. Kristine Mann was a close professional colleague of Harding and Bertine. Analysands were referred back and forth among the three of them, especially at times when one of them was studying in Zurich. Jung wrote about Kristine Mann's unconscious material in "A Study in the Process of Individuation" (Jung *CW* 9:525–626). When Kristine Mann died of cancer in 1945, the Club library was named in her honor. The library has assembled a press archive of Jung and Jung's work starting in the early 1900s and has amassed a large collection of related material on mythology, anthropology, psychology, and comparative religion. Many unpublished manuscripts can be found in this library.

Other important Jungians in New York were Ann and Erlo van Waveren. Ann was originally from the Midwest and married Erlo, a Dutchman living in New York. From the early 1930s they had analysis with Jung during their yearly visits to Zurich, and they continued their annual trips to Switzerland until their respective deaths in the 1970s. Ann was offered membership into the group of New York analysts, but Erlo was not accepted as a member because he did not have any academic credentials. Ann refused to join the analysts as long as Erlo was turned down. They both had practices and saw clients in a Jungian-oriented way for over forty years, and they were definitely part of the Jungian community. There was a long-standing tension between the Van Waverens and Drs Mann, Bertine, and Harding, as the Van Waverens were not considered "proper analysts." When the van Waverens died in the late 1970s, they left a legacy which became the basis of the van Waveren Foundation. Olivier Bernier, a student of the van Waverens, became the director of the foundation which has helped to sponsor numerous significant Jungian projects.

The van Waverens were instrumental in another fateful encounter, as Mary and Paul Mellon came to them for analysis in 1936. At the encouragement of the van Waverens, the Mellons consulted with Jung during his 1937 visit in New York and the following year attended the Eranos conference in Ascona, Switzerland. Jung then confirmed that he would have time to see the Mellons in analysis, and so they stayed on in Zurich. The Mellons returned to the United States after the outbreak of World War II, during the period of the "phony war" in 1939. Prior to leaving Zurich Mary Mellon discussed her idea of having Jung's *Collected Works* translated and published in English. Minimal contact was possible during the war, but in 1945 the Mellons and Jung resumed their negotiations to form a Foundation. The Foundation was to publish Jung's works and the work of important poets, artists, art historians, philosophers, and theologians in English. Before the Mellons were able to return to Zurich and finalize the negotiations, Mary Mellon died tragically in *status asthmaticus* in the spring of 1946. In her memory, Paul Mellon created the Bollingen Foundation, named after Jung's tower in Bollingen. The first volume of the *Collected Works* to be published in English in 1953 was *Psychology and Alchemy*. The Bollingen Foundation subsidized the publication of Jung's writings in order to make them available to the general reader. Many other important philosophical and artistic works were published by the Bollingen Foundation until it was dissolved in the early 1980s. At that time the publication of Jung's books was taken over by Princeton University Press.

At the conclusion of World War II Harding and Wheelwright had their apocryphal meeting off the coast of Maine to carve out areas of influence in the United States. Both New York and San Francisco founded medical societies for analytical psychology in 1946, which were ratified in a letter from Jung. In 1954 the psychologists in New York formed their own group called the Society for Analytical Psychologists. When both physicians and psychologists realized that they had common ground in the practice of Jungian analysis, they merged to form one professional society, the New York Association for Analytical Psychology. The NYAAP became one of the founding members of the International Association for Analytical Psychology at its inaugural meeting in Zurich in 1958.

C.G. Jung Foundation

Interest in Jung's psychology continued to grow, and the Analytical Psychology Club had neither the financial resources nor the personnel to meet the growing need. On 29 February 1960 Dr Eleanor Bertine,

Miss Estelle Bertine, Dr Eugene Henley, Dr Esther Harding, Dr Margaret Nordfeldt, and Mrs Frances Wickes had a meeting and summarized their plans as follows: "To promote the idea that some sort of organization might be created that could receive monies tax free, by gift or legacy, to be used by a Jung Foundation for the furtherance of Jung's ideas in this country by any means considered effective and feasible" (Lee 1983). The stated purposes of the new Foundation were:

- To train analysts or assist in establishing . . . a school for analytic training;
- To arrange for lectures by leaders in the field for students and for the public;
- To give fellowships or scholarships for study;
- To establish and maintain a library for students and/or the public for research in analytical psychology;
- To publish lectures, articles or other documents in the field of analytical psychology;
- To establish a clinic.

The C.G. Jung Foundation was incorporated on 22 September 1962 and became operational in the following year. The New York Foundation is basically a lay organization with membership open to any individual regardless of prior experience, either academic or analytic.

The founders were all Club members, but friction developed between the aims of the Club and those of the Foundation. Both the strong public thrust of the Foundation and the training of analysts were not activities which suited the needs of the Club. The public lecture program of the Foundation, which had been thought of as a teaching program for candidates, did not answer the demands of the lay public, who had less technical interests. The activities of the Foundation very quickly overshadowed those of the Club. The Foundation lacked financial backing and urgently needed a physical location, whereas the Club had its home at the Kristine Mann Library. By 1965 the growth of the Foundation was such that a full-time executive director with secretarial staff was needed. Two activities which the Foundation entered into were the publication of books and a low-fee clinic. Book publishing was not a money-making proposition, and other commercial publishers began to publish Jungian writings, so that after a few years the Foundation decided to get out of the publishing business. A low-fee clinic was set up with Dr Werner Engel as director in 1975, and it continued until 1990. Since that time a "low-fee referral service" has continued to be offered by the Foundation.

A significant event was the establishment of the Archive for Research in Archetypal Symbolism (ARAS), an enormous collection of pictures and commentary on their archetypal significance from numerous cultures and ages. The collection was begun by Olge Froebe-Kapteyn in Ascona at the behest of Jung in the 1930s and had been supported by the Bollingen Foundation. When the Bollingen Foundation was phasing out its operations, the New York Jung Foundation was offered the ARAS collection, if it would provide housing and continued care for its development. Mrs Jesse Frazer, a long-time archivist and Club member, was given responsibility for the collection. Mrs Jane Pratt agreed to underwrite and guarantee the costs for the first ten years of its existence, so that ARAS became an integral part of the Foundation in the late 1960s. Paul Mellon also lent support to ARAS with a generous grant which has helped to put ARAS on a firm financial footing. Eventually, ARAS separated from the Foundation and formed its own national board and administration. The collections are continuing to grow and are made accessible by means of books and the latest computer technology. Charles Taylor has been a long-time president of the ARAS board and has been an enthusiastic and tireless supporter of ARAS.

The estates of Eleanor Bertine and Esther Harding, who died in 1970 and 1971 respectively, provided an endowment for the Foundation which enabled them finally to buy a five-story brownstone house in midtown Manhattan which is its present home. Since May of 1975 the Analytical Psychology Club, ARAS, the professional association, the Kristine Mann Library and the Foundation, along with a book store, share the space.

At the inception the Foundation saw itself as a national information center for Jung's psychology. The professional analytic training in New York was subsumed by the Foundation, a situation that produced continual conflict between analysts and lay members. Eleanor Bertine's original idea, as well as that of the other founders, was to give analysts authority to run the Foundation with assistance from non-professional members. However, over time analysts were outnumbered and the by-laws were changed to curtail their influence on the board. Initially no one anticipated the degree of separation which would develop between the analyst community and the Club. As in every other Jungian center which started with a Club, the separation of the analysts from the Club was painful. In 1973 the C.G. Jung Training Center became separately chartered in the state of New York. In the 1980s the Bingham Trust agreed to fund the Training Center for several years and to match any funds that the Institute could raise on its own. It is fortunate that the

Institute and ARAS separated their funds from those of the Foundation; Charles Taylor and Philip Zabriskie were responsible for separating the previously commingled funds. When the Foundation lost money in the late 1980s, both the Institute's and ARAS's endowments continued to grow.

When the Jung Foundation opened in 1963 there was no comparable institution in the United States. Its mandate was to be a public information resource for the whole nation, and for the first few years it did serve that function. The early boards had representatives from San Francisco and Los Angeles, in addition to New York members. The international Jungian community also looked upon the Foundation as the center of American influence, and the IAAP sent a representative to Foundation meetings for many years. In the late 1970s and early 1980s when other areas began to develop Jungian training programs and lay "Friends of Jung" groups, the Foundation lost its national character. Within metropolitan New York and the Eastern seaboard the membership had grown to over 1300. The Foundation was the central focus for public program activities associated with analytical psychology in the New York area. The Foundation was also the publisher of the journal *Quadrant*.

The Foundation required outside donations to underwrite its growing number of programs, one of which was a Mid-Life Center in the late 1980s. Taking advantage of its location in the heart of Manhattan, it aimed the Mid-Life Center programs at business people in mid-life transition who might gain from the insights of analytical psychology. Unfortunately, the Center became the focus of an acrimonious dispute within the Foundation board, a controversy that lasted three years, during which the endowment steadily declined. The upshot was that there was a change in the executive directorship, the Mid-Life Center was dropped, and the financial health of the Foundation was perilous to the point that sale of its remaining asset, the building, was under consideration. Though owner of record, the Foundation shared ownership of the building with three other bodies, the Analytical Psychology Club, the Archive for Research in Archetypal Symbolism, and the professional association of analyst members. Arguments over the fate of the building were heated. Only part of the board of the Foundation wanted to sell the building to cover past debts and operating expenses. Other bodies owning the building and the remainder of the board disagreed. There were complicated legal and tax implications involved with either decision. The faction of the board which wanted to sell fought the remainder of the board with legal means and called for a vote of the entire membership of the Foundation. The drama reached the pages of the *Wall Street Journal*. Finally, in 1997, it came to a general vote of the membership, which overwhelmingly favored remaining in the building. Now the Foundation is but a shell of its former self: all programs have been scaled down; the book store is smaller; *Quadrant*, having suspended publication for several years, reemerged in a simpler format. The Foundation definitely lost its national character and now functions as a local center for public information on analytical psychology. The building still houses ARAS, the Analytical Psychology Club, and the professional association, in addition to the Foundation.

The New York Jung Institute

Although a professional association was formed in 1946, the training program was informal until the establishment of the Foundation. The first candidates graduated in 1963. Before the Foundation existed training consisted of a long period of personal analysis and supervision of cases with another analyst, after which the prospective analyst would be invited to join the professional group. There was no special requirement for admission beyond a degree in psychology or medicine. For example, Alma Paulsen-Hoyer began her analysis with Esther Harding in 1934. When she mentioned her desire to become an analyst, she was told to first obtain a Ph.D. in psychology. She received a scholarship from the estate of Beatrice Hinkle, who had died shortly before, and this allowed her to study in Zurich. It took her ten years to qualify, and in 1953, after a semester in Zurich, she was admitted into the New York Association. While Alma studied in Zurich, it was unclear whether she would stay there or return to New York for further training. All the early analysts had comparable stories with many variations. When the Foundation was formed and the New York Institute became a part of it, the training center had its own board which governed policies with regard to training and which was separate from the Foundation board. The professional group became the New York Association for Analytical Psychology (NYAAP) in 1963. The group remained relatively small, and the analysts were more like a family than a professional association.

Inappropriate and unprofessional intimate relationships were formed by some senior analysts with patients and candidates. In the 1960s and 1970s this pattern was possible, although not approved of by the Jungian community. Analysts rationalized this behavior by the pattern set forth by Jung in his forty-year relationship with Toni Wolff. Jung did not recommend this pattern for others but stated that it was his fate to live his life this way. In the early 1980s sexual liaisons within the

New York professional group were strongly protested by the younger analysts. Newly certified analysts, Maurice Krasnow, Charles Taylor, and Beverley Zabriskie contacted ethicists, lawyers, and confronted their senior analysts. A dialogue took place which was creative for both sides. The senior analysts involved realized the error of their ways, and a genuine transformation took place. The negative effect of disregarding the boundaries in analysis was acknowledged. Since that confrontation Jungian analytic training in New York has become more professional. However, there still have been isolated ethics violations by individual members, but the subculture of ethical misconduct, which threatened to undermine the whole fabric of the training process, has disappeared. New York was not the only group facing this issue, as serious ethical misconduct occurred in Zurich, San Francisco, and Los Angeles in roughly the same time period.

One of the unique features of training in New York has been the requirement of all candidates attending a two-year, once-a-week group therapy. This developed out of a two-year, leaderless group therapy experience of six senior analysts from 1960 to 1962 who found it so useful personally that they made it a requirement of the training program. Christopher Whitmont, one of those six original senior analyst members, recognized how much conflict there was between members, and how individual analysis did not prepare one for dealing with professional interpersonal conflict. Personal analysis helped with the personal intrapsychic and interpersonal issues, but it did not necessarily help the individual to relate within a group.

The NYAAP has produced a number of leading Jungians in the United States. Both Edward Edinger and Christopher Whitmont trained in New York, as have Sylvia Perera and Beverley Zabriskie. One of the most widely read Jungians in America today is Edward Edinger. His first book, *Ego and Archetype*, published in 1972, is considered a classic in Jungian circles. Edinger, a medical doctor from Yale, had his analysis with Esther Harding, which he described in most positive terms; he became a member of the New York professional association in 1956. He was on the original training board, as well as the original Foundation board, and was an analyst and supervisor to many of the candidates. As an introverted thinking-sensation type, he has written with clarity about much of the religious and alchemical symbolism which occupied Jung for so many years. Many people compare his writings to those of Jung but find him much easier to read. Edinger attributed this ability to clearly express Jung's complex ideas due to his strong sensation function, which enabled him to sustain a focus on specific ideas. Edinger's life work was to explore Jung's thought in depth and intensity, and to present it to those who shared his passion. In 1976 Edinger moved to Los Angeles where he became a leader within the Society of Jungian Analysts of southern California. He died in Los Angeles in July 1998.

Christopher Whitmont followed a different path to Jung. He was born into a Viennese Jewish family and raised in the shadow of Freud. He studied medicine in Vienna before coming to the United States prior to World War II. He always had a strong interest in alternative medical approaches, and for fifty years he practiced and studied homeopathy in addition to medicine and analytical psychology. After World War II he returned to Germany and had analysis with Gustav Heyer, a known member of the Nazi party. Whitmont thought that his analytic work with Heyer was superior to the training analysis he had received in New York. Whitmont was a favorite analyst of many candidates, and many generations of students did their training with him. Christopher Whitmont died in New York in December 1998.

Theoretically, analytical psychology in New York has stayed close to its roots in Jung's works. The ethical issues which surfaced during the early 1980s made analysts realize the value of keeping appropriate boundaries in the consulting room, and "frame" issues were emphasized until they became generally adopted. Fordham's Jungian developmental school took on a different form in New York. Early developmental issues have been theoretically described in archetypal terms in Donald Kalsched's publication *The Inner World of Trauma* (1996), rather than in the language of object-relations theory.

Membership in the professional association is around one hundred, and there is an active training program which attracts individual candidates from as far away as Canada. Three women analysts of a recent generation, Beverley Zabriskie and Sylvia Perera, have had an impact on the dissemination of analytical psychology with their work on clinical application of mythological themes, Celtic and Egyptian, and Ann Ulanov has written several books on the relationship between psychology, religion, and feminine psychology.

SUMMARY

The history of analytical psychology in New York goes back to the very beginnings of the discipline. For the first twenty-five years women practitioners dominated the field. They had very strong positive transferences to Jung, and they lived and practiced in an environment which protected Jung. In the early days there was little contact between

Freudian psychoanalysts and Jungians, and only in the past fifteen years has a relationship between analytical psychology and psycho-analysis developed. The legacy of those early years still remains, and in spite of many efforts it has been a slow process for the New York Jungians to establish themselves in the wider mental health community. A very strong Analytical Psychology Club has been a vital organiza-tion for over half a century. Again, it had a preponderance of women members. When the training of analysts was formally instituted in 1963, it was a branch of the newly established C.G. Jung Foundation, which had the grandiose scheme to serve as the center for all Jungian activities in the United States. When the Foundation overreached it-self in the 1980s, the fallout within the New York Jungian community was profound. Legal battles ensued to determine who was to blame for the large financial losses at the Foundation.

For the first decade of formal training beginning in 1963 there was an intimate and sometimes too close relationship between the trainers and the students. In the early 1980s boundary violations were brought into the open and dealt with, and healing took place within the larger professional community. Stricter boundaries between analyst and patient, and analyst and candidate were instituted. At present there is a thriving Jungian professional community in New York. In spite of adversities New York has a well established Jungian community with a history that it can justly be proud of.

5 Analytical psychology in northern California

EARLY HISTORY

Although San Francisco is situated at the western end of the American continent, it has developed into an important regional center since the days of the Gold Rush of 1849. Immigrants from Europe and Asia have entered this port city, and by the beginning of the twentieth century, with its emerging universities, Stanford and University of California, it was well on its way to becoming the major cultural and intellectual center of the West. It was fertile ground for analytical psychology to take root in such a promising environment.

It is not clear what prompted people from the San Francisco area to seek out Jung. It is known that Chauncey and Henriette Goodrich went for analysis with Jung and Toni Wolff in the early 1920s. The Goodriches, descendants of an old California family, were friends with Cary Baynes and Frances Wickes, important early students of Jung, who influenced the shape of analytical psychology in America. Chauncey Goodrich influenced his sister Elizabeth and her husband, James Whitney, both general practitioners, to go to Zurich for analysis. The Whitneys returned in 1927 to begin practicing Jungian analysis as the first depth psychologists in the Bay area. The first Freudian analysts arrived in the 1930s as émigrés from Europe. Henriette Goodrich never practiced analysis herself, but she retained a life-long interest in analytical psychology, and was influential and very helpful when Jane and Jo Wheelwright and Joseph Henderson returned to San Francisco and started their respective analytic practices. James Whitney Sr. died shortly after returning from Zurich. His wife, Elizabeth Whitney, had a long and outstanding career as an analyst in the Bay area until the late 1950s, and her influence on the development of analytical psychology in San Francisco was profound. Elizabeth and James Whitney had a son named James who also became a doctor and analyst.

The year 1927 was significant for additional reasons. Dr H.G. "Peter" Baynes of London, who was Jung's first assistant, spent a sabbatical year in Berkeley and Carmel, lecturing, writing, and giving analytic consultations. He influenced a number of professionals to go to Zurich and enter analysis with Jung. One such person was a young Joseph Henderson, who later became a founder of the Society of Jungian Analysts of northern California and an internationally recognized analyst and author.

STRUCTURE

In 1939 a new phase commenced. Dr Joseph Wheelwright and his wife Jane returned to the United States from their training in London and Zurich. They both had had analysis with Jung, and Jo had finished his medical studies in London. They settled in San Francisco, and formed an Analytical Psychology Club, modeled after the Zurich and London Clubs. Both Jo and Jane had been members of the Analytical Psychology Club in London, where Jane was also the secretary. Under her guidance an attempt was made at that time to form a loose association. On account of World War II and other developments after the war a confederation of all Analytical Psychology Clubs never happened.

In 1938 Joseph Henderson moved to New York where he set up a practice, and in 1940 he returned to his roots in San Francisco. The Hendersons and the Wheelwrights had become close personal friends in London where the two men had studied medicine together at St Bartholomew's Hospital. The two were completely opposite psychological types, with Henderson the introverted intuitive thinker and Wheelwright the extraverted intuitive feeler, viewing the world from markedly different perspectives. As they were close friends, they were able to use their differences creatively. This ability to accept differences would play an important role in the culture of the C.G. Jung Institute of San Francisco later on. With the arrival of Henderson, professional members realized the possibility of forming a professional organization separate from the Club. Thus, in 1943 the Medical Society for Analytical Psychology (MSAP) was formed. As in other similar situations, the lay members of the Club felt abandoned by the professional analysts, even though the analysts continued their membership in the Analytical Psychology Club.

Developments in San Francisco were quite unique and, except perhaps in London, there was no parallel situation in the Jungian world, where almost all the founding members were physicians. The only non-physician in the original group was Jane Wheelwright who was accredited as a lay analyst by the vote of her colleagues. This gave the newly formed MSAP a respectability, which most Jungian groups of that era did not have, in the eyes of other physicians who dominated the field of psychotherapy in America. During World War II Joe Henderson and Jo Wheelwright worked closely with Freudian analysts at the Rehabilitation Department of Mt Zion Hospital, evaluating military personnel returned from the Pacific theater. This collaboration represented the foundation for respect and even friendship. Wheelwright became an early member of the Langley-Porter Neuropsychiatric Institute, where he served on the faculty for over thirty years. Henderson joined the faculty of Stanford University's Lane Hospital in San Francisco, where he taught until the medical school relocated to the Stanford campus in 1959.

From the outset the interest in Jungian training was greater among psychologists than among physicians. Two psychologists, Elizabeth Howes and Sheila Moon, had analysis with Elizabeth Whitney and had also seen Dr and Mrs Jung in Zurich. Drs Howes and Moon and their professional work were strongly influenced by a Christian viewpoint. In 1944 a decision had to be made as to whether they should be a part of the newly forming professional group. The two women elected to go their own way and in 1955 formed the Guild for Psychological Studies of which Mrs Emma Jung was a founding sponsor. To this day the Guild has functioned as a separate organization, presenting lectures and workshops to interested participants. Elizabeth Howes continues her activity in the Guild, although age and illness have lessened her involvement in its daily operation. Sheila Moon died approximately a decade ago.

This early cleavage was significant because it established analytical psychology in northern California as a clinical discipline, and individuals with a predominantly Christian orientation found a niche in the Guild. The separation of the Guild from the MSAP, as well as the fact that most of the professional members were physicians, led to criticism that the San Francisco Jungians were more interested in their medical persona than the deeper values of analytical psychology. Los Angeles Jungians felt a greater affinity to the Guild and often gave lectures at its workshops.

In 1948 four psychologists, who had their analyses with the medical analysts, were accepted as trainees within the professional group. These four immediately formed the Association of Clinical Analytical Psychologists as a counterpart to the medical group. In those days the rivalry in the United States between medicine and psychology was acute, and each discipline felt the need to have its own organization. However, both groups quickly realized that analysis should not be restricted to a single discipline. Jung had always emphasized the value of mythology, anthropology, religion, and other disciplines in the practice of analysis, and the newly formed Jung Institute in Zurich accepted graduate students from diverse fields.

FOUNDERS

Elizabeth Goodrich Whitney (1885–1966)

Elizabeth Goodrich Whitney was born in 1885 into a New England family. As a graduate from Vassar College, she attended both Johns Hopkins and Stanford Medical Schools. Both she and her husband, James Whitney, had medical practices in the San Francisco area. Following the Goodriches' example, they went to Jung for analysis in the early 1920s. In 1927 they began to practice as Jungian analysts, and Joseph Henderson was one of Elizabeth Goodrich Whitney's first patients. James Whitney had a serious illness in mid-life and gave up his practice shortly thereafter. Elizabeth Whitney practiced until 1958 when she suffered the first of a series of strokes which left her increasingly mentally and physically impaired. She died in 1966. One son, James Whitney Jr., the first analyst trained in San Francisco, also died tragically early in 1966 of a dissecting aneurysm. Dr Elizabeth Whitney has been described as "a wonderful listener and a wonderful analyst" by Joseph Henderson (1996). Elizabeth Osterman, another early Jungian analyst in San Francisco, has described her in relationship to the early Jungian society as, "one that enabled our society to become one of the few in the world that has not yet split or lost its ascendance" (Osterman 1996). Osterman was referring to the marked individual differences in psychological type between Wheelwright, extraverted intuitive feeling, and Henderson, introverted intuitive thinking. According to Osterman, it was the presence of Elizabeth Whitney and her ability to transcend the opposites which allowed the differences to coexist. Dr Whitney provided the feminine ground which enabled the San Francisco Society to have a solid foundation. Dr Whitney had a small cottage in the country where she happily spent most of her weekends and vacations with family and professional colleagues. Her influence on the founding of the Society of Jungian Analysts of northern California is often overlooked, as she preferred to stay in the background.

Joseph B. Wheelwright (1906–1999)

"Jo," as he was known to most people, was born on 6 June 1906 in Boston to an old New England family. He encountered great difficulties as a college student at Harvard and left after three years, but not before meeting his wife-to-be, Jane Hollister, who was a student at Bryn Mawr. Jane came from an old ranching family near Santa Barbara, California. There Jo met Jane's uncle, Lincoln Steffens, a famous left-wing journalist; he influenced them both profoundly, and as a result the Wheelwrights traveled to China and Soviet Russia in search of their destiny. Not finding it, they landed in Zurich on Jung's doorstep. Jung's psychological types became a cornerstone of their marriage and professional work, as their opposite typologies had been both problematic and creative for them. Jo, the extreme extravert, attended St Bartholomew's medical school in London, where he met Joe Henderson. The Wheelwrights and Joe Henderson belonged to the Analytical Psychology Club in London, and after graduation the Wheelwrights returned to San Francisco in 1939 where they began organizing the Jungians into lay and professional groups.

During the 1940s Jo made friends with a number of Freudians, including Erik Erikson. Jo had a position on the staff at the newly opened Langley-Porter Neuropsychiatric Institute, where he befriended many other psychoanalysts. His seminar for the psychiatric residents over the next thirty years introduced many future analysts to Jung, and by the time he retired he had reached the rank of full professor. Because of their life-long interest in psychological types, Jo and Jane, along with Horace Gray, MD, an internist who became a Jungian analyst, created a test for psychological types, called the Gray–Wheelwright type test, which is used by many institutions to delineate individual differences in personality. Today it is less popular, as other more sophisticated tests of psychological type have been developed, such as the Myers–Briggs, which is the most widely used test of psychological type today.

The Wheelwrights were instrumental in forming the philosophy of the training program in San Francisco, as it evolved from 1945 onwards. Both of them passionately believed that the character of the individual was paramount, and they strongly supported personal, interpersonal, and clinical values over and against academic requirements. Their influence on the San Francisco training is still felt today in the emphasis on individual growth and development. On the one hand this has been very positive, because it allowed candidates to progress at their own pace, but on the other hand intellectual curiosity and creativity have sometimes not been fostered.

During his long and productive professional career Jo Wheelwright spent, according to his own calculations, 70 percent of his time with Freudians. He became a member of the prestigious Group for the Advancement of Psychiatry, known as GAP. Through GAP he met and befriended many of the most prominent Freudian psychoanalysts of the day. In the 1960s Jo was the editor of a book entitled *Sex and the College Student*, which was quite popular at the time. This, along with his extreme extraversion, led some Jungians to doubt his commitment to analytical psychology.

Jo traveled regularly to London and Zurich and was always involved internationally with the Jungian community. In 1966, at a time when it was unlikely for an American to become president of the IAAP, he was elected as a compromise candidate when two other candidates could not win a majority. He served two terms and was active in promoting and enhancing the international community of analytical psychology. After finishing the presidency he retired from his private practice, traveled extensively, and continued his involvement in international matters as an elder statesman. He became a consultant to the Inter-Regional Society of Jungian Analysts IRS) in 1973, which was probably his most significant project after his presidency. At that time only three societies existed in North America, two in California and one in New York, but new individual analysts were beginning to move into new geographical areas in the United States and Canada. Jo promoted the idea of forming some kind of loose association for these individual analysts, so that trainees could get a wider range of analytic training experiences. As soon as a group in a region became large enough, he encouraged it to separate and become a member group of the IAAP. Jo's notion of group development was sometimes realized, and at other times groups remained as satellite groups within the Inter-Regional Society.

In 1989 the Wheelwrights retired to live full-time on a portion of the Hollister ranch near Santa Barbara where Jane grew up. The ranch is extremely remote, and they did not have a regularly functioning telephone. The Wheelwrights, in retirement from the professional scene of Jungian psychology, rarely spoke with anyone connected with their former professional lives. Jo developed blindness in old age. In the spring of 1999 Jane had a small stroke, and the Wheelwrights moved to a retirement facility in Santa Barbara. Jo died suddenly on 22 June 1999.

Joseph Henderson (1903–)

Joseph Henderson was born on 31 August 1903 in Elko, Nevada, the second of three children of a pioneer family with roots in Virginia and

California. As a result of an eye infection suffered at birth, his outward vision has been limited to one eye; this injury, though, may have accentuated his natural introversion, turning one eye perpetually to his inner experience. As an adolescent he attended Lawrenceville School in New Jersey where his mentor was Thornton Wilder, the well-known American dramatist. After graduating from Princeton with a degree in French literature, he returned to San Francisco to begin his career as a journalist, writing book, movie, and theater reviews. Not happy in this career he sought out analysis with Elizabeth Whitney in 1927. Through Dr Whitney he was introduced to Peter Baynes, Jung's first assistant, when he spent a year's sabbatical in the San Francisco area. With Baynes' encouragement Joe Henderson made preparations to see Jung in Zurich in the future.

In 1929 Joe spent a year in Zurich in analysis with Jung and Toni Wolff. As a result of his analytic experience he decided to enter medical school at St Bartholomew's in London, rather than in the United States, so that he could continue to see Jung during the academic breaks. In 1934 he married Helena Darwin Cornford, great granddaughter of Charles Darwin and the daughter of Francis Cornford, the noted Cambridge don, author of *From Religion to Philosophy*, and translations of Plato. At medical school Henderson met and befriended Jo Wheelwright, a fellow medical student, and they became life-long friends and colleagues.

The Hendersons moved to New York in 1938 where Joe Henderson began his practice as a Jungian analyst. With the approach of World War II Henderson moved his wife and daughter back to San Francisco in 1940 and joined the Wheelwrights, Dr Elizabeth Whitney, and Dr Lucille Elliot, to form the professional society in northern California. During the war Henderson joined the Mt Zion Rehabilitation Clinic where Jungians and Freudians worked together in the evaluation of military personnel returning from the Pacific. He also began teaching a seminar on dreams at the Stanford Lane Medical School in San Francisco, which he continued until 1959 when the medical school moved to Palo Alto. Many of the early candidates were attracted to the training at the Jung Society through their contact with Henderson at Stanford.

In 1960 Henderson was the only non-Swiss asked to contribute a chapter to *Man and His Symbols*, a book authored and edited by C.G. Jung. Henderson's chapter, titled "Ancient Myths and Modern Man," describes his research into the archetype of initiation. He continued writing on this subject in *The Wisdom of the Serpent* (1963), where he provided the psychological commentary and Maud Oakes presented the mythological material. In 1967 he published *Thresholds of Initiation*, summarizing over thirty years of research on the same topic.

In 1962 Henderson was elected first vice-president of the IAAP and was clearly in line to become president of the Association. However, he chose to withdraw from the politics of the organization, because he sensed that it would interfere with his writing.

At the same congress in Zurich in 1962 Henderson presented a provocative and thought-provoking paper on the cultural unconscious, a layer of the psyche between the personal and archetypal. He continued his research on this theme in *Cultural Attitudes in Psychological Perspective*, published in 1984, wherein he outlined four basic attitudes, the social, philosophical, aesthetic, and religious. Later a fifth attitude, the psychological, was added.

In recent years Henderson has focused his attention on the Archive for Research in Archetypal Symbolism (ARAS). So far two have been published utilizing images from the archive, and Henderson has written many of the psychological commentaries on the images. He was the chairman of the national ARAS committee and now is its honorary chairman.

As a founding member of the Society of Jungian Analysts of northern California, Henderson served twice as president and was on the training committees many different times over his fifty years as a member. At the time of writing Joe Henderson continues to have an active practice of analysis three weeks per month – a ritual he began at age sixty-five. He is now a very lively ninety-six years old!

In addition to the books mentioned above, a collection of Henderson's papers was published as *Shadow and Self* (1990). He has also published numerous movie and book reviews in many Jungian journals, especially the *Journal of Analytical Psychology*, the *San Francisco Library Journal* and *Psychological Perspectives*.

Joe Henderson is a very modest man who is not driven by narcissism and power. No other Jungian analyst in the world has the respect of so many of his colleagues. His influence on the San Francisco Jungians is enormous, and until recently almost every training candidate has had either supervision or analysis with him. Joe Henderson has been one of the mainstays of the training seminars of the San Francisco Institute, teaching both clinical subjects, and such diverse subjects as alchemy, dreams, the culture of the American Indian, initiation, culture and anthropology, and basic concepts of analytical psychology. On the international level he is seen as one of the pre-eminent, first-generation students of Jung. He is truly one of the most creative and original members of that first generation who analyzed with Jung and Toni

Wolff. He has been very open and welcoming to new influences in the field, unlike many others of his generation who would not let a word of Jung be changed. His influence on analytical psychology goes deep.

SOCIETY OF JUNGIAN ANALYSTS OF NORTHERN CALIFORNIA

In 1950 the Association of Clinical Analytical Psychologists united with the Medical Society of Analytical Psychology to form the Society of Jungian Analysts of northern California. The differences between the two factions were minimized, and for most of the following half-century there has been relative harmony between the disciplines. However, on more than one occasion moves were initiated to form a national medical Jungian association for governmental and insurance reasons. Such efforts have not materialized because whenever the potentially divisive issue was raised, the non-medical analysts protested vigorously so that it had to be dropped.

The northern and southern California Jungian groups quickly realized that they needed to deal with the respective projections upon each other. San Francisco Jungians were perceived as overly invested in their medical persona, and the Los Angeles Jungians were seen as being too identified with Jung and having no connection to the professional environment in which they practiced. The early San Francisco analysts came from long established American families of Anglo-Saxon origin, whereas the Los Angeles community consisted of mostly German-Jewish refugees. In 1952 the two groups met for a conference in Santa Barbara, and thereafter annual spring meetings became a tradition which continues to the present. Many changes have taken place over the years, as outlined in the chapter on southern California.

C.G. JUNG INSTITUTE

The early training seminars were held in the library of the Wheelwrights' office. On 13 July 1964 the C.G. Jung Institute was created as a non-profit organization; subsequently the training was restructured, a low-fee out-patient clinic was formed, and a building to house these activities was purchased. At the time there was already a professional body, the Society of Jungian Analysts of northern California (SJA), and consequently each analyst became a member of two organizations – the Society and the Institute. Professional training matters were central to the SJA, whereas the low-fee clinic, public programs, and the library became part of the Institute, overseen by a Board of Governors which includes four to six non-analyst members. There were eighteen charter members at the time of incorporation of the Institute. In the 1960s Jung's work became much better known, and interest in Jung's psychology began to mushroom. By the end of the 1960s public workshops and lectures on analytical psychology attracted large audiences, and the enthusiasm for Jung's theories brought many new candidates from medicine and psychology into training.

By that time the persona of the Institute was well established to enable it to accept individuals at the master's level in a clinical field. The original constitution provided a category for "exceptional persons," and from that point on candidates at all levels of clinical education have been accepted on equal terms for analytic training. It was important for an applicant to have appropriate clinical experience and a license to practice in the state of California. As the term "clinical" is often misunderstood, it may be warranted to clarify its meaning. In Switzerland and other European countries, "clinical" often means observing patients on a mental ward, or having lecture demonstrations on clinical syndromes, but does not include actual, supervised experience treating patients in a psychotherapeutic setting. In the United States "clinical" means that a student in training learns to conduct psychotherapy and undergoes supervision of the therapeutic work. The latter is the mandatory prerequisite for candidacy at the San Francisco Institute. While many other training centers require that the candidate have a clinical degree by the conclusion of training, San Francisco and the Society of Analytical Psychology London (SAP) are the Jungian Institutes in the world where this type of background is a prerequisite for analytic training.

In 1972 a most significant event occurred for the San Francisco Institute. In celebration of the eightieth birthday of Frances Wickes, a pioneer analyst in New York, friends and former analysands established a foundation in her name. Over the years the foundation distributed small grants, but in 1972 the board decided to dissolve it. The Wickes Foundation Committee – which included Professor Henry Murray, the distinguished Harvard psychology professor; William McGuire, the executive editor of the *Collected Works* in English; and Dr George Hogle, a former analysand of Frances Wickes, who had become a member of the San Francisco Jung Institute – was faced with the question of what to do with the remaining capital. A very thorough investigation of possible uses of the money was made, and – with George Hogle standing aside because of a conflict of interests – the foundation made a terminal grant of $1,500,000 to the C.G. Jung Institute of San Francisco. With the grant the San Francisco group bought its present residence for $150,000 and with the remainder established an endowment. For the following several years the financial stability of the Institute was assured by the earnings from the endowment as well as by contributions from interested lay people. The existing programs of the Institute grew rapidly, and new ones were developed. New staff members were employed to manage the library, public programs, the clinic, and overall administration. When members had new ideas, there were ample resources and receptivity to implement proposals. Those were the "halcyon days" of the San Francisco Jung Institute!

CHANGING VIEWPOINT OF JUNGIAN ANALYSIS

A large issue overshadowed this generally positive picture in San Francisco. Boundaries between analysands and analysts were not always maintained. Moreover, whenever boundary violations occurred, especially sexual ones, they were generally overlooked. In 1950 a significant individual, John W. Perry, MD, had joined the San Francisco group after having received a Rockefeller grant to study for a year in Zurich and after completing his psychiatric residency. Perry's father was the Archbishop of the Episcopal Church in Rhode Island, and Jung had stayed with him at the time of the Harvard Tercentenary in 1936. In 1953 John Perry published a book, *The Self in Psychotic Process*, for which Jung wrote the introduction. Perry was continuing the work on schizophrenia which Jung had begun at the Burghölzli fifty years previously. In San Francisco John Perry worked with acutely psychotic patients, demonstrating how archetypal themes were manifested; he developed methods for the treatment of selected acutely psychotic patients, without the use of anti-psychotic medication. This work was extremely exciting and began to receive attention both nationally and internationally. Mental health practitioners of all persuasions were attracted to this work, and Perry was sought after as a mentor and analyst. Perry lectured widely and introduced many future Jungian analysts to analytical psychology. In the late 1960s Perry led a research project at Agnew's State Hospital in San Jose on this approach, and a short while later a center named "Diabasis" was established in San Francisco to continue the work. It had funding from both the city of San Francisco and private sources. Hopes were high, but the problems of treating patients without medications, and the anxieties it engendered in the staff, brought the program to a standstill after several turbulent years. It became clear that patients required much more than containment and a non-pharmacological treatment of their unconscious. Meanwhile John Perry had developed a devoted following, and in his private analytic practice he enacted his belief that the powerful sense of union, *coniunctio*, which occurs between patient and analyst in an exploration of the unconscious, could be physically consummated. Over the years he became sexually involved with female analysands. In the early 1970s he was put on probation by the California State Medical Board, but, in spite of the warning, continued his practice of having sexual relations with female clients. In 1981 Perry was brought before the Ethics Committee of the San Francisco Jung Institute where his behavior toward female clients was investigated. The committee decided to place him on "indefinite suspension," which was a painful process and difficult decision, because Perry was valued as an analyst, teacher, lecturer, writer, and because he had one of the most creative minds in the San Francisco Institute. Eventually, his connection to the Institute was severed when he was forced to surrender his medical license to the State Licensure Board of California.

The looseness of boundaries around sexual issues and the lack of separation between social and professional relationships were problems which were being faced generally by many Jungian training centers. A reevaluation of the more informal approach that Jung had espoused and the first-generation Jungians had continued, was urgently needed. By the early 1980s new influences were beginning to be felt within the Jungian movement. Many younger analysts were drawn to the work of Robert Langs, an American psychoanalyst, whose work on the frame issues in analysis counteracted the earlier tendencies. As with many new ideas, the frame concerns became an obsession for some analysts. One of the most vociferous proponents was William Goodheart, who spoke to Jungian colleagues all over the United States; soon every American society was acquainted with "frame" issues within the analytic relationship. As the frame issues have been attended to, the Langsian influence has abated.

Heinz Kohut was a second major influence. His new "self-psychology," as described in his book *The Restoration of the Self* (1977), was developed in the 1970s. His work was introduced into the *Weltanschauung* of the San Francisco analysts by David Tresan and Herbert Wiesenfeld, through comparison of Kohut's "self" and the Jungian Self.

A further influence came from Michael Fordham who, in 1979, was invited to San Francisco as a visiting lecturer for a month. Many San Francisco analysts were drawn to Fordham's model of personality development which was heavily influenced by Melanie Klein and D.W. Winnicott. Fordham's model, with its emphasis on analysis of infantile fantasy through frequent weekly sessions on the couch, and focus on the transference/countertransference relationship, stimulated much interest among San Francisco Jungians.

Some analysts continued to follow a model closer to that of Jung, but adapted to the clinical focus of most San Francisco analysts. Others used concepts from self-psychology to fill the clinical gaps which were not specifically addressed in Jung's writings. Another strand of analytical psychology, e.g., James Hillman's "archetypal psychology," had little impact on the practice of San Francisco analysts, probably because of their strong clinical bias, even though the San Francisco Institute exhibited all the different attitudes which Andrew Samuels described in *Jung and the Post-Jungians* (1985).

The tendencies toward the integration of analytic theory and method from outside the Jungian field have continued into the 1990s, and the differences thrive within the San Francisco Institute. While disaffected members have resigned or joined other societies, usually the Inter-Regional Society, there has been no move toward division or the formation of an alternative Institute.

ACTIVITIES OF THE C.G. JUNG INSTITUTE

In San Francisco the Society of Jungian Analysts of northern California functioned as the professional arm while the C.G. Jung Institute maintained the programs and the relationship to the public. In the early 1980s then-president James Yandell questioned the need for two organizations, as the membership was the same in both. The result was an amalgamation of the Society into the Institute in an effort to have only one legal entity. The Society of Jungian Analysts of northern California no longer exists as an organization, and all activities occur under the aegis of the Institute.

Training

The training program consists of four years of weekly didactic seminars, a case conference, education in group process, yearly evaluations, and at least a hundred hours of individual supervision of analytic work. The first two years of seminars cover the core concepts of analytical psychology, whereas during the last two years the candidates are free to arrange their own elective courses. The yearly evaluations serve to assess the candidate's progress and maturity. Training concludes with a case report and a presentation to a Certifying Board.

For over forty years the Certifying Board consisted of an equal number of San Francisco and Los Angeles analysts. When the Joint Certifying Board was instituted, it was unique in the Jungian world. No other Jungian group had outside evaluators pass judgment on its candidates. The initial reason was the small size of both societies, but over time it was recognized that sharing evaluation was beneficial for both the candidates and the analysts doing the evaluations. In spite of major differences in outlook the Joint Board has always worked well until recently when a specific Joint Board did not function properly and a temporary suspension of the practice occurred. In the interim San Francisco has invited analysts from other institutes to help with its evaluations. The Joint Board and the yearly California North/South Jungian Conference have promoted a general working relationship between the two societies.

In an effort to lessen the authority problems within training, several key provisions were instituted at the beginning. First, the evaluation committee memberships are rotating so that one new person would come onto a committee, and the one who had served the longest would rotate off. Consequently, no individual analyst would acquire power over the training process. Second, there are no training analysts; this category, common to many training institutes, was never instituted in San Francisco. Candidates could see any qualified analyst of the Institute for their personal analysis. From the outset the personal analysts were not permitted to speak about their candidate's analysis to the evaluation committee. This rule was instigated in an attempt to have the candidate's analysis be more like other analyses rather than it being seen as a "training analysis." Third, any qualified analyst with five years of experience automatically becomes eligible to be a control or supervising analyst in the training program.

Changes have occurred in the make-up of the San Francisco Jung Institute, as fewer medical doctors apply for training, and with the general movement in psychiatry away from psychotherapy to a biological–pharmacological approach. Currently applicants come either from the fields of psychology or social work, with the occasional psychiatric nurse practitioner or marriage and family counselor. Women predominate among the present applicants and candidates, representing a shift away from the early days when applicants were mainly male medical doctors. Three to eight new candidates are admitted per year. The San Francisco Jung Institute has approximately 125 active members and fifty candidates in various stages of training.

Child analysis

From the beginning the Wheelwrights hoped to have a child training program in analytical psychology instituted in San Francisco. When Dora Kalff began her yearly visits to California during the 1960s and 1970s, many analysts and candidates were inspired to learn about Sandplay therapy, and several analysts began using the technique with children. Child analysis was given another viewpoint when Michael Fordham visited in 1979. His model of child analysis was very different from the one espoused by Sandplay therapists. In San Francisco, as in other centers around the world, the two approaches diverged more than they complemented one another. Both approaches have continued to be presented in training seminars for candidates. No specific training for child analysis has been instituted, allowing individual analysts to find their own way to work with children. Again, in the tolerance for individual differences lies the hope and the promise for integration in the future.

Clinic

When the Institute was incorporated in 1964 it received its non-profit status by virtue of its low-fee clinic. Many of the analysts and candidates saw one or two patients at reduced fees. As time passed many analysts whose practices became more demanding withdrew from seeing clinic patients. When Hal Batt, an analyst, became clinic director, he introduced an internship program for pre-doctoral psychology students, and many of them subsequently entered training at the Institute. Candidates who wish to have more Jungian exposure see patients at the clinic.

Public programs

The San Francisco Institute was the first Jungian Institute to organize a significant public seminar program. From modest beginnings at Stanford Hospital in San Francisco in the late 1950s, the program grew to be a major part of the Institute by the 1980s. It was not unusual to have audiences of 500 at lectures by well-known speakers. The public programs required the largest amount of energy of all the Institute functions. In 1989 several members protested the inflation of the public programs which no longer represented the Institute's philosophy. Consequently the public programs were downsized, and more local analysts were enlisted to participate in them. The internal changes at the Institute coincided with a drop in public interest. Staff was reduced, and gradually the program has become a more integrated part of the Institute. At the present time the selection of speakers in the public program is no longer a staff function but is handled by a committee of analysts under the direction of Tom Singer.

The San Francisco Library Journal

In 1979 John Beebe, after graduating as an analyst, decided to start a book review journal called *The San Francisco Library Journal*. At the time nothing comparable existed in the Jungian world. From very modest beginnings it has become one of the leading journals in the Jungian community and is published four times per year with extensive reviews of important books and movies relevant to Jungian psychology. The *Library Journal* expresses a broad spectrum of viewpoints, and its diversity is one of its strongest assets. It now enjoys a higher circulation than any other Jungian journal in the world. Beebe has announced his retirement after twenty years, and the new editor is Steven Joseph, a San Francisco analyst, with Dyane Sherwood as the associate editor.

Archive for Research in Archetypal Symbolism (ARAS)

The San Francisco Jung Institute acquired a complete copy of the New York ARAS collection. Educational public programs using the ARAS collection are well attended. For many years Joe Henderson has been the national honorary chairman of ARAS and has encouraged research activities relative to the ARAS collection. In San Francisco a lay group, called the Friends of ARAS, has formed to support the collection. The ARAS collection is open to interested outside scholars as well as to members of the Institute.

Current status of the San Francisco Institute

The San Francisco Jung Institute has long been considered one of the most organized and respected Jungian institutes in the world. From the very beginning it established good relations with psychoanalysis. The Wheelwrights, Joseph Henderson, and Elizabeth Whitney worked well together to found the early professional group. At the time of writing there have been no serious splits within the professional group, and an air of respect generally prevails among the membership. From the outset there have been monthly dinner meetings of the membership, so that there is ample opportunity for members to know each other in a less structured setting. As time has passed, it is clear that the influence of Joe Henderson has been the predominant one, and his quiet presence has provided a steady rudder while members have charted the Institute's course.

Many members of the San Francisco Jung Institute have established national and international reputations in the field of analytical psychology. Two of its members held the presidency of the IAAP, Jo Wheelwright and the author of this volume, each for a period of six years. Joseph Henderson was a first vice-president, and co-author in Jung's *Man and His Symbols*. John Perry was a leading figure in modern schizophrenia research before his lack of professional ethics ran his career aground. Don Sandner, a leading figure in the world of analytical psychology with a scholarly interest in shamanism, was the author of an important book on the Navajo Indians in the American Southwest, an area that Jung himself visited. Elizabeth Osterman, Bertha Mason, and Kay Bradway were in the vanguard in opening up the psychological world of the feminine to new audiences. John Beebe started the influential *San Francisco Library Journal*, and through his work with psychological types and movie reviews has become an international figure in the Jungian community.

A new pilot program for foreign students has recently been instigated in San Francisco, making it the first institute outside of Zurich to formally admit students from a foreign country. The purpose of the International Student Analytical Psychology Pilot Program is to give students from countries which do not have a functioning institute a chance to immerse themselves in analytical psychology for two years, together with the candidates in training. In 1998 the first student, a psychiatrist from Korea, completed two years of an immensely successful experience. The second foreign student is from Bulgaria and, if the pilot program is successful, it is hoped that the atmosphere of the San Francisco Institute will forever be changed. The program was initiated by Jean Kirsch, and other institutes are now planning similar programs.

What are the problems facing the San Francisco Institute? Perhaps the biggest danger facing the Institute today is its own success. During the past fifty years it has established a structure where it is possible for members to become complacent. There is a sense that someone will always do the task, and that no one individual needs to take responsibility. The membership has grown to such an extent that the individual can sometimes feel unimportant. The success and the size of the organization can actually stifle creativity. A second issue is parochialism. Sometimes the self-congratulatory feeling exists that everything can be found within the confines of the San Francisco Institute, and that outside influence is not welcome. Thirdly, the only active founder, Joe Henderson, is well into his nineties, and although he has receded into the background, his presence is still strongly felt. By and large, the San Francisco Jung Institute has had a remarkable fifty years and has been widely acknowledged as one of the leading Jungian centers in the world.

6 Analytical psychology in southern California

EARLY HISTORY

One might wonder how and why analytical psychology took root in sprawling Los Angeles, a city made up of interlocking communities with no real center. The sense of an urban center had only recently been established, whereas early development of analytical psychology usually took place in large metropolitan areas with a long history of culture. It was Nazism and the exodus of Jews from Europe in the late 1930s that changed the face of Los Angeles permanently. Many Jewish and non-Jewish refugees were drawn to the then paradisiacal desert which lies beneath the modern city of today. Among them were many European Freudian psychoanalysts, and in November 1940 the first qualified Jungian analysts, James and Hilde Kirsch. Analytical psychology began with the arrival of the Kirsches, followed in 1941 by Max and Lore Zeller. Kate Marcus, who had a long Jungian analysis and had studied hand analysis with Julius Spier in Germany, arrived in 1944. Spier's book, *The Hands of Children* (1955), had a foreword by Jung.

Although southern California appeared to have no Jungians prior to 1940, it happened that an American woman from Los Angeles, Mary Wilshire, had gone to see both Freud and Jung when the two were still colleagues in 1908, then had returned to see Jung again in 1917 and had come back to Los Angeles to practice therapy. Though she claimed to be neither Freudian nor Jungian, she did appreciate Jung's point of view. In the 1940s she gave a lecture at one of the early meetings of the Analytical Psychology Club, but her influence on the development of analytical psychology in the region was minimal (Spiegelman 1963).

By the spring of 1944 there were twenty people who had the requisite 150 hours of analysis to form an Analytical Psychology Club. Fritz Künkel, the founder of "We Psychology," was also a founding member, but he resigned soon thereafter because he wanted more group work along with individual analysis. He remained on friendly terms with the Jungians and introduced many people to analytical psychology. The Club grew slowly, and by 1952 there were thirty-eight members. In 1950 twenty people from Los Angeles were in analysis in Zurich, and they were so impressed with the lecturers at the Jung Institute that they established an educational fund to invite analysts from Zurich to lecture in Los Angeles. Rivkah Schaerf, who was later to marry Yechezkel Kluger, was the first to visit in 1951, followed by Marie-Louise von Franz, Barbara Hannah, Michael Fordham, Gerhard Adler, C.A. Meier, and many others. Most of the well-known, first-generation analysts came to Los Angeles at some time, and these visits generated much enthusiasm and excitement. In 1950 a professional group formed within the Analytical Psychology Club which, in 1953 separated from the Club to become the Society of Jungian Analysts of southern California.

FOUNDERS

James Kirsch (1901–1989)

Of all the original members James Kirsch had a true pioneering spirit. He was born in Guatemala on 21 July 1901, the son of a German-Jewish merchant, who sent the family back to Berlin in 1906 so that young James could have a good European education. James graduated from Heidelberg University in 1922 with a medical degree and practiced psychiatry in Berlin. In 1928 he met Jung and in the following year began an analysis with him, traveling periodically from Berlin to Zurich. He was a founding member of the C.G. Jung Society of Berlin. When the Nazis came to power in 1933, James immediately left for Palestine. Based upon a dream in which he foresaw brown-shirted hordes, he strongly urged all his relatives, friends, and patients to do likewise. Among the latter was Hilde Silber, a widow with two small children, who followed him to Palestine, where they became a couple. They were not happy in Palestine. Zionism had lost its appeal for James who had been an ardent supporter in his university days. In 1935 Hilde and James Kirsch emigrated to England where he became one of the founding members of the Jungian professional group in London. In 1940, at the height of the Battle of Britain, the Kirsch family emigrated to the United States. They had planned to settle in New York, but after a visit to relatives in San Francisco James stopped over in Los Angeles, liked what he saw, and brought the rest of the family there. The Zellers arrived in the following spring (1941), and together the two families began the groundwork to set up practices in Jung's psychology. In 1942 James began a weekly seminar series at his home, a practice he continued until shortly before his death in 1989. In these seminars various texts of Jung were analyzed in great detail. In the early days many of Jung's works were not yet available in English, and James would translate and interpret them. In later years he studied some of Jung's more difficult alchemical writings in an almost Talmudic fashion.

In 1944 James Kirsch spent seven months in New York preparing himself for the medical license examination, which he passed. However, when it came time to do an internship, he balked because he saw what had happened to Otto Fenichel, a well-known Freudian analyst in Los Angeles. Fenichel, in similar circumstances, had begun an internship in mid-life, during which he died of a heart attack. An American internship was a necessity to practice in the state of California. The lack of a proper license contributed to James Kirsch never becoming a part of the rapidly developing medical or psychotherapeutic community in Los Angeles.

James Kirsch was a founding member of the Analytical Psychology Club in 1944 and of the Society of Jungian Analysts of southern California in 1953. As soon as post-war travel was possible in 1947, Kirsch returned every year to Switzerland for two months to continue his analysis with Jung and Toni Wolff, and, after their deaths, with Dr Liliane Frey and Professor C.A. Meier. This pattern continued for forty years. Kirsch was a frequent lecturer both in the United States and Europe on such diverse subjects as Moby Dick, Dante, Jack London, Jung and anti-Semitism, dreams, and the individuation process. He was the author of two books, *Shakespeare's Royal Self*, the initial publication of the C.G. Jung Foundation of New York, and *The Reluctant Prophet*, an analysis of the dreams that led a nineteenth-century German rabbi, Hile Wexler, to urge his congregation to leave Germany. In his later years James Kirsch returned to his Jewish heritage and wrote extensively about Rabbi Nachman of Bretzlav. He died on 17 March 1989 after a brief illness. The Los Angeles Institute has named the main lecture room in his memory.

This biographical data would be incomplete without mentioning James Kirsch's impact on the development of analytical psychology in Los Angeles. He was an ardent follower of Jung and saw himself as his representative wherever he went. Along with his immense scholarship there was an orthodoxy to his interpretation of Jung's viewpoint which produced conflicts for some of his analysands and students. He made no room for inclusion of non-Jungian ideas. Thus, his presence as a leader of the Jungian movement in Los Angeles meant that the following generation of analysts were expected to accept his orthodox Jungian position.

Hilde Kirsch (1902–1978)

Hilde Kirschstein Silber Kirsch was introduced to Jung's analytical psychology in 1933 when she found herself alone with two small children, after the death of her husband, at a time of deep political and economic unrest in Germany. She began an analysis with James Kirsch in Berlin, and then followed him to Palestine. In 1933 she managed to obtain an appointment with Jung, even though he was fully booked, and subsequently returned for repeated periods of analysis until 1939. When Hilde and James emigrated to England in 1935 she became a member of the Analytical Psychology Club. She was a nursing mother in 1937 when Jung sent her an analysand, Michael Fordham, without forewarning her of Fordham's call. She had no intention of becoming an analyst at that time, but Fordham's arrival on the scene changed that forever.

When the Kirsch family arrived in Los Angeles in 1940, Hilde continued to work as an analyst, even though she had no formal degree beyond high school. Much more introverted than her husband, she devoted herself to her analytic practice and neither lectured nor wrote much. Owing to her strong intuitive and feeling functions, she became an extremely popular analyst. Many academically oriented persons preferred to work with her, and she was sought after by candidates in training. She did prepare one seminar based on Jung's "Zarathustra" seminars which became a perennial favorite for analytic candidates and analysands, drawing people from far away. Although outwardly quiet and reserved, she exerted a powerful influence behind the scenes of the Jungian community. She was the glue that held the early Los Angeles group together, and without her it might have developed more slowly.

Hilde Kirsch was instrumental in introducing Sandplay therapy to the United States by inviting Dora Kalff to lecture and conduct workshops. Through her friendship with the dancer Mary Whitehouse, Hilde was instrumental in furthering the use of body work in conjunction with analysis. Also, she was very interested in developing analysis for children, and the Los Angeles Jung Institute has named its children's center in her honor. Her death from cancer in 1978 left a gaping hole among the Los Angeles Jungians.

Max Zeller (1904–1978) and Lore Zeller (1914–)

Max Zeller, another German Jew from Berlin, had been friends with Hilde Kirsch since 1932. This friendship continued until their respective deaths in 1978. He had received a degree in jurisprudence in Germany but was not satisfied with work in that field. He began a psychoanalysis with Otto Fenichel, but after two years – because of a dream – he transferred to Kaethe Buegler, the first Jungian analyst in Berlin. In 1938 Max also worked analytically with Gustav Heyer in Munich for a number of months. Heyer was a medical doctor and, at the time, a leading associate of Jung's. Heyer encouraged Zeller to emigrate and aided him in this process by giving him a letter of certification, which allowed him to practice as an analyst in another country. While waiting to emigrate to the United States, Zeller was interned in a concentration camp outside of Berlin in 1938, and was extremely fortunate to be released after five and a half weeks. He and his wife, Lore, ten years his junior, fled first to London and then to Los Angeles to join the Kirsches who had relocated there. Finally, once in Los Angeles, Max Zeller was able to open his practice as a Jungian analyst and, along with the Kirsches, he was instrumental in shaping the Jungian community which was to develop. He was a founding member of both the Analytical Psychology Club and of the first professional society. Max Zeller, a feeling type, was much loved by his analysands and colleagues.

James Kirsch and Max Zeller had an uneasy relationship, which lasted for the rest of their lives. Although they saw each other frequently over many years, spent vacations together, and at different times lived in the same house, they never became intimate friends. For instance, speaking in German, they never could become comfortable addressing each other with the intimate *Du*; they would try but always revert to the more formal *Sie*. On the other hand, since Max was extremely close with Hilde, he and James over time were able to live with their differences.

Lore, a sensation type, was a charter member of the Analytical Psychology Club which formed in 1944. Later she was instrumental in having spouses included in many of the professional meetings. Although Lore never became an analyst, she has been connected to the Jungian world since 1936, and her remembrance of the early days is quite extraordinary. When her husband Max was no longer able to function as an analyst and lecturer, she took over the organization of the Bruno Klopfer Workshop, a residential workshop in analytical psychology held in Asilomar, California every two years.

As with so many analytic groups at the beginning, the Los Angeles society's social, collegial, and analytic relationships were all intertwined.

Lore, as the younger non-analyst, had analysis with both James and Hilde Kirsch at different times. Hilde was at least as much a confidante of Max as she was of her husband James, and many analytic secrets were exchanged under the aegis of collegial consultation between these friends and marriage partners. These incestuous relations were finally broken in 1957 when the Zellers spent a year and half in Zurich. Reparation payments from the West German government made their sabbatical possible. When the Zellers returned to Los Angeles, it was inevitable that the formerly close Kirsch–Zeller bond would have to undergo a stressful period. Apparently many of Max's former analysands did not return to him after his sabbatical, and the network of referrals to each other stopped functioning and became the symbol of the conflict. Over time the rift healed, and the relationships among the four of them resumed on a new and more conscious level with better attention to boundaries. Max, however, suffered a series of strokes in the mid-1970s which gradually debilitated him. He died in 1978 at the age of 74. Since Max's death Lore has come more into her own with her long experience with Jungians and analytical psychology. At the time of writing Lore continues to be active in the Institute Book Store, the Club, and the magazine *Psychological Perspectives*. In 1983 the library of the Los Angeles Jung Institute was named the "Max and Lore Zeller Library" in their honor.

SUMMARY

The foregoing facts contribute much to the picture of the spirit of analytical psychology in Los Angeles. First, the founders were all of German-Jewish extraction who had to start new lives in Los Angeles under wartime conditions. Second, none of the founders had an appropriate license, which isolated them from the medical, psychiatric, psychoanalytic, and psychological circles. A third factor was that all the founders had had their lives and their analyses interrupted by the war, and none of them experienced a normal termination. They were completely cut off from contact with Jung until 1946, and so the idealization on Jung remained fixed. A fourth factor was the post-war accusation of Jung's alleged anti-Semitism. Here was a society of German-Jewish refugees, themselves traumatized by the Nazis, having to defend Jung against charges made by Freudian psychoanalysts, among others – all against the backdrop of witch-hunting in the film industry of Hollywood in the late 1940s and early 1950s. The tension between Freudians and Jungians in Los Angeles was enormous. In addition, the manner in which analysis was practiced in those days left fluid boundaries between analysts and patients. Most analysts had consulting rooms in their homes, and there was frequent social contact in addition to analysis. This combination of factors made for an extremely close, incestuous group. It also set the stage for major flare-ups when a member wished to separate from the group. The German-Jewish influence dominated Jungian psychology in Los Angeles in the early days and subliminally affected the group for many years thereafter. New members, like Margaret McClean, Kieffer Frantz, and Malcolm Dana joined in the 1950s, and the chemistry of the group slowly changed.

SOCIETY OF JUNGIAN ANALYSTS OF SOUTHERN CALIFORNIA

The first meeting of the Society took place on 11 January 1953, and the founding members were James and Hilde Kirsch, Max Zeller, Kieffer Frantz, Jay Dunn, Kate Marcus, Margaret McClean, and Malcolm Dana. Frantz and McClean were psychiatrists, Dunn was an osteopathic physician, and Malcolm Dana had been a minister and small college president. The academic and professional personae of the founders were extremely varied, and their connections to medical and psychological clinics and institutions were minimal. Concurrently, Kieffer Frantz was the driving force behind a clinic for low-fee patients. Another important development was the annual meeting of Los Angeles and San Francisco analysts beginning in 1952.

As in other Jungian centers the professional society began to distance itself from the Analytical Psychology Club and took over many of the educational functions of the Club, such as seminars, workshops, and lectures. The Club members experienced a sense of abandonment from the professional members, although comparatively in Los Angeles the analysts continued to be more involved with the Club than in many other Jungian centers. The professional society grew slowly and continued to attract members from outside the usual academic and clinical circles. In the mid-1950s a breakthrough occurred when Bruno Klopfer, a prominent Rorschach researcher and professor of psychology at UCLA, became a professional member. Through him clinical psychologists became interested in entering the training program, and the society began to take on a more professional identity. Starting in 1959 Klopfer inaugurated a biennial two-week residential workshop in analytical psychology at Asilomar, California, which attracted participants from all across the United States. At that time it was the only venue in the United States which offered such a program. Many future analysts had their first exposure to analytical psychology through this program. The seminar leaders were mainly from the Los Angeles and San Francisco Jung societies. After Klopfer retired, Max Zeller, a frequent lecturer, assumed the leadership of the program until his health no longer permitted it. In 1975 Lore Zeller took over; however, in the years following, the uniqueness of the Klopfer workshop was over-shadowed by many competing programs in the United States and Europe. Lore continued to run the program until 1995, by which time the once-innovative program had run its course.

C.G. JUNG INSTITUTE OF LOS ANGELES

In 1967 the C.G. Jung Institute of Los Angeles was founded to co-ordinate the activities of the Analytical Psychology Club, handle public relations, and serve as a training center. The Los Angeles Institute has continued to grow and develop. In 1970 William Walcott began the journal *Psychological Perspectives*, a magazine devoted to analytical psychology in relationship to culture, politics, the arts, and poetry. It is published two times per year, financially supported by the Los Angeles Institute, and has established itself as an important voice in the Jungian world. The current co-editors are Gilda Frantz and Margaret Johnson. Another important project is "Matter of Heart," a film archive produced by Suzanne and George Wagner, who have interviewed many of the first-generation analysts who had known and worked with Jung. A documentary film, *Matter of Heart*, which includes excerpts from many of these interviews, has been shown commercially all over the world. Full-length interviews of each of the twenty-four individuals are being made available commercially. This project has been ongoing for over twenty years.

The initial orientation of the Jung Institute was closely aligned to Zurich. James and Hilde Kirsch had spent considerable time in ana-lysis and training in Zurich. The connection between the two cities was further strengthened by the continuous stream of visiting analysts from Zurich as guest lecturers supported by the Analytical Psychology Education Fund of the APC. The toings and froings between Zurich and Los Angeles heavily influenced the way Jung and analytical psy-chology were received in Los Angeles. Emphasis on the inner world of archetypal images and the individuating process was paramount, whereas the adaptation to the extraverted world was considered less sig-nificant. The combination of the close ties to Zurich, the aforementioned idealization of Jung, and the weekly seminars by James Kirsch, all conspired to make Jung appear larger than life. Whether this idealization of Jung had to do with the unresolved transferences of the founders, or whether Switzerland became the adopted homeland for these dispossessed German-Jews, or some combination of the two, Jung and Zurich became central to the early students of analytical psychology in Los Angeles.

LOS ANGELES AND SAN FRANCISCO: PROFESSIONAL COOPERATION

In the 1940s there were only a few Jungians in America, and it was only natural that the analysts from Los Angeles and San Francisco should have contact. However, the attitudes of the two burgeoning societies could not have been less alike. The Los Angeles analysts had mixed professional qualifications in their new country, whereas the San Francisco founders were all physicians and members of long-established American families. Projections from one group to the other were strong and avidly held to be true. The Los Angeles analysts were seen as mystical and unrelated to the "collective," as the host culture was referred to in those days, whereas the San Francisco analysts were seen as caught up in the persona and were accused of having sold out to the "collective." The Kirsches and Max Zeller were reluctantly accepted as associate members of the San Francisco group in 1944.

In 1952 the two groups cautiously planned a joint meeting in Santa Barbara, California to explore areas of mutual interest. They hoped that a meeting between the two societies could lessen the mutual projections. The initial meeting proved to be fruitful, and the two societies decided to get together on a yearly basis from then on. The annual event became known as the North–South Conference, and it was the first-ever meeting between two Jungian societies. A trust developed between the two groups, and they decided to create a joint board with equal representation to evaluate candidates from both sides. As the number of analysts was small, it was helpful to combine forces for this most important training function. By the mid-1960s candidates and spouses were allowed to attend the annual meeting, which was held in different venues in California. In the 1970s analysts from other parts of the country began to attend, and the conference developed into a National Meeting for a few years. But the two groups missed the meetings of the North–South Conference, and it was reinstituted and once more flourished.

The joint evaluation of candidates has gone on for over forty years. The differences in approach between the members of the two societies have produced tensions, and any disagreements could always be worked out. However, in the past few years the discrepancies between the two groups became unresolvable. As a result, the long tradition of joint certification has been temporarily suspended, while the two societies independently question their respective philosophies and practices. Perhaps there is no longer a need for joint certification, as both societies have grown in size.

RECENT DEVELOPMENTS

The intense identification with Jung by the founding members produced strong reactions in the next generation of candidates. Many carried the same strong sense of allegiance toward Jung, as did the first generation of analysts. Many others had a contrary reaction to this over-identification with Jung and in the 1970s began to explore other psychotherapeutic theories. First they became attracted to the writings of the London Jungians headed by Michael Fordham. It was not long before the psychoanalytic works of Kohut, Klein, Bion, and Grotstein, among others, influenced these Los Angeles Jungians with diverse interests. Furthermore, after the deaths of Hilde Kirsch and Max Zeller, and with James Kirsch retreating into the background, there seemed to be a readiness for new energy to emerge.

In the mid-1970s Edward Edinger arrived in Los Angeles from New York. Although Edinger brought with him the knowledge and experience of a classical Jungian, he did not have a personal analysis with Jung. His analysis with Esther Harding in New York had been a very positive experience for him. However, Edinger's intellectual focus was on the works of C.G. Jung and Marie-Louise von Franz, and his published books reworked Jung's ideas into a language which seemed easier to grasp than Jung's. His publications include the subjects of alchemy, William Blake, Goethe's *Faust*, Melville's *Moby Dick*, Christianity, images in the Old Testament, and others. He has also published lectures on Jung's *Aion* and *Mysterium Coniunctionis*, which have made them more accessible to the general reader. His first book *Ego and Archetype*, published in 1972, has been a well-received basic text on Jung's analytical psychology. Edinger strongly believed that Jung was the most important individual since Jesus Christ, and once said, "Jung's psychology offers not only a method for the psychological healing of individuals but also a new world view for Western man which holds out the possibility for healing the split in the contemporary collective psyche" (*New York Times*, as quoted in the Obituary of Edward Edinger, 2 August 1998). For over twenty years Edinger influenced many Los Angeles analysts who have shared this point of view. As Edinger had such deep convictions about the value of Jung's work, he could not comprehend why candidates would want to read anyone else. Edinger had no understanding or patience for those who reached out to psychoanalysis. Many candidates were interested in the new developments in psychoanalysis which had relevance for analytical psychology, and this led to an enormous tension within the Los Angeles Jungian community. In the decade of the 1990s, the division between those who adhere closely to the words of Jung and von Franz and those who wish to incorporate psychoanalytic concepts into Jungian practice has widened. Whether the rift is so wide that it will cause a split within the Los Angeles Society is an open question. Edinger died after a long battle with cancer in July 1998. What effect his death will have on the opposing points of view within the Institute is open to conjecture. The sentiments on both sides are strong. At the time of writing these differences have not been settled.

SUMMARY

Analytical psychology has developed in Los Angeles from a small German-Jewish émigré enclave to a substantial professional Jungian community. Currently the Society of Jungian Analysts of southern California includes approximately seventy members (the majority having been certified within the past six years), and twenty-five candidates. The Institute, founded in 1967 without an endowment, has managed to survive and grow throughout this period. The Institute components include its own ARAS collection, the Hilde Kirsch Children's Center, the Max and Lore Zeller library, the James Kirsch lecture room, the Kieffer Frantz Clinic, the journal *Psychological Perspectives*, the archive film project "Matter of Heart," and numerous ongoing projects. There is an active training program with many candidates. It is difficult to ascertain how the theoretical differences in the membership will influence the overall shape of the Institute in the future.

7   Developments in the United States and Canada after 1970

In this chapter the development of analytical psychology in the United States and Canada after 1970 will be outlined. The story becomes more confusing as small institutes and study groups begin to develop all across the country. The study groups formed around a central organization called "CenterPoint," which had the endorsement and encouragement of Esther Harding and Edward Edinger. Small study groups formed all across the country where Jung and other Jungian authors would be read and discussed. CenterPoint presented a national annual meeting with a featured speaker and published an ongoing newsletter *In Touch*. However, CenterPoint has always been separate from the development of professional training, so that it will not be discussed further. It is important to note that many thousands of Americans have been introduced to the writings of Jung and Jungians through the CenterPoint program.

On the side of professional development there was no training available outside of California and New York before 1974. Individuals who did not live or work in those two areas had either to go to Zurich or to one of the existing training institutes in New York or California. Some individuals traveled great distances each week to do the training in the United States; however, the majority of people interested in Jungian training went to the Jung Institute in Zurich, graduated from there, and then returned to the United States. By the early 1970s the need for more training institutes was obvious. Groups formed in other parts of the country, and I shall briefly chronicle their development according to when they became recognized by the IAAP. How the many American groups began to relate to one another will be discussed as part of the Council of American Societies of Jungian Analysts, known as CASJA.

INTER-REGIONAL SOCIETY (IRS)

The C.G. Jung Institute in Zurich had opened its doors in 1948, and from the very beginning attracted American students. In Zurich there was the possibility of meeting Jung, as well as having analysis with one of Jung's close associates. At the time it was considered the most desirable path to becoming a Jungian analyst. Most of the early graduates returned to New York and California. By the late 1960s some of the graduates were settling in such diverse places as Chicago, Seattle, Dallas, and Minneapolis. What would happen to these single analysts as they returned to cities without a Jungian presence? How would they establish a Jungian community and train future analysts? What would happen if the single analyst in an area were analyst, supervisor, teacher, and possibly the analyst of the significant other? The issue of incest has always been a consideration when a new group formed. All depth psychology groups have had to deal with this issue. The large distances between individual members often precluded the formation of new groups.

This was the situation in the early 1970s as the first wave of graduates from Zurich arrived in places distant from established centers. June Singer in Chicago and James Hall in Dallas were the only Jungian analysts in their respective cities. Each of them was facing a need for training facilities closer to home, and had begun preparing prospective candidates through special study courses. June attended a Jungian conference in Texas as a presenter, as did James Hall and Murray Stein. The three analysts discussed their common difficulties in providing analytic training in the middle of the United States. Out of that discussion came the idea of establishing a training program with certified Jungian analysts who were not associated with either the East Coast or the West Coast Jungian centers. They invited several experienced analysts to meet with them to explore this possibility. An organizational meeting was held in St Louis in 1973, and the original three were joined by William Willeford of Washington State, Linda Leonard of Denver, Colorado, Thomas Kapacinskas of South Bend, Indiana, and Arwind Vasavada, who had recently moved to Chicago from India. Also present – by invitation – were elder analysts: Jo Wheelwright of San Francisco, who had recently retired as president of the IAAP, and Werner Engel, past president of the New York Association for Analytical Psychologists. These two were asked to come to the initial meeting to serve as advisors on the founding of a new Institute. Both Drs Engel and Wheelwright lent their support from the beginning. Two Zurich candidates, Louise Bode and William Walker, were also invited to this first organizational meeting, as the organizers felt that it was advisable to gain input from future training candidates as well as seasoned analysts in the development of a training program.

This small group of seven analysts and two candidates was at the beginning of a large undertaking. First, they had to convince the existing societies in the United States that they were not just being "rebellious," as they needed to obtain approval from the existing societies in California and New York (Walker 1980). Jo Wheelwright went to the three existing groups and discussed the creative aspects of such a training. Wheelwright made the following statements in support of the IRS Training Program: (a) the IRS would lessen the incest in all the newly forming groups; (b) as each individual group within the IRS developed a critical mass, the developing group would break off from the IRS and form an independent group within the IAAP; (c) eventually, the IRS would self-destruct as each new group would in time become independent. June Singer does not recall that item (c) was ever discussed during the organizational meeting of the IRS. She believes that Jo may have come up with this creative idea in response to possible fears that were voiced that the IRS in some way might become a threat to the existing training centers.

Secondly, and significantly, the IRS would not develop training groups in areas with already established Institutes. The IRS was to be utilized as an outreach program to develop training programs in new areas. They were not seen as an alternative training to already established programs. If that point had not been made clear, there is no way that San Francisco, Los Angeles, or New York, would have approved of the new training society.

Thirdly, they had to agree on what constituted adequate training to become a Jungian analyst. Following the Zurich model they proposed broad requirements in order to include all the varying philosophies. In that regard the requirements for admission to training were liberal so that many kinds of candidates could be included. A terminal degree in medicine, psychology, social work, counseling, and pastoral psychology was required. A "special persons" category was also included to allow for that rare individual who did not have the appropriate degree but who was deemed a suitable analytic candidate.

At the IAAP Congress in August 1974 the IRS was accepted as a new member with the name of the Inter-Regional Society of North America. The name of the new society included "of North America" because in addition to Americans both Canadians and Mexicans would be eligible to be members of this group. A most important clause in the IRS constitution was that members of any other Jungian society could join the IRS, as long as they attended one meeting every two years. This left a loophole for any analyst from any other society, for whatever reason, to join the IRS with no questions asked. As members in good standing, they were eligible to become part of IRS. Over time this has presented major political problems.

Although not brought up specifically at that first meeting, concerns were being raised about what was going on in the training program of the IRS. There were disconcerting rumors that numerous boundary violations were occurring between women candidates and their male supervising analysts. Since this was a new training group with relatively little experience in these matters, this sensitive issue was of great concern. It has been difficult for the IRS to resolve these matters, and they have been slow to adopt a code of ethics.

It is necessary to interrupt this history of the IRS to report on another event which had some significance for the development of analytical psychology in the United States. What was happening to those solo analysts who did not join the IRS in 1974 or shortly thereafter? One important member, Mary Ann Mattoon in Minneapolis, decided not to join the IRS at that time. She preferred to have her candidates train in the old way towards individual membership in the IAAP. This was an option open to any individual anywhere in the world, but it required the acceptance of the group or groups from the country where the applicant lived. The conditions for individual membership were easier to fulfill, and Mattoon's trainees had met those requirements. However, there was much opposition from the IRS, which felt that if the path of individual membership in the United States were left open it would undermine the *raison d'être* of the IRS. A compromise was reached between the IAAP and the IRS in 1978; individual applicants from Minnesota were accepted into the IAAP without objection, but in the future the door to individual membership from the United States would be closed. Each analyst in the United States must belong to a society. Over the years there have been some instances where American members of the IAAP did not wish to belong to any particular society, but after the above agreement came into effect it was necessary for individuals to find a suitable professional society or withdraw their membership from the IAAP.

In 1980 the Chicago Society of Jungian Analysts became the first society to claim independence from the IRS, and its history will be described elsewhere. In 1981 the following sub-groups were formed under the aegis of the IRS: Vancouver–Seattle, New Mexico–Colorado, Texas, Illinois, Pittsburgh, Toronto. Regional boards were set up to screen prospective trainees before being brought before the national board of the IRS.

A second important issue began to emerge at that time. Many non-clinical applicants were applying for training and coming in under the "exceptional persons" clause. Applicants from a state which allowed practice as a Jungian analyst with no licensure requirements could train as long as they did not break any state regulations concerning the practice of Jungian analysis. The "exceptional person" clause was replaced by a non-clinical category of training. This two-tier training had important, long-term consequences for the development of the IRS. The following motion was ratified at an IRS meeting in 1980:

> The Society recognizes that the cultural significance and the clinical applications of analytical psychology are of equal importance and acknowledges the necessity for analytical psychologists who hold clinical degrees to be practicing legally in those fields and to be related acceptably to other professional groups to which they belong.
>
> Therefore, in general, applicants who hold clinical degrees will be expected to have before taking the Diploma Exam a degree that permits independent analytical-type practice in their intended place of residence and to be licensed if required by their place of practice.
>
> Non-clinical applicants (i.e. those who do not hold clinical degrees and who were formerly called "exceptional persons") will be expected as a requirement of their acceptance into the training program to sign an agreement not to use any wording which might infringe on a legally defined field of practice. All applicants will designate themselves in such a fashion as not to break any law relating to practice in their state of residence or practice.
>
> The minimum requirement for a non-clinical applicant will be a M.A. degree or its equivalent.
>
> All applicants will abide by the code of ethics of the Society.

In addition to training many non-clinical candidates, the new graduates returning from Zurich found the atmosphere in the IRS congenial. Zurich was one of the few places in the world where non-clinicians could train to become Jungian analysts, so that most of the American students from the 1980s on were non-clinicians. Originally, Americans had been drawn to Zurich as a Mecca, but now they were going because it was the one of the few remaining Jungian trainings, in addition to the IRS, which did not require a clinical degree. As a result of the influx of graduates from Zurich, the percentage of non-clinical members in the IRS increased the tension between the two factions. In 1984 the issue was raised again at one of their biannual meetings. The wording of the qualification requirements was changed to state that "each candidate be judged on individual merit," and "the categories of clinical and non-clinical be abolished" (Walker 1980). Clinical competence and knowledge of transference were to be judged during the admission interviews. The IRS has continued to clarify and amplify what constitutes a good candidate over the years. No new categories have emerged.

The issue between clinical and non-clinical reminds one of the fights that the American Psychoanalytic Association had with the International Psychoanalytic Association which led to the former withdrawing from the latter for forty years. In 1936 the American Psychoanalytic Association wished only medical doctors to be eligible for membership. This went against the principles of the International, which included lay analysts. Freud wrote his essay on "The Question of Lay Analysis" (Freud 1936) to defend non-medical persons and their value as analysts. After so many years – with some irony – the American Psychoanalytic Association has now become a leader in including non-medical persons for training. In analytical psychology the net is much wider, and both in the IRS and in Zurich any person with a Master's degree in any subject is eligible to become an analyst. The candidate must demonstrate solid clinical competence by the end of the training. The issue of clinical versus non-clinical is a most important one and is potentially divisive for the Jungian movement both in the United States and the rest of the world.

Other professional societies, besides Chicago, have emerged out of the IRS as independent groups and have become members of the IAAP. They include the Pacific Northwest Society of Jungian Analysts, the Dallas Society of Jungian Analysts, the Ontario Association of Jungian Analysts, the New Mexico Society of Jungian Analysts, and the Philadelphia Association of Jungian Analysts. The Minnesota contingent, which began independently from the IRS, is now a regional sub-group of the IRS.

The Inter-Regional Society has continued to grow, and recently new sub-groups have formed in Buffalo and in the Southeast.

As any IAAP member can join IRS, some members from both San Francisco and New York have joined its ranks. This provision allows members who do not like what is taking place in their local society to join IRS and avoid the conflicts closer to home. It is a subtle form of splitting, and this loophole is not appreciated by other American societies. Because of this membership clause, the IRS can appear to act as a quasi national organization, as no other American society has this geographical outreach.

The IRS has also started accepting training candidates from areas where there is an existent professional society. Recently a candidate turned down by a local group was accepted for training by the IRS. This had not been the original intent of founding the IRS, but to stop the IRS from doing so would be restraint of trade, legally. If the local society were to protest the IRS decision regarding a candidate, the counter argument would be that individuals have the freedom to train wherever they want, and that the choices should not be limited to the local group. The IRS has stated that it will not run training seminars in communities served by IAAP-approved Institutes. However, it will consider all qualified applicants "without regard to race, gender, religion, sexual orientation, or geographic place of residence" (Minutes of IRS Meeting, April 1997).

In conclusion, it is clear that the IRS, created when there was a large vacuum in training possibilities within the United States, has now become a large, shifting in nature, professional society, which has many unique characteristics. The lack of definite geographic boundaries, acceptance of persons without a clinical license, and crossing of national borders, has given the IRS a mercurial presence which the other more geographically defined groups do not possess. The predominance of non-clinically trained analysts gives it a more loosely defined persona, but at the same time it is represented by a number of well-known Jungians in the United States.

NEW ENGLAND SOCIETY OF JUNGIAN ANALYSTS (NESJA)

In 1973 five Zurich graduates returned to the Boston area and began practicing as Jungian analysts. At that time the unwritten rule in the IAAP was that five members could start a new group and begin training. None of them had degrees in a clinical discipline; they had degrees in economics, anthropology, and rabbinical studies. In 1974 the Boston group applied for membership in the IAAP, and the New York Association for Analytical Psychology vetoed their application on the grounds that they were too inexperienced. The Boston group applied again in 1977 at the Rome Congress, and the New York Association again intended to block their admission but relented. The Boston group was admitted as the New England Society of Jungian Analysts.

In view of their lack of clinical emphasis, they had almost no contact with the rest of the large and established psychotherapeutic and psychoanalytic community in the Boston area. For many years they recreated their Zurich training and attempted to replicate that experience for their candidates. One big part of the Zurich inheritance was to follow one's introversion and not to be concerned with collective issues. For a long time the Boston group participated only reluctantly in national Jungian concerns, and its position at meetings was to slow down change as much as possible. One had the impression that the founding members were holding on to their image of Zurich of the 1970s, whereas the real Zurich had changed considerably. As new members were admitted, both from Zurich and from their own training, the atmosphere in the NESJA began to change. They became more involved in the extraverted world of analytical psychology; furthermore, some of the new members were psychologists and related more to the psychotherapeutic milieu around them. The NESJA has grown and now includes approximately sixty members. They have hosted two national Jungian meetings since 1985, and in general have been more participatory in national Jungian concerns. In spite of all the changes, they have been the most reluctant society among the Americans to ratify having an ethics code for their members. After several years of internal debate they finally passed an ethics code in 1997. This is in keeping with their Zurich heritage which has had a similar debate and struggle about having an ethics code.

In the past ten years the NESJA has changed markedly because of two people who have had contrary approaches to analytical psychology. On one side is Robert Bosnak, a Dutch lawyer who trained in Zurich. He has been extremely active in the larger political world, maintaining contact with world leaders. He has organized seminars on dreams and HIV in Russia and has been active in the former East Germany, Australia, Japan, and other places too numerous to mention. He has written popular books for the lay public. On the other pole is Joe Cambray, who has forged a strong connection with psychoanalysis in Boston and elsewhere. He now teaches at the Harvard Medical School hospitals and has become an integral part of the Boston psychotherapeutic scene. He replaced John Beebe as the American editor of *The Journal of Analytical Psychology*, and on account of this position he has deepened the professional connections between the psychoanalytic and analytical psychological worlds. His professionalism, tact, and enormous energy have begun to transform the NESJA, so that it is now no longer a reluctant member on the American Jungian scene. The NESJA is now a fully participating American Jungian society, and has ceased to be just an outpost of Zurich. Naturally, there are still strong ties to Zurich, but the identification with it is palpably less.

CHICAGO SOCIETY OF JUNGIAN ANALYSTS

In 1980 Chicago was the first professional society to separate from the IRS and form an independent group within the IAAP. This was not surprising since one of the important leaders in the IRS, June Singer, was also the founder of the Chicago group. Moreover, Chicago had already begun to train its own candidates prior to the founding of the IRS in 1974, so that it had a head start on the other IRS regions.

The present Chicago Jung Institute had its beginnings in 1965 through the pioneering efforts of Richard Singer and his wife June. After graduating from the Zurich Jung Institute, they returned to Chicago and began a small reading seminar on Jung. As there were no analysts in Chicago at the time, the Singers could not require a prerequisite of analysis for membership in a Jung group. Tragically, Richard Singer died from a sudden and massive heart attack in February 1965, and June Singer had to take over the mantle in running the Jung group. Fortunately, Arwind Vasavada arrived in Chicago from India and quickly established a following, not only among Jungians but among others in the city of Chicago. In 1966 the Jung Group had its first open lecture and prominent people like Esther Harding and Robertson Davies were among the speakers. During the 1970s three analysts arrived from Zurich: Tom Kapacinskas, Murray Stein, and Tom Lavin; they were to play a major role in the development of a training program. However, recognizing the need for more local analysts, the Board of Directors, as early as 1970, turned its energies to raising money to send selected candidates to Zurich for analytic training. Soon, a part-time executive director was hired to establish "pre-training seminars," which later were to become the Institute's Analyst Training Program (Nolan 1997).

From its very beginning the Chicago group has emphasized education, and the programs have been open to the public, lay and professional alike. From its modest beginnings, the public educational program in Chicago has become one of the biggest of any Jungian organization in the world. Over the years several well-attended conferences have been held on topics germane to analytical psychology. The shadow side of this mixture of public and professional audiences has been a lack of clearly defined boundaries between professional and personal relationships. As in other Jungian centers this boundary issue has also been a problem for Chicago.

June Singer was certainly the inspiration of the expanding group, but there were other supporting members of the cast. After the unexpected death of her husband she was professionally alone with the rapidly emerging group. She turned to the New York Jungians, becoming a member of the New York group; she was also made a member of the Board of the C.G. Jung Foundation in New York. This brought her in touch with Vernon Brookes, Werner Engel, Esther Harding, and William Kennedy.

Given June Singer's situation, there was an inevitable blurring of boundaries between the professional and personal aspects of her life. During this same period of the early 1970s June Singer, amazingly enough, found the time and energy to write a book *Boundaries of the Soul* (1972) in which she described Jungian analysis in a way that was readily understood by American readers. Her reputation as a Jungian author and analyst was established. When the Chicago Society was accepted as a member of the IAAP in 1980, June decided that this was a good time to leave Chicago; she moved to Palo Alto, California, where she taught at the Institute of Transpersonal Psychology, continued her writing, and practiced analysis. This move took a great deal of courage, and it was admirable for her to leave the Chicago group which she had worked so hard to develop. She could feel comfortable in leaving the Windy City, because by that time the Chicago Society of Jungian Analysts had increased both in size and quality with an influx of analysts from Zurich and of graduates from the IRS. June Singer is a lifetime honorary member of the Chicago group. In California she became an active member of the San Francisco Institute as well as being involved with the Gnostic church in Palo Alto. She has written on many subjects, such as gnosticism, androgyny, physics, and archetypes. In 1995 she retired from private practice and moved back to Ohio with her second husband, Irving Sunshine.

The Chicago Institute purchased its first home in Evanston, Illinois, just north of Chicago, in 1976. In 1979 it started a Jungian book store which has been a very successful part of the Institute. In 1982 Peter Mudd, while still a candidate, became the Executive Director, and after finishing his training in 1986 also became the Director of Training, a post he held until 1995. Holding both those powerful positions within the Institute was problematic, so it was important for him to give up the training directorship. On 31 December 1999 Peter Mudd resigned from the position of Executive Director.

By 1992 the Chicago Institute had clearly outgrown its earlier home, and it was time to find a larger space to house the library, book store, and hold public seminars. There were now eleven staff people, and the budget had grown to $800,000 per year (1991). A new larger facility was found which could more adequately serve the community. It also houses fifteen psychotherapy offices, and their rent helps to defray the increased costs. Currently there are approximately fifty professional members.

June Singer has not been the only Chicago analyst to publish books. Another prominent analyst in Chicago, Murray Stein, has been one of the most productive and creative of a younger generation of Jungian writers. Stein, with a master's degree in divinity from Yale, received his diploma from the Jung Institute in Zurich in 1973 and returned to Houston, where he was an analyst with the C.G. Jung Educational Center. In 1976 he moved to Chicago and helped June Singer with the organization of the IRS and later the Chicago Training Program. He was elected president of the Chicago Society in 1978 and remained in that position until 1985. He is a prolific writer, having written on such diverse subjects, as *In Midlife, Jung's Map of the Soul, Jung's Treatment of Christianity, Practicing Wholeness, Transformation: Emergence of the Self*, and edited an important clinical book, *Jungian Analysis*, which is now in a second edition. In addition, together with Nathan Schwartz-Salant, he has run a publishing house, named Chiron, which has consistently published clinical Jungian titles since 1983. During the 1980s Chiron also held a yearly conference at Ghost Ranch, New Mexico, where clinical papers on a particular theme were presented and later collected in an annual volume.

Members of the Chicago Institute have also been extremely active internationally. In 1992 the Chicago Institute hosted the triennial International Jungian Congress. Murray Stein was the honorary secretary of the IAAP from 1989 to 1995, followed by one term as second vice-president, and he now holds the position of the president-elect. He has traveled and lectured widely, including China, Mexico, Europe, South Africa, and Japan. Former Chicago Institute president, Lee Roloff, has been active in helping the Southern African Association of Jungian Analysts in Cape Town develop its training program. Tom Kapacinskas has visited the newly independent Lithuania several times, teaching analytical psychology to a group of psychotherapists. One Lithuanian, Grazina Gudaite, a psychology professor from Vilnius, has spent a year in the training program of the Chicago Institute.

In conclusion, it is evident that the Chicago Jung Institute is one of the most lively and energetic of all Jung Institutes in the world. It has grown at a rapid pace, and as a result there have been growing pains. The move into the new Institute building has not been without tremendous financial and organizational pressures. However, the vitality of the Institute is obvious, and, located in the heartland of America, it is a focal point for a large geographical area.

ONTARIO ASSOCIATION OF JUNGIAN ANALYSTS

Toronto, Canada, has long had an active Jungian organization under the stewardship of James Shaw. A Canadian by birth, Shaw lived for many years in New York where he had had a lengthy analysis with Esther Harding. When he returned to Toronto in the late 1960s, he organized a Jung Center and brought in well-known Jungian speakers, including Esther Harding, Joseph Henderson, Adolf Guggenbühl-Craig, and Edward Edinger. Jungian analysts have always looked forward to the experience of speaking in Toronto, which is a very congenial host city, and the audiences there were responsive to the ideas of analytical psychology. A significant and active member of the Jung group in Toronto was the novelist Robertson Davies, whose novels have had wide impact on the English reading public. One novel, *The Manticore*, is the story of a person going to Zurich for analysis. Jim Shaw retired in 1991, but not before establishing a strong tradition in Jung's work.

During the 1970s three individuals from Toronto went to the Jung Institute in Zurich for training. When they returned, they joined the IRS and were among the early members of that group. They have played a major role in the development of analytical psychology. Two of the three, Marion Woodman and Frazier Boa, were brother and sister. Boa had been making movies in Hollywood, whereas sister Marion had a degree in English Literature. The third member, Daryl Sharp, had previously been in the publishing business and also worked at Spring Publications in Zurich with Jim Hillman. Upon his return from Zurich to Toronto, Sharp started a Jungian book publishing company and called it Inner City Books. It had the sole purpose of publishing books by Jungian analyst authors. Marie-Louise von Franz supported the idea and became the patron of the publishing venture. It had a modest beginning, but when Marion Woodman's *Addiction to Perfection* was published in 1982, sales skyrocketed; it established Inner City Books. Now several new titles come out every year, and it is the only Jungian book publishing house which relies exclusively on Jungian analysts for its material. Marion Woodman has published a number of other books on subjects such as mythology, eating disorders, the role of the body, and the feminine. Her work has a special appeal for women with issues around body image, its relationship to food, anorexia, and bulimia. Her brother, Frazier, went on to make a documentary on dreams, using Jung's theories, and having Marie-Louise von Franz interpret the dreams. Ten half-hour segments were made with von Franz's commentary; they demonstrate the objective nature of the unconscious. These films have been enthusiastically shown around the world, to much acclaim.

The Ontario Association of Jungian Analysts finally became an independent society and a member of the IAAP in 1995. It is still a relatively small society with fewer than twenty members and has a lively public seminar program. Most of the members are graduates from Zurich, while others have trained in American Institutes. Frazier Boa died of cancer a few years ago.

PACIFIC NORTHWEST SOCIETY OF JUNGIAN ANALYSTS; JUNGIAN ANALYSTS – NORTH PACIFIC

The Pacific Northwest Society of Jungian Analysts (PNSJA), as a group, was an outgrowth of the IRS. It encompasses the states of Oregon and Washington in the United States and British Columbia in Canada. It became independent in 1986, and its history has been rather turbulent. Many of its members trained through the IRS, but several members trained in Zurich; others, such as Russell Lockhart and Janet Dallett, transferred from Los Angeles. The Pacific Northwest is a very beautiful part of the United States and Canada to live in, and its lack of congestion increases the attractiveness of the area. Shortly after becoming an independent society, conflict over the nature of training arose. Some wanted a more structured training program, whereas others, particularly Russ Lockhart, wanted a program based on the mentor model. He wanted one person, the mentor, to be the supervisor and teacher throughout the training of the individual candidate. Most of the others wished to have group seminars, and committee evaluations, with a more typical analytic training model. A second issue was that several newly graduated analysts returned from Zurich, where they did not receive as much clinical training as is typical in America. The more clinically oriented members wanted the recent graduates from Zurich to have one to two years of supervised clinical work before they could be admitted as full members. The combination of the mentor model and the increased clinical requirements for Zurich graduates caused a deep cleavage in the society, and no healing was possible.

PNSJA split and a new group formed called Jungian Analysts – North Pacific (JANP). This new group accepted the Zurich graduates without further clinical training, and a modified mentor model was installed. There was a brief honeymoon period which lasted only months as the new group began to organize its training program. By then Ladson Hinton, a senior psychiatrist analyst trained in San Francisco, arrived on the scene, and took over leadership of the new group. They accepted their first trainees, and a seminar program was begun. Legal battles with regard to unprofessional conduct of one of the members caused a deep division within the newly formed group. Time, money, and energy were sapped as a result of the legal struggles so that the training program has slowed down considerably.

The remaining members in PNSJA established a more traditional training program for its candidates. Most of its members reside in Oregon, and an important member, John Allan, lives in Vancouver. Robin Jaqua in Eugene, Oregon, has been the director of training, and has embarked on a film project, named MacKenzie Oaks Films, producing teaching documentaries on analytical psychology.

Now that the fight between the two societies is over, a healing process is beginning to take place. Ideologically the differences between the two groups is not that significant, and now that the mentor model has been seen to be impractical for both societies they can begin to agree on most issues.

OTHER INDEPENDENT AMERICAN JUNGIAN SOCIETIES

As there is no national American Jungian association, each individual society, as it develops and desires to become autonomous, needs to present its documents to the IAAP. There are many small societies emerging in different parts of the United States. The rest of this chapter will discuss those which have already formed or are in the process of forming.

Society of Jungian Analysts of San Diego

The earliest of the small societies to become independent was San Diego, California, which became an autonomous society in 1980. Located 120 miles south of Los Angeles, all of its original members had their training there. It started out small and has remained a small society of seven members.

C.G. Jung Analysts Association of the Greater Washington, DC Metropolitan Area

The Washington group is another small society with nine members at the present time. Most of its members either trained in New York or came from Zurich. It has been in existence since 1989.

New Mexico Society of Jungian Analysts

The New Mexico group has developed out of the IRS. It became independent in 1989. New Mexico has a special appeal for Jungians because of its closeness to the American Indian culture and its beautiful natural scenery. As a result many of the members of this group have trained elsewhere, such as Zurich, San Francisco, Chicago, and New York. Many different theoretical points of view have been brought to bear in the training of candidates. The various influences have not always mixed well, and at certain times enormous battles have ensued. The training of candidates is ongoing, and New Mexico offers an active public program.

Philadelphia Association of Jungian Analysts

This is a society which has become independent only in the last three years. It is a small group.

Dallas Society of Jungian Analysts

The Dallas Society is also a small group which has separated from the IRS and functions at a low level of activity. No candidates are being trained in Dallas.

PROFESSIONAL GROUPS – NOT YET APPROVED

Pittsburgh

A symptom of one of the most vexing problems that has faced the American Jungians is the history of analytical psychology in Pittsburgh. The first Jungian analyst in Pittsburgh was Harriet Machtiger, a psychologist who trained in London at The British Association of Psychotherapists – Jungian Section (BAP). Through her BAP training she was heavily influenced towards British object-relations psychoanalysis. Upon her return to the United States in the mid-1970s, she developed a close working relationship with psychoanalysts in Pittsburgh. As the only Jungian in Pittsburgh she had many professional therapists coming to her for analysis and training in analytical psychology. Several psychologists became accredited through the IRS training program. Strong personal feelings among the four Jungian analysts in Pittsburgh resulted in the formation of two separate factions. At times the two competing groups had Jungian public lectures on the same night.

In 1993 Harriet brought together four other analysts from around the country with whom she wanted to form the nucleus of a new independent Jungian group within the IAAP. Her colleagues were chosen on the basis of ideological compatibility rather than geographical proximity. The issue was discussed by the American Jungian representatives at a CASJA meeting, who did not want to approve of a group where all the members lived at such a great distance from one another. The two groups continue to have their separate programs. To this day each side seems resigned to the status quo, and it has not reached national attention again. Neither group in Pittsburgh is large enough on its own to form an independent society within the IAAP.

What happened in Pittsburgh is typical in the history of depth psychology training. A negative transference–countertransference reaction is not contained within the analytic relationship. Instead, the emotional interplay is acted out in a more or less public setting, and the whole group becomes involved in the struggle. Each side has its adherents, and neither side will concede anything.

Houston

A very interesting history for analytical psychology developed in Houston. In the late 1950s Ruth Thacker Fry, a woman of financial means from Houston, studied in Zurich but did not graduate. She returned to Houston and founded the C.G. Jung Educational Center, despite the fact that there were no such centers anywhere. She received a letter from C.G. Jung who approved of her outreach program to the general public. Over the years the Center has been run mostly by lay people, but an analyst has been brought in as director whenever possible. At present the director is James Hollis, an analyst. They have been able to bring in major Jungian speakers from all over the world. Both James Hillman and Adolf Guggenbühl-Craig made their American debut there, and Sir Laurens van der Post lectured there several times. Frank McMillan, who later endowed the professorship in analytical psychology at the University of Texas A&M, was first introduced to Jung through the Houston Center. Another person connected with the

Houston center was Carolyn Fay, who has provided the funds for an annual lecture series at Texas A&M, now in its tenth year.

COUNCIL OF AMERICAN SOCIETIES OF JUNGIAN ANALYSTS (CASJA)

In most European countries there exists a national organization of analytical psychologists. When there are enough analysts in a country, a national umbrella organization is formed with satellite institutes in the major training centers. If a split occurs within a national society, the second group is also national in nature, such as is the case in England and Italy. The American and Canadian situations have been different, in that neither country has been comfortable with a national umbrella organization. The Canadian attitude is quite understandable as there are so few analysts across the country. However, even though approximately a quarter of the Jungian analysts (over 500) in the world live in the United States, there has been no authoritative national body here. The rest of this chapter will describe the circuitous path that the United States has taken towards a national organization, and some of the issues that have arisen among the groups.

The earliest mention of any national or territorial claims was made in 1945 when Esther Harding and Jo Wheelwright discussed how to carve up their respective spheres of influence. The Mississippi river was considered the dividing line between the two. No further mention of any national organization occurred until 1962, when the C.G. Jung Foundation of New York, headed by Esther Harding, thought of itself as *the* national center. Although at the time it had national representation on its board, it never truly functioned as a national body.

The seeds for a yearly national meeting were planted in 1972. From 1952 on there had been an annual North–South California meeting. In 1972 Edward Edinger, living in New York, asked to be invited to the North–South meeting as a guest. He liked the meeting, and in the following years many others from New York and the rest of the country and Canada attended the annual meeting as well, and the old North–South meeting gradually took on a national character. Although the meeting itself became all-American, no political or training issues of a national nature were discussed. Whenever an attempt of that sort was made, it would immediately be dismissed by the group. However, these meetings did allow for a general collegiality among American and Canadian analysts.

In 1978 when a concern emerged regarding the territorial boundaries of the rapidly expanding IRS, a network of connections to organize a meeting on the subject was already in place. Representatives from the five existing societies and an IAAP representative met for a weekend in New York (see IRS history, pp. 104–9). The meeting was very spirited; James Hall, the first and long-time president of the IRS, denied that the IRS had any plans to become a national organization, and he could not understand the concerns of the other societies. The outcome of this meeting was the realization that representatives from each society should meet on a yearly basis at the national meeting. Over time this confederation came to be known as CASJA. The meetings have grown larger as new societies have been included.

From the very beginning the discussions were informal, and it was clear that the body was to be advisory and would not interfere with the autonomy of any single society. Los Angeles and Boston had doubts about even this level of commitment to this fledgling organization without power. Issues which have come before CASJA include the training programs of each society, questions about territoriality, as well as power and prestige problems related to each society. An example of a territorial issue occurred when the IRS wanted to organize a satellite training in Sacramento, California, seventy miles from San Francisco. Representatives of the San Francisco society objected to such an institute, and the proposal was dropped. Similar concerns appeared when the San Diego society was formed 120 miles from Los Angeles. However, that proposal was approved. As a result of these territorial problems an amendment was voted on that "no new society should be formed less than 200 miles from an already existing training program." In view of the fact that CASJA had no official authority, it remained a strongly worded recommendation.

Realizing that so many Americans were training in Zurich in the mid-1980s, it was decided to pay half the fare for a Zurich representative to attend the yearly CASJA meetings. In view of the fact that between five and ten analysts have returned to the United States every year from Zurich to swell the ranks of American Jungian Institutes it was deemed important that a Zurich representative be present to have a better understanding of the issues facing the graduates when they return to the United States.

What to call this informal national organization was always a puzzle. Finally, with the help of Charles Taylor, former provost of Yale University and present chair of the National ARAS, the name Council of American Societies of Jungian Analysts (CASJA) was agreed upon. CASJA continues to meet at least yearly. Although no formal vote can be taken on issues, a sense of how the different societies feel about a question certainly becomes clear.

Some extremely important topics have come before CASJA – e.g., when the Pittsburgh conflict arose, the two sides presented their respective positions at a CASJA meeting. It was important for the other American societies to hear first-hand what the issues were.

Many new and small American societies are emerging, such as the one in Atlanta and one in South Carolina. The question is how long the United States can go on without having a more authoritative national umbrella organization. Issues like insurance payments for psychotherapy, accreditation for analysts, possible licensing issues, transfer of candidates from one Institute to another, and other concerns need to be dealt with on a national level. The local groups will probably have to yield some autonomy in order to unite and keep abreast of these issues. At the present time the IAAP is the only legal entity to deal with such questions, and that can seem distant and far away. Meanwhile the IRS is moving into new areas, developing new satellite institutes, and carrying on as a quasi-national entity.

ANALYTICAL PSYCHOLOGY AND ACADEMIA

The role of Jung in academia has been problematic all over the world, but nowhere more so than in the United States. Jung's emphasis on the non-rational, the unconscious, mystical experience, has left Jung generally out of the academic mainstream until recently. Now the pendulum has swung away from materialism, and an objective study of the phenomena which interested Jung and analytical psychology has taken on greater significance. To take a comprehensive look at Jung and academia is beyond the scope of this section. However, it is important to see how analytical psychology seeped into the universities, and what a powerful effect it had on the development of analytical psychology in the United States.

After World War I Jung's writings became quite well known in the United States. His books on *Psychological Types* and *Psychology of the Unconscious* were widely read by the lay public. Jung was invited to speak at the Harvard Tercentenary in 1936 and again at Yale in 1937 to give the Terry Lectures on "Psychology and Religion." However, behaviorism was at its peak and there was little interest in Jung's work in academic psychology. The situation in psychiatry was not much different. In the late 1930s a wave of European Freudian psychoanalysts emigrated to the United States, and psychoanalysts became the chairmen of all the psychiatric departments in the United States. The antipathy towards Jung was great, and so, with very few exceptions, Jungians were not allowed to teach in the medical schools.

The exceptions were Bruno Klopfer at UCLA and Joseph Henderson and Jo Wheelwright in San Francisco. Klopfer, a German-Jewish refugee, had studied Rorschach and had become a leading exponent of the test. At UCLA he was a clinical professor of psychology, taught the Rorschach test, which was extremely popular at the time, and Jungian psychology. Many of his graduate students in psychology eventually went into Jungian training, including Marvin Spiegelman, Hayao Kawai, Harold Stone, and many others. In 1959 he founded the Bruno Klopfer Workshop at Asilomar, California, which was the only intensive course in analytical psychology at the time and attracted students from all over the country.

Jo Wheelwright became an instructor at the newly opened Langley-Porter Neuropsychiatric Institute in 1941. This institute was and is part of the University of California Medical Center in San Francisco. He taught analytical psychology to psychiatric residents and psychologists for over thirty years. Many students have entered training by way of this route. Many other analysts have continued the tradition of teaching and supervising residents and psychologists at Langley-Porter. Today there are numerous Jungians on the faculty and staff of Langley-Porter. Joseph Henderson followed a parallel path at Stanford Medical School while it was located in San Francisco. He gave a seminar on dreams to the psychiatric residents for fifteen years. When the Stanford Medical School moved from San Francisco to Palo Alto, Tom Kirsch continued the tradition of teaching at Stanford from 1968 until 1998. Now there are many other Jungians on the staff of Stanford as well.

Many American members now have part-time teaching positions in various university settings. This has been a remarkable change from thirty years ago, when teaching positions for analytical psychologists were scarce. The most significant full-time position in analytical psychology has been the endowed professorship in analytical psychology at the University of Texas A&M. Frank McMillan, a wealthy businessman, endowed the position at the University ten years ago, and the first and only recipient has been Dr David Rosen, a psychiatrist and Jungian analyst. David Rosen and his students have been undertaking research projects in analytical psychology, and theses dealing with analytical psychology have been written. A yearly lecture series, supported by Carolyn Fay, takes place each spring on the campus of the university. Afterwards the lectures are published in book form.

Another significant academician is Dr Harry Wilmer in Salado, Texas. Wilmer, an academic psychiatrist and psychoanalyst, was the director of a "hippie" unit at Langley-Porter in San Francisco in the late 1960s. He saw the value of Jung's idea and entered a Jungian analysis and was made an individual member of the IAAP in 1974. He had transferred to San Antonio, Texas, where as a professor he continued his research on marginal groups and their dreams. He took over the directorship of the Institute of the Humanities in Salado, Texas and made it into a forum for analytical psychology as well as wider cultural interests.

Recently, academia has become less hostile to the viewpoint of analytical psychology. There no longer exists great antipathy towards anything Jungian. It can now be taught at the university like any other subject.

8 Analytical psychology in Germany

EARLY HISTORY

The story of Jung and analytical psychology in Germany is intimately connected with the general history of Germany in the twentieth century. One cannot speak about twentieth-century Germany without mentioning Nazism and Hitler. Jung personally, and analytical psychology in general, were closely connected to the Nationalist Socialist regime; much has been written about this period in Jung's life. Both Jung's detractors and his apologists have argued for over a half century whether Jung was a Nazi and/or was anti-Semitic. These are related and overlapping issues which will be discussed.

From today's perspective it is sometimes difficult to imagine the importance that Germany held for pre-World War II Europe. Having been united for the first time in the late nineteenth century by Bismarck, with Berlin as its capital, Germany was a leader in science, philosophy, music, and the arts. Both Freud and Jung thought that if psychotherapy was to survive, it would be vital that "analysis" in Germany be strong (Roazen 1974). For example, the first psychoanalytic institute was not in Vienna, where Freud lived and worked, but was founded in Berlin in 1920. The structure for most training institutes, Freudian or Jungian, goes back to the model of the Berlin Psychoanalytic Institute, which included analysis, supervision, and training seminars. Until the Nazis banned Jewish practitioners and Freud's books in May of 1933, the Berlin Psychoanalytic Institute was the leading Freudian Institute in the world (Ehlers 1985).

Gustav Richard Heyer (1890–1967)

The medical doctor Gustav Richard Heyer from Munich was the first significant person in Germany to be attracted to Jung's psychology.

Most students of Jung's psychology in Germany went to see Heyer in Munich for analysis and training. He had married Lucie Grote, a gymnastics teacher and breathing specialist, at the end of World War I in 1918. She had been instrumental in their creating a combined physical and psychological therapy. They had both done a short training analysis with Jung in the mid-1920s. Several future Jungian analysts saw Lucie for body work, including Margit Frank of New York, and even today there are well-known body therapists in the United States, such as Marion Rosen, who can trace the origin of their work to therapeutic experiences with Lucie Grote-Heyer (Rosen 1995:54–55). Dr Heyer developed a close friendship with Jung and was one of the few outside the family who addressed Jung with the more intimate "*Du*" in German. When Jung took over the controversial presidency of the General Medical Psychotherapy Society, he chose Heyer to be his deputy for the first year. Jung also wrote an introduction to his book *The Organism of the Mind* (Heyer 1934). Heyer was a regular lecturer in the early years of Eranos in Ascona, Switzerland. In 1936 Heyer and Jung got into an argument at the annual meeting which changed the nature of their relationship (personal interview, Charlotte Eschmann). In 1937 Heyer joined the Nazi party and in 1939 was asked to come to Berlin to teach and see patients at the Goering Institute. Lucie Heyer divorced him in the mid-1930s, in part because of his political leanings. He remarried, but he and Lucie remained friends and colleagues.

To illustrate the confusion of the times, Max Zeller, one of the later co-founders of the Jungian Society in Los Angeles, was in analysis with Heyer in 1938, just before being interned in a concentration camp. Zeller, a Jew, prohibited by law to practice in Germany, was given a letter of recommendation by Heyer allowing him to practice in another country. In the letter dated September 1938 Heyer stated: "I esteem equally highly his gifts as a psychotherapeutic practitioner and his character as a man. I recommend him most warmly and wish him much success in the future" (translated by Lore Zeller). It was this training certificate which allowed Zeller to practice as an analyst when he finally settled in Los Angeles in 1941. In the 1930s Lore Zeller had worked with Lucie Heyer. The Zellers never found a trace of anti-Semitism in Heyer. However, as a member of the Goering Institute, Heyer was willing to write publicly in an ostensibly anti-Semitic fashion against "Jewish" influence.

In 1941 Heyer reviewed the German edition of Jung's writings on "Psychology and Religion" in the *Psychiatrische–Neurologische Wochenschrift*. Heyer attacked Jung for his "western-democratic audience" and his criticism of totalitarianism, which Heyer rightly understood as Jung's criticism of National Socialism.

After the war Jung denounced Heyer for his Nazi affiliation. Heyer attempted to speak to Jung about this, but Jung would never meet with him again. Christopher Whitmont, originally an Austrian Jew – who anglicized his name – and a long-time practitioner in New York, saw Heyer for analysis in the early 1950s and tried to arrange a meeting between the two but without any success. Heyer claimed that it was Jung who recommended that he join the Nazi party, and that Jung shared with him similar ideas about the Nazis (Lockot 1994). However, a document exists at the Bundesarchiv (National Library) in Berlin, written by Heyer and dated 29 February 1944, which gives another picture.

> I did my training analysis with C.G. Jung in whose teachings the breakthrough was made from 'alien' construct. Yet today I cannot underwrite everything he published. Several things differentiate us, for instance, that he is more researcher than physician; that he does not value my inclusion of the feminine into psychotherapy, and besides such scientific differences there also are different attitudes to political situations.
>
> (translated by Lore Zeller)

These political differences were a definite source of tension between Jung and Heyer. It shows that Heyer's politics were in spite of Jung, rather than because of Jung. Heyer was deeply immersed in Nazism, but he withdrew his membership from the Nazi party sometime in 1944. Shortly after the war in November 1945 Jung wrote to Friedrich Seifert in Munich that he would have nothing further to do with Heyer because of his Nazi affiliation (unpublished letter from Jung to Seifert, dated 21 November 1945). Toni Wolff wrote in a similar vein to Seifert about Heyer. After the war Heyer moved back to rural Bavaria where he continued to practice and write until his death in 1967. Except for Christopher Whitmont, there are no other Jungians who saw Heyer in analysis after the war. According to Whitmont, Heyer was an excellent analyst, and the analytical work with Heyer was crucial for his development. Heyer became active in the Lindau Conference, a yearly meeting for German-speaking psychotherapists, where many other Jungians lectured over the years. Heyer's daughter was contacted during the writing of this book and stated that she had burned all of her father's papers.

Kaethe Buegler (1898–1977)

The second person in Germany to become interested in Jung's psychology was Kaethe Buegler, a medical doctor, half Jewish, who was supervised in her work by Heyer in Munich. In 1927 she went to Jung for analysis, and returned to Berlin in 1929 where she practiced as an analyst until the early 1970s. James Kirsch, Heinz Westmann, Max Zeller, and other German Jews from Berlin had many years of analysis with her. Buegler had a long-standing love relationship with Heyer, who was able to protect her throughout the Nazi period. It must not have been an easy time for her. In 1946 she attempted to establish an independent Jungian training but did not succeed so soon after the war. Jung did not support this venture, and it disbanded in 1949. She continued to work as an individual Jungian analyst in Berlin. When other Jungians became a part of the new German Psychoanalytic Institute she considered it too Freudian, and she remained separate. Her own orientation remained that of a classical Jungian.

JUNGIAN ORGANIZATION

The C.G. Jung Society of Berlin was founded on 24 December 1931 with Mrs Eva Moritz as president. On the executive committee of the Society was Adolph von Weizsäcker, Wolfgang Kranefeldt, a prominent Jungian both before and after the war, and about a dozen others who made up the membership which was registered in Berlin. Kaethe Buegler and others of Jewish descent were not mentioned in the official document (Lockot 1985:51). Adolph von Weizsäcker analyzed with Emilii Medtner and Jung, and in 1933 he interviewed Jung on the radio for the Nazi government.

The Jung Society had an active lecture program where Heinrich Zimmer, the great Indologist, lectured several times on "The Psychology of Yoga"; many other famous German scholars of the time also lectured there. It is important to note that at that time in Berlin there were several young Jewish Jungians who were to become influential later in other countries: Gerhard Adler in England; Ernst Bernhard in Rome; Werner Engel and Heinz Westmann in New York; James Kirsch in Palestine, England, and Los Angeles; Erich Neumann in Palestine, later Israel; Max Zeller in Los Angeles (see chapters on the respective societies). The Jung Society, without its Jewish members, continued to meet regularly, and Goering wanted the Jungians to become part of his Institute in 1936. Jung advised against this, and the Society continued to be allowed to meet until 1939, at which point the Gestapo began to exert influence on the Jung Society and required that Nazi party members be included on the Executive Committee. Professor Gustav Schmaltz and a Professor Koerner, who were Nazis, were made Board members. Schmaltz had analyzed with Emma Jung and had run a study group in Düsseldorf. Heyer did not join in the meetings of the Jung Society, and it dissolved as the war began. During the war Jungian activities were limited to the Goering Institute.

INTERNATIONAL GENERAL MEDICAL SOCIETY FOR PSYCHOTHERAPY

The next part of this history is one that has haunted Jung, Jungians, and psychoanalysis. The story is complex, and it has taken many years to get the facts approximately correct. There are two recent books, *Psychotherapy in the Third Reich* by Geoffrey Cocks (1997), and *Erinnern und Durcharbeiten* by Regine Lockot (1985, published only in German), which have painstakingly researched the subject. A brief summary follows.

In 1926 a General Medical Society for Psychotherapy was founded in Germany. It was specifically a German organization, but foreigners were invited to attend its annual congresses. Ernst Kretschmer, a famous professor of psychiatry, became the president in 1930. Jung was made vice-president the same year. In 1933 their congress was scheduled to be held in Vienna, where Freud, Adler, and Jung were to give lectures. When the Nazis took power, they refused to allow the German Society to hold this congress and would not approve travel expenses for the German members. Kretschmer became extremely uncomfortable with the power tactics of the Nazis; he resigned to return to his professorship at the University of Tübingen, which he retained until retirement some twenty years later. He was not Jewish, as has often been rumored, but was born a Catholic. Matthias Goering, also a professor of psychiatry, and a first cousin of the future Reichsmarschall Hermann Goering, was made leader of the nazified German delegation. By this time Freud's and Adler's books had been banned. Jung as honorary vice-president was next in line to be president and was asked to take the post. Jung agonized over the decision, and after many months of negotiations accepted subject to the following conditions: (1) that the society would change its name to become the International General Medical Society for Psychotherapy, and (2) that German Jews could remain as individual members of the Society. Jung later stated in many different places that eventually he made the decision to take the presidency because he could not let his German colleagues down. From his perspective at that time it was essential for psychotherapy to survive in Germany.

The following event is the one which has indelibly marked Jung and Jungians to this day. In 1933, as the new president of the International General Medical Society for Psychotherapy, Jung wrote an introduction to the resuscitated *Zentralblatt*: "Genuinely independent and perceptive people have for a long time recognized that the difference between Germanic and Jewish psychology should no longer be effaced, something that can only be beneficial to the science" (Jung *CW* 10:533–534). Jung went on to discuss differences between Aryan, Chinese, and Jewish psychology. These racial and national characteristics were topics which had interested Jung for many years, and so the ideas expressed were not new. The real question has been why he wrote these statements at that particular moment. As we analysts know, timing is critical in analysis, and the same holds true for politics. What was Jung expressing by writing this statement as his introduction to his presidency? Was he still reacting to the break with Freud? One could answer in the affirmative in view of the fact that Jung had been quite wounded in his relationship with Freud. The "secret committee" had been formed in 1912 around Freud in an effort to isolate Jung and to make sure that Freud would not be hurt again. In the *History of the Psychoanalytic Movement*, Freud referred to Jung as a mystic who had left the discipline of psychoanalysis. Continual efforts had been made in the ensuing twenty years to discredit Jung's views. Jung felt isolated, alienated, and not read in relationship to Freud and Alfred Adler. Jung saw this as an opportunity to promote his psychology which had a forward-looking, spiritual aspect to it over and against the regressive, materialistic viewpoints of Freud and Adler, and in an important country of Europe. In the same issue, which was supposed to go to German members only, a statement by Goering was included, acknowledging the scientific validity of Hitler's *Mein Kampf* and the expectation that the members had studied it. The juxtaposition of the two statements caused a huge international furor.

In a Zurich newspaper in 1934, Gustav Bally, a former Berlin psychoanalyst, who had been forced to emigrate to Switzerland, attacked the emphasis that Jung was placing on the distinction between Jewish and German science, a common theme among Nazi intellectual apologists. For his part, Jung replied to Bally by citing his "disappointment" at the publication of the Goering pledge of allegiance to Hitler in the *Zentralblatt*, and also noted that he was president of the International

Society and had nothing to do with the German Society. Furthermore, he noted that his distinctions between different racial and ethnic groups were a part of his ongoing research and that there was no value judgment implied. As both Bally and Jung lived in Zurich, they had occasion to speak to each other, and afterwards Bally was comfortable with Jung's position. Others, including James Kirsch and Erich Neumann, who were then living in Palestine, questioned Jung's relationship both to Nazism and to anti-Semitism. In Jung's response he stated that people did not understand him and, of course, he was not anti-Semitic or pro-Nazi. The public just did not understand his work (letter Jung–Kirsch, dated 26 May 1934).

Jung's presidency was a three-year term, but he reluctantly agreed to remain as president until the political turmoil was over. Between 1934 and 1936 there were many articles written in the *Zentralblatt* favorable to Jung's analytical psychology. In 1934 Jung sought again to distinguish between the Jewish and "Aryan" unconscious, stating that: "Freud did not know the German soul, and neither do any of his blind adherents. Has not the shattering advent of National Socialism, upon which the world gazes with astonished eyes, taught them better?" ("The State of Psychotherapy Today", *CW* 10). This passage has provoked much discussion from many quarters and has often been read by non-Jungians as anti-Semitic and pro-Nazi. My own opinion is that Jung was making a statement of how deeply these racial and ethnic issues can go – i.e., they have an archetypal root. What was needed was an understanding of the collective unconscious forces at work in the German psyche at that moment. However, I can also see how this statement of Jung's might be seen as an admiration for what National Socialism was doing for Germany. Jung had a certain fascination with the changes going on in Nazi Germany, and he saw the archetypal image of Wotan at work. By 1936 Jung was contemplating National Socialism with a more critical eye: "The impressive thing about the German phenomena is that one man, who is obviously 'possessed,' has infected a whole country to such an extent that everything is set in motion and has started rolling on its course to perdition ("Wotan," Jung *CW* 10, para 381: 185).

At the time of Jung's sixtieth birthday in 1935 a whole edition of the *Zentralblatt* was devoted to his psychology. Having banned both Freud and Adler, the German psychotherapists were seeking to exploit Jung's international and "Aryan" credentials for their own professional purposes. The Nazis themselves were ambivalent about Jung.

In 1936 an important event for psychotherapy and analysis occurred in Germany. It was the establishment of the German Institute for

Psychological Research and Psychotherapy, headed by Professor Matthias Goering, commonly known as the Goering Institute. It marked the beginning of professionalization of psychotherapy in the Third Reich. Jung's role in the affairs of psychotherapy in Germany diminished once this institute was established. His major preoccupation from 1936 until 1940, when he resigned as president of the International General Medical Society, was with the international congresses and controversies surrounding them. The controversies mostly had to do with the attempts of the German members of the General Medical Society to assert their numerical dominance within the International Society. Jung was eager to have other European countries form national groups to counteract the influence of the dominant German group. He was successful in getting other European countries to form their own national groups, and yearly congresses were held until 1938. In 1936 an English group was admitted and had as one of its leaders, Erich Strauss, a Jew, whom Jung had supported over the objections of Goering and the German group.

The tenth and last congress was held in Oxford in the summer of 1938. By that time the Nazis had stepped up their persecution of the Jews, effectively banning them from professional life. Jung led a group which put forth an outline called "common points of view," which purported to be a statement upon which all psychotherapists could agree. One can see Jung's basic tenets of psychotherapy in this statement. Jung was able to have an Englishman, Dr Hugh Crichton-Miller, as vice-president in exchange for holding the next international congress in Germany. Up to this point Jung and Goering had a collegial relationship, but Jung was becoming increasingly impatient with Goering's "simple psychology." Jung's influence within the General Medical Society diminished. Goering succeeded in having the new axis countries become members of the Society, and Jung increasingly became a figurehead president. In September 1940 delegates from both the axis and neutral European countries met in Vienna, and it was decided to place the General Medical Society under German direction for the remainder of the war and to move the headquarters from Zurich to Berlin. C.A. Meier, Jung's assistant, who had replaced Heyer as deputy in 1934, Jung, and Crichton-Miller were essentially replaced.

After the war the International Society was reconstituted, but by this time Jung had his first major heart attack and had retired from many of his professional duties. Another Swiss, Medard Boss, the existential "Daseinanalyse" psychoanalyst, became the new leader of the organization, and it took on a direction where analytical psychology was no longer central.

Jung's participation as president of the General Medical Society for Psychotherapy, and his statements in 1933 and 1934 to that organization, has left an indelible mark on his professional stature. In today's world of psychotherapy one cannot be a Jungian without having to answer to the charge that Jung was both a Nazi and anti-Semitic. Jung's long-standing interest in racial and ethnic traits, and his statements on these subjects with reference to Jewish psychology, have long been interpreted as his, at least, devaluing Jewish traits. His statements on the over-materialistic values of Jewish psychology, and its corrosive effect on the spiritual nature of the psyche, were made in the 1930s; the timing of these statements could not have been worse. The debate that has raged over what Jung meant by these statements goes on unabated. Every time that the issue is raised anew, clarification and amplification of Jung's statements are made, but the issue refuses to die. At the encouragement of Andrew Samuels and others, Jungian analysts themselves have examined the topic at International Jungian Congresses, and written about it in books and articles. Psychoanalysts have used it as a reason not to study Jung; other intellectuals use it to discredit Jung. Every candidate and analyst, Jew or non-Jew, has to come to terms with this aspect of Jung for him/herself, and at present roughly a third of Jungian analysts in the world do have a Jewish background. Everyone looks for a "smoking gun" to prove that Jung was really a Nazi way back when. It is not there. What Jung did not do is openly and publicly repudiate the Nazis before the war. That criticism could be made of many other influential people. There is still the expectation that Jung, as a depth psychologist, should have known better.

This subject is one that has been very close to me. My parents, both Jewish, were in analysis with Jung all through the 1930s. My father and Jung had a correspondence on the subject, where Jung adamantly denies any anti-Semitic and Nazi affinities. My mother stated that it was through her work with Jung that she first began to understand what it meant to be Jewish. Neither of them felt a trace of anti-Semitism in their work with Jung during the 1930s. A number of other Jewish people saw Jung during that period, and they all have stated that they could not find any anti-Semitism in the work. Nevertheless, it has been pointed out to me that Jung could have been very fair on an individual level, and yet on the collective level presented another point of view. My father made the point that before the war Jung only saw the rational element in the Jewish religion, but that after the war Jung experienced the mystical or numinous element of Judaism, which changed his attitude towards the Jewish psyche. There is no question in my mind that Jung's relationship to Freud and Sabina Spielrein played a role in how Jung related to the Jewish question, especially during the 1930s. Jung was still feeling the wound in relationship to Freud. Furthermore, Jung felt that his views were being put down by Freud and Freudians, and with the rise of National Socialism he saw an opportunity to advance his own theories. On the other hand, the National Socialists needed Jung more than Jung needed the National Socialists. Jung's prestige gave Germany's psychotherapy a legitimacy that it would not otherwise have had. Psychoanalysis, and mainly Jewish psychoanalysts, had been predominant in Germany prior to 1933, and with the exodus of all Jewish practitioners the ranks of psychotherapists had been decimated. The Nazis were eager to have someone of Jung's stature supporting them.

It is my opinion that we shall never have a fully satisfactory answer to Jung's role in the International General Medical Society for Psychotherapy, and it becomes important to decide how relevant it is now. Do Jung's theories promote racist tendencies? Is the hypothesis of the collective unconscious racist? These are hypotheses that are open to scientific enquiry, and they present the scientific researcher with fundamental questions about human nature. I do not believe that they have a racist bias. Therefore, we should try and proceed in an objective manner to understand the psyche and its contents. After a long delay we as Jungians have delved into this difficult aspect of Jung's association with National Socialism. There were complex motives for Jung becoming involved with the Nazis, and it is all too easy in hindsight to fault Jung for his involvement. No one knew the extent of the destruction that Nazism would ravage on the world.

THE GOERING INSTITUTE

The German Institute for Psychological Research and Psychotherapy was founded in May 1936. With Matthias Goering as head, it was granted favorable status within the Nazi political structure until the end of the war. The task of the Institute was to create the "New German Psychotherapy," with its emphasis on conveying to the patient the newer higher values and the great common destiny of the German peoples. The curriculum was run on the model of the Berlin Psychoanalytic Institute, but psychoanalytic theory was not recognized. The governing body consisted of representatives from the three groups gathered within the Institute: Fritz Künkel and Edgar Herzog for the Künkel group (also known as the Adler group); Eva Moritz, Wolfgang Kranefeldt, and Adolph von Weizsäcker for the Jungians; and Felix Boehm, Carl Müller-Braunschweig, and Harald Schultz-Hencke for the Freudians and neo-Freudians. Psychoanalysts were allowed to practice as long as they were not Jewish. The governing body changed over the course of the nine years of the Institute's existence; however, Goering was always the director, because he had the connections to the powers within the Nazi party. Künkel, who had lost an arm in World War I, remained in the United States while on a lecture tour in 1938. He moved to Los Angeles; he became essentially Jungian and was a close friend of James Kirsch. Several Jungian analysts, including Jack Sanford of San Diego, were introduced to Jung through Künkel.

In 1936 Goering and the psychoanalysts wanted the Jungians to merge with the Institute, but Jung warned Moritz, the head of the Jungians, not to do so. Jung feared that the Jungians would not be able to have their point of view accepted (Cocks 1997:158). As a consequence individual Jungians continued to teach at the Goering Institute.

In 1939 Heyer moved from Munich to Berlin and taught courses on the relationship of the body and the unconscious. Other Jungians teaching at the Institute included Eva Moritz, Julius Schirren, Gustav Schmaltz, Wolfgang Kranefeldt, and Olga von König-Faschenfeld. They taught basic courses on dreams, psychological types, and interpretation of fairy tales. Kaethe Buegler worked as a therapist at the Goering Institute throughout the war years but did not teach any courses.

The Goering Institute played a significant role in the war effort, conducting research on war neuroses, alcoholism, and homosexuality. Satellite centers were established in other cities in Germany. Besides Berlin, the most active center was in Munich. The Goering Institute was the main training ground for all psychotherapists during the Third Reich and professionalized psychotherapy. On 27 April 1945 the Russians captured the Goering Institute building and brought an end to its operation. In the process of relinquishing the building to the Russians, while trying to escape, Matthias Goering was shot by a Russian officer. The ending tells the story of the Institute in a nutshell.

It is significant for Jungians that after the war Harald Schultz-Henke and Werner Kemper, two prominent members of the old Goering Institute, became the founders of the Deutsche Psychoanalytische Gesellschaft (DPG), the neo-Freudian Institute. Eventually the Jungians became a part of the DPG in the same way as they had previously been a section within the Goering Institute.

So far the Goering Institute has been discussed in relationship to Jungians but not to Jung. After the Goering Institute was founded

Party at the C.G. Jung Institute in Zurich, 1954
Front row, seated on floor, Katie Hillman, C.A. Meier; first row, seated left
to right, Franz Riklin, unknown, Kurt Binswanger, unknown, Rivkah
Schaerf-Kluger, Emma Jung, C.G. Jung, Jolande Jacobi, Liliane Frey;
second row, seated right to left, Aniela Jaffé, Yechezkel Kluger, James
Hillman – Barbara Hannah is in the middle of that row. The rest are
unknown (photo by Oskar Hogstetter, Zurich)

Professor C.A. Meier celebrating his ninetieth birthday in Zurich (photo
from author's collection)

Marie-Louise
von Franz in the
1950s (picture
courtesy of Lore
Zeller)

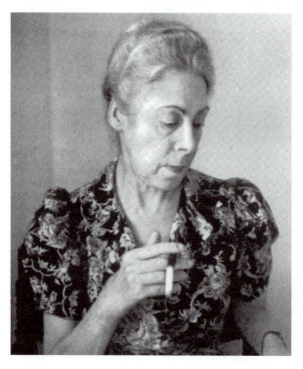

Toni Wolff
in the 1940s
(picture courtesy
of Inge Holle)

Adolf Guggenbühl-Craig 1998 (picture courtesy of the author)

Michael Fordham in the 1980s (picture courtesy of Harriet and Dick Friedman)

Esther Harding in the 1930s (picture courtesy of the Analytical Psychology Club of New York, Michelle Mckee)

Kristine Mann in the 1930s (picture courtesy of the Analytical Psychology Club of New York, Michelle McKee)

Eleanor Bertine in the
1930s (picture courtesy of
the Analytical Psychology
Club of New York,
Michelle McKee)

Frances Wickes in the
1960s (picture courtesy of
the Analytical Psychology
Club of New York,
Michelle McKee)

Edward Edinger in the 1980s (picture courtesy of Lore Zeller)

Heinz Westmann
in the 1970s (picture
courtesy of Ilse
Westmann)

Seminar room, Bailey Island, Maine, 1936 (picture courtesy of the
Analytical Psychology Club of New York, Michelle McKee)

C.G. Jung, Bailey Island, Maine,
1936 (picture courtesy of the
Analytical Psychology Club of New
York, Michelle McKee)

Joseph L. Henderson (picture
courtesy of the author)

Joseph B.
Wheelwright
(picture courtesy
of Wheelwright)

Henderson and Wheelwright on the Italian Riviera, 1977 (picture courtesy
of Joseph Henderson)

Zarathustra Seminar, Los Angeles. Front row, left to right, William Sanford, Janet Dallett, Suzanne Wagner, Deborah Wesley, Rose Emily Rothenberg, Hilde Kirsch; back row, left to right, Russel Lockhart, Max Zeller, Charles Zussman, James Silber, Wyler Green (picture courtesy of Lore Zeller)

Max and Lore Zeller, 1950 (picture courtesy of Lore Zeller)

James Kirsch in the 1980s (picture courtesy of the author)

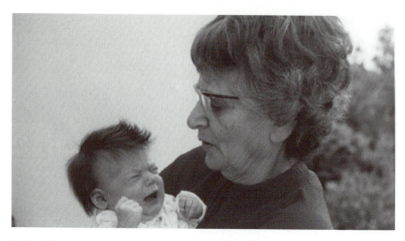

Hilde Kirsch in the 1970s (picture courtesy of the author)

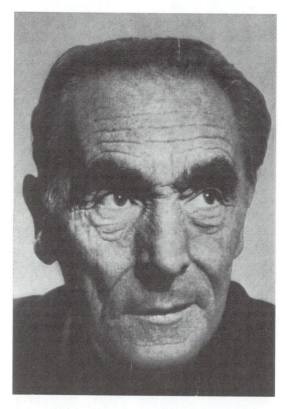

Gustav Richard
Heyer in the 1950s
(picture courtesy of
Raymund Schaeffer)

Ernst Bernhard in the 1940s (picture courtesy of Mario Realfonzo)

Elie Humbert and his wife Myrtha in the 1980s (picture courtesy of Myrtha Humbert)

Erich Neumann in the 1950s (picture courtesy of Dvorah Kutzinski)

Rivkah Schaerf-Kluger in the 1960s (picture courtesy of Lore Zeller)

Gusti Dreifuss and Geula Gat, 1998 (photo from author's collection)

IAAP Congress, 1958. Front row, left to right, Max Zeller, K.W. Bash, Erich Neumann, Bertel Sommer, Ania Friedland, Mary Briner, Peter Walder, Christopher Whitmont, Kurt Binswanger; back row, left to right, unknown, Dora Bernhard, Ernst Bernhard, Robert Moody, Gerhard Adler, Franz Riklin, Murray Jackson, Gordon Prince (picture courtesy of Lore Zeller)

IAAP members in San Francisco, 1996. Left to right, Thomas Kirsch, Clarissa Pinkola Estes, Renos Papadopoulos, Eli Weisstub, Jean Kirsch, Andrew Samuels (picture courtesy of the author)

IAAP members Andrew Samuels and Thomas Kirsch, 1996 (picture courtesy of the author)

IAAP Executive Committee, 1998. Left to right, Vesna Luger, Christian Gaillard, Luigi Zoja (picture courtesy of the author)

Aniela Jaffé (picture courtesy of Robert Hinshaw)

Sigmund Hurwitz (picture
courtesy of Robert Hinshaw)

Liliane Frey (picture courtesy
of Robert Hinshaw)

Ute and Hannes Dieckmann (picture courtesy of Ute and Hannes
Dieckmann)

H.G. "Peter" Baynes
(picture courtesy of Diane
Jansen)

Jung was no longer involved, except to give one seminar there in 1937, which brought money into the coffers of the Institute. By 1938 Jung was pretty disillusioned by Goering and was strongly opposed to axis countries like Hungary, Italy, and Japan becoming members of the International Medical Society. There was no correspondence between Jung and Goering after 1940, as by then Jung had distanced himself completely from the Nazis.

The question lingers as to why Jung spent so much time and energy with the Nazified Goering Institute. As a neutral Swiss he thought that he could help German psychotherapy and analysis survive, aid individual Jewish doctors, and have a forum for his own views on the psyche. The fact that he was in such close contact with the Nazis during that period has led to all kinds of preposterous claims about the extent of his collaboration with them. Jungians ever since have had to confront this difficult issue. It is inexplicable that otherwise intelligent people have not bothered to find out the facts of the situation. His association with the Nazis during that period, no matter how objectively analyzed, almost always raises the twin issues of Nazism and anti-Semitism against him.

POST-WORLD WAR II

Berlin

The emigration of many analysts, the question of the role of some analysts during the war, and a divided Berlin, made the revival of analytical psychology in Berlin and the reconstituting of a Jungian group difficult. Kaethe Buegler no longer wanted to be associated with an institute where different schools of psychotherapy were represented. In 1946 she decided to form her own study group in Jung's psychology. However, Jung did not support her in this endeavor, which was ill-timed, and the group disbanded in 1949. Schultz-Hencke emerged as a dominant influence in Berlin, and synthesized the work of Freud, Adler, and Jung into one comprehensive theory – namely, his own. When Schultz-Hencke wished to become a member of the International Psychoanalytic Association (IPA), he came into conflict with Felix Boehm and Carl Müller-Braunschweig, two non-Jewish psychoanalysts who had remained in Germany, worked at the Goering Institute, and won out in obtaining IPA approval. Boehm and Müller-Braunschweig formed the Deutsche Psychoanalytische Vereinigung (DPV), whereas Schultz-Hencke and the DPG never received IPA accreditation. Schultz-Hencke went on to develop a neo-Freudian institute with a similar structure and with many of the same people who had been part of the Goering Institute.

On 11 September 1948 Kretschmer, together with Künkel, revived the old Allgemeine Aerztliche Gesellschaft für Psychotherapie (est. 1926). Following an invitation from Wilhelm Bitter the representatives of the different psychoanalytic schools, Müller-Braunschweig (Freud), Schultz-Hencke (Neo), Schmaltz (Jung), Seif (Adler), Michel (Künkel-pupil), Mitscherlich (substituting for Adolph von Weizsäcker), founded the Deutsche Gesellschaft für Psychotherapie und Tiefenpsychologie (DGPT). To this day it still exists as an umbrella organization for thirty institutes in Germany. Von Weizsäcker was the first post-war president, and Wilhelm Bitter was managing director. Those who had trained at the Goering Institute had the option of becoming members. The goals of the DGPT were to establish psychotherapy on solid theoretical, academic, and financial principles for all psychotherapists, medical and non-medical. Currently Kurt Höhfeld, a Jungian analyst from Berlin, heads the organization.

In the immediate post-war era, Julius Schirren, the one remaining Jungian from the Goering Institute, headed up the Jungian section of the new Neo-Freudian Institute. Schirren, a man who had begun medical studies without ever completing them, had become an artist and painter after World War I and developed an interest in Jung's writings. It is said that "he took a long walk around the lake with Jung," and that is how it is rumored that he became a Jungian (interviews with Hannes Dieckmann and Regine Lockot). Most likely he had an "autodidactic analysis." Schirren, as the head of the Jungian section within the new institute, and Kaethe Buegler, who refused to be a part of that institute, were staunch enemies. In the immediate post-war era, Jung supported the Jungians being a part of the Schultz-Hencke Neo-Freudian Institute, much to the disappointment of Buegler. According to Dieckmann (personal communication), Schirren was a very intuitive man with a good connection to his unconscious.

As Schirren was the only Jungian at the Neo-Freudian Institute, those who were interested in Jungian psychology had to have analysis with him. By the early 1950s a group of four medical doctors with training in psychiatry, including Hannes Dieckmann, Hans-Joachim Wilke, Eberhard Jung, and Rudolf Blomeyer, began analysis with Schirren and trained at the Neo-Freudian Institute. Psychoanalysis was the subject of all their courses, and it was difficult to include any classes in analytical psychology. To be Jungian at that time had a very dubious connotation. At first these four students, who were called the

"Gang of Four" after the Chinese communist leaders, had to meet privately at Dieckmann's house to study analytical psychology. They had little formal didactic training in analytical psychology, and in order for them to graduate from the Neo-Freudian Institute they all had to present psychoanalytic cases. When Dieckmann first applied for membership to the IAAP, he was told that he needed further training before he could qualify. Consequently, Dieckmann had a second analysis with Jolande Jacobi, traveling to Zurich three times a year. He was the only one of the four who came under any direct influence from Zurich. Schirren died in the late 1950s and never became a member of the IAAP.

The "Gang of Four" began to teach at the Neo-Freudian Institute, and gradually students became interested in analytical psychology. All the students had to follow the same curriculum, which included courses in both psychoanalysis and analytical psychology. The only difference was that the Jungian students had a Jungian analysis, whereas the Freudian students were in analysis with Freudians. The "Gang of Four" were made individual members of the IAAP in 1962. These four individual IAAP members were instrumental in forming a group in Berlin which grew rapidly. Later this Berlin group was part of the national German Society which became a group member of the IAAP in 1968. The Berlin section of the German Society currently has a membership of close to two hundred. Since 1973 they have published a journal, *Zeitschrift für Analytische Psychologie*, edited by Hans-Joachim Wilke since its inception, which is a clinical Jungian journal in the German language with English abstracts. The Jungian training at the Neo-Freudian Institute, by virtue of one curriculum for all students, continues to have a strong psychoanalytic influence.

Since 1977 the Freudian and Jungian sections have been divided and candidates attend separate seminars. Students can choose courses from either track, but in order to graduate they have to pass an examination given by their own institute. The Berlin contingent is the largest within the German national group, and the German Society is the single largest Jungian professional organization in the world. Since the unification of Berlin, many analysts have been teaching in the former East Germany and other Eastern bloc countries.

On an international level the Berlin group has been the most visible of the German institutes for the rest of the Jungian community. The Berlin group made its mark internationally when the "Gang of Four" presented a detailed study on "countertransference" at the international congress in London in 1971. The group had been involved in this project for many years, and the presentation was very well received by the participants of the congress. At that same congress Hannes

Dieckmann was elected to be the second vice-president of the IAAP, in a closely contested election. He served on the executive committee for eighteen years and eventually as president for two terms, from 1983 to 1989. For many years the Berlin Jungians had wanted to host an international Jungian congress, but the memories of its political past did not allow it to become a reality until 1986. The presence of the congress in Berlin helped to heal old wounds.

An important reason for the growth of all depth psychology in post-war Germany was the generous coverage for analytic therapy by the semi-public and many private health insurances (and from the early 1970s onward also for behavior therapy). Since the mid-1960s, after an empirical retrospective study conducted by Annemarie Dührssen and others for the Allgemeine Ortskrankenkasse in Berlin had shown the cost reductions for medical treatment of psychotherapy patients, an application format has been in effect that permits analytic treatment up to two to three times weekly for up to three hundred sessions. Thus, German patients have enjoyed a very humane inclusion of psycho-therapy in the health system, and psychotherapists have always had more than enough patients. A new psychotherapy law which came into effect on 1 January 1999, together with economic difficulties (un-employment rates, the unavoidable costly modernization of former Eastern Germany), appears to threaten this financial arrangement due to sinking fees and probable structural changes.

The government is now requiring that all forms of therapy have to prove scientifically that they are effective. Analytical and behavior therapy have already been approved by governmental authorities, but there is a fear of new demands. As of 1 January 2000 quality assurance measures according to World Health Organization guidelines will be required. It is unclear what added burdens will be placed on psycho-therapy and psychotherapists, but it is likely that intrusions into ana-lytic therapy will increase.

The Jungians, especially in Berlin, have formulated a protocol to demonstrate the effect of Jungian analysis on absenteeism in the work-place, alcoholism, psychosomatic disorders, number of other doctor visits, and various parameters of health. The first study in the early 1990s was retrospective in nature and did show much improvement in these parameters, but now careful prospective studies are underway. These studies have been jointly funded by research grants from private foundations, the IAAP, and private donations from the German ana-lysts. A Jungian analyst in Berlin, Wolfram Keller, is the leader of the research project and is assisted by several candidates.

Stuttgart

The first association in analytical psychology in Germany, called the Südwestdeutsche Vereinigung für C.G. Jung, was organized in Stuttgart and was established in 1957, which was several years before the foundation of the Berlin group in the 1960s. Jung took a personal interest in the Stuttgart group and had a strong personal connection to its founder, Wilhelm Bitter. Bitter had frequent contact with Jung over the last twenty-five years of Jung's life.

Wilhelm Bitter (1893–1974)

Wilhelm Bitter was born in the Rhineland in 1893 to a Protestant mother and a liberal Catholic father. He was brought up in a largely Catholic region and he and his family did not fare well. He studied business, economics, and political science, and lived in London and Geneva. In the late 1930s he returned to Germany to obtain a medical degree in Berlin and underwent a four-year psychoanalysis with Felix Boehm, who was one of the few remaining psychoanalysts in Germany. In 1942, as a businessman and a politician, Bitter attempted to broker a peace between the Nazis and the Allies, which failed, and as a consequence he had to leave the country. He fled to Switzerland with the help of some influential connections. In Zurich he had a Jungian analysis and a chance to study with Jung.

After the war Bitter returned to Stuttgart where, in 1948, he founded the first Institute for Psychotherapy and in the same year a group called, "Arzt und Seelsorger" (physician and caretaker of souls), which brought together physicians, theologians, historians, political scientists, and depth psychologists to discuss subjects of mutual concern. Many theologians were introduced to Jung's thought, and through Bitter they met with Jung – who had a special interest in having contact with theologians – in Zurich. Bitter was also a founding member of the Deutsche Gesellschaft für Psychotherapie und Tiefenpsychologie (DGPT), an umbrella organization for all depth psychologists.

Following Jung's suggestion, Bitter founded the Südwestdeutsche Vereinigung für C.G. Jung (the Southwest German Association for C.G. Jung) in 1957. Three years later this association became the first German group to be accepted as a member group in the IAAP, and it developed into the Stuttgart Jung Institute in 1971. Bitter also founded the first *"Pychotherapeutische Klinik"* (psychotherapeutic clinic), with 102 in-patient beds, in Germany based on Jung's principles in 1967.

Having lived outside Germany for many years, and being political by nature, Bitter recognized the dangers of National Socialism early on. He was never drawn to it and tried unsuccessfully to speak with former Nazis like Heyer about their views. In a *Festschrift* honoring Wilhelm Bitter on his seventy-fifth birthday, Gerhard Zacharias characterized Bitter in the following manner:

> National without being nationalistic, a depth psychologist who does not stick to a single denomination, theologically oriented without confessional purification, used to economic thinking without falling prey to materialism, acting politically without an ambition towards power.

> (Zacharias 1968)

The Stuttgart C.G. Jung Institute

A study group interested in Jung's psychology already existed in Stuttgart prior to World War II and was active between 1930 and 1937. It was headed by a friend of Jung's named Stockmayer (Buder 1963). The Stuttgart-based individual members became part of the newly formed Deutsche Gesellschaft für Analytische Psychologie (DGAP). In 1962 the Stuttgart group was the first German society to join the IAAP.

The Stuttgart group did not become an official Jungian training institute within the German Society until 1971. The leaders behind the formation of the Stuttgart Institute were Helmut Eschenbach, a medical doctor and former student of Wilhelm Bitter, and Johanna Läpple, a psychologist. Both had been deeply influenced by Bitter's symbolic approach to the psyche. Helmut Eschenbach and his wife, Ursula, also a medical doctor, had been members of another institute, the Stuttgart Akademie für Psychotherapie und Tiefen-Psychotherapie (Stuttgart Academy for Psychotherapy and Depth Psychotherapy). They were reluctant to leave this academy in order to form a separate Jung Institute. The Stuttgart Institute modeled itself after the Zurich Institute, and there were frequent guest lecturers from Zurich. In part, this was due to the geographical proximity of the two cities but primarily with a shared viewpoint on analytical psychology. On the other hand, the Stuttgart point of view was different from that of psychoanalytically oriented Berlin; thus, a friendly tension has always existed between the two institutes, although they are both member institutes of the Deutsche Gesellschaft für Analytische Psychologie (DGAP).

Theodor Seifert arrived in Stuttgart in 1967 and became a member of the Stuttgart group, after having graduated from the Zurich Institute and having had analysis with Marie-Louise von Franz. Helmut Eschenbach was president of the Stuttgart group for the first year, followed by Theo Seifert, who was president for the following seven years. Seifert's warm and extraverted feeling has provided a container for the continued growth and development of the Stuttgart Institute. Today the Stuttgart Institute has 180 members and continues to emphasize courses on dreams, individuation, the relationship between psychology and religion, and interests closely aligned with Jung. In addition to his activities with the Stuttgart Institute, Theo Seifert has been deeply involved in planning and organizing programs of the Lindau Psychotherapy Weeks (Lindauer Psychotherapie Wochen).

The Stuttgart Institute has an active training program for the analysis of children and adolescents, which promotes training in Sandplay and has a strong emphasis on symbolic development. The child training is as developed as the adult training, and students are required to do 600 hours of supervised training and therapy with children.

Theoretical differences have arisen in the Stuttgart Jung Institute between archetypal psychology, as represented by Wolfgang Giegerich, and others who were influenced by the research data coming from academic and government circles. Because of the strong collective pressures from government for research on analytical psychology, Giegerich decided to be on his own, and he moved near Munich. The combination of the collective pressures and the conflict around archetypal psychology led the Stuttgart Institute to subtly shift the focus of the course work. The curriculum developed more didactic material based upon clinical issues and lessened the emphasis on mythology and religion. In spite of many challenges and pressures, the Institute continues to have a very active training program and represents a counter pole to a more psychoanalytically oriented philosophy.

The practice of analysis in Stuttgart is faced with problems for three reasons. One, there are too many analysts in Stuttgart at the present time, and the government has prohibited new analysts from starting a practice there in order to force new analysts to move to less crowded areas. Two, although the national health insurance still should pay 140 DM per session, the actual payment for each session has been reduced to 80–100 DM (around $50), depending on regional conditions. The economic changes were caused by the unification of East and West Germany. Three, payments by the health insurance have been widened to cover medical doctors and psychologists with analytical and behavioral training. Insurance companies thought that 3000–4000 therapists would apply for reimbursement, but instead 11,000 therapists want to be licenced under the new regulations, thus diluting the money available for analysis. Consequently, there is a fear that some therapists will not be able to survive economically under these conditions. It appears that today there is a greater motivation to study in an analytic institute independent of its theoretical orientation because the training is accredited by the government for the therapist to receive reimbursement.

Munich

The relationship between Jung and depth psychology in Munich was a complex one. The first Jungians in Germany were from Munich through the influence of Gustav Richard Heyer, the former close friend of Jung, who became a Nazi during the Hitler period. In the early 1920s Heyer was working at the Second Medical Clinic at the university in Munich and was teaching psychotherapy for psychosomatic disorders. He influenced Kaethe Buegler, another young physician, who went to Jung for analysis in 1927. She left for Berlin in 1929, never to return to Munich. In those early years Jung visited Munich several times to lecture at the "Men's Meetings" of the Physicians Association, at the "*Kulturbund*," as well as the Richard Wilhelm Society. Richard Wilhelm taught the *I-Ching* to members of his society, and it was partly through these contacts that Jung and Wilhelm became friends. At the memorial service for Richard Wilhelm Jung gave the eulogy in the Kurt-Wolff Haus in Munich. When Kaethe Buegler left for Berlin, she had the impression that there was a keener intellectual interest in Jungian psychology in Munich than in Berlin. She described Munich at that time as spiritually half-way between Vienna and Zurich (Buder 1963).

Other individuals became interested in Jung's psychology during the 1930s. Friedrich Seifert and Manuela Jäger went to see Jung and Toni Wolff for analysis, traveling to Zurich several times a year for a number of years. Friedrich Seifert was a professor of philosophy at the Technische Hochschule für Philosophie und Psychologie in Munich. Seifert was in the army during the war and was strongly anti-Nazi. In November 1945 Jung wrote to him asking him about the activities of other German Jungians during the war, soliciting his opinion about them (Jung–Seifert, unpublished letter, dated 21 November 1945). Seifert has been described as a brilliant but difficult man, who was unable to form a lasting Jungian group. He died in 1963.

Manuela Jäger was another important Jungian in Munich during the 1930s with an interesting story to tell (personal interview with her daughter, Mrs Brigitte McLeod, a Jungian herself). Manuela Jäger met Jung in Munich at a conference where he noticed her and invited her to sit beside him at the dinner. As a result of this meeting she began an analysis with Jung, and he eventually transferred her to Toni Wolff. The analysis with Toni Wolff did not work, and Manuela Jäger returned to Munich. During the war she did not want to work in the factories, which was the usual role of women in those times, and instead she went to Berlin and trained as a psychologist at the Goering Institute. There she befriended an idealistic Freudian, John Rittmeister, head of the out-patient clinic at the Institute. Before the war Rittmeister had lived in Switzerland and had written an article critical of Jung and his mystical leanings. Jäger planned to attend a social gathering where Rittmeister and many of his friends were present. However, on that particular night she was ill, which saved her life, because all the others who attended that gathering were later killed by the Nazis. Rittmeister himself was accused of espionage and executed in 1943. After the war Jäger went back to Zurich for analysis with Emma Jung and then returned to Munich to practice as a Jungian analyst. Her daughter became a Jungian child analyst.

The Institut für Psychologische Forschung und Psychotherapie, the Goering Institute, had a small branch in Munich until 1945. After the war it became the Reichsinstitut für Psychologische Forschung und Psychologie, a combined institute for depth psychology, which included a Jungian track, headed by the Seiferts. After the Seiferts died, the Jungian section was dissolved. The last Jungian to be certified by the Reichsinstitut was Raymund Schaeffer, and when other Jungians attempted to receive accreditation as Jungian analysts they were not accepted.

For approximately fifteen years there was no Jungian accredited training in Munich until the arrival in the 1980s of two medical doctors, Helmut Remmler, and Barnim Nitsch, who had received their individual training by traveling to Zurich for analysis and control work. To become certified as analysts they had to pass an examination at the DGAP. Joanne Wieland-Burston arrived from Zurich and joined the others in forming a small Jungian Institute in Munich. Remmler died in 1998. At the present time there are approximately twenty students in Munich.

Jung's initial recognition in Germany was in Munich and he visited there frequently during the late 1920s and early 1930s. Because of the war, analytical psychology almost vanished from Munich. However, in recent years, there has been a resurgence of interest in analytical psychology, and there is a small training institute.

Other institutes

In recent years new study groups and smaller institutes have developed in Cologne and Bremen, as well as Dresden, Leipzig, and other cities in the former East Germany. Many German analysts teach on a regular basis in the former East Germany, and Jungian interest groups are at various stages of development.

Publishing

The *Zeitschrift für Analytische Psychologie*, published by the Berlin Institute for over twenty years, has been a respected clinical journal in the German language with summaries of articles in English. It is similar to the format of the *Journal of Analytical Psychology* in English.

Another journal, *Gorgo*, founded in 1979 by Wolfgang Giegerich, an independent member of the IAAP in Germany, is a psychological Jungian journal which emphasizes archetypal psychology and imaginal thought. It presents a Jungian viewpoint with a cultural emphasis and German translations of articles from the journal *Spring*. Giegerich has close connections with many Swiss Jungian analysts. He received his Ph.D. in the United States, analytical training in Stuttgart, and has scrutinized and elaborated many major themes of analytical psychology over the past twenty years. His writings have pursued basic themes of Jung, and he has integrated them with Hegel's dialectical thinking. Much of his writing is in English, and his reformulation of Jung's ideas in relationship to Hegel's provoked much attention within certain Jungian circles. In the fall of 1998 Giegerich led a discussion of his work on the Internet, which was provocative, stimulating, and well received.

SUMMARY

Germany has played an important role in the history and development of analytical psychology. Prior to the mid-1930s the history of Jung in Germany was evolving at a pace commensurate with other major Western countries. The rise of National Socialism interrupted the development of analytical psychology in Germany, as all the Jewish analysts emigrated to other countries. During the Nazi period the Goering Institute institutionalized the training of psychotherapy, and the Jungians, like the other schools, benefited professionally from its existence. After the war, the Jungians were able to reconstruct a professional society with the non-Jewish members who had remained. However, the development was different from that of other major Jungian centers, because there was no longer an Analytical Psychology Club, and there were no longer any Jewish members. German Jewish members who emigrated became some of the most significant Jungians in the world.

Since World War II, with the financial support of the German government, depth psychology, including analytical psychology, has grown rapidly into a strong institution. The unification of the two Germanies has brought about many changes and, together with the psychotherapy law of 1999 which strengthened the influence of clinical psychologists and their faculties, will surely impact the development of analytical psychology in the future.

The role of Jung in the professional developments of psychotherapy in Germany has been discussed. Jung's contact with the Nazis from 1933 through 1940, and his statements from the first years, has been problematical. Having studied the issue for close to forty years, my attitudes have changed as more information has become available. At first I, along with other Jungians, defended Jung completely, as it was all an attack by the Freudians to discredit Jung. As more information has become available, my defense of Jung has changed. Jung was a very complex person, and his attitudes towards Jews underwent many changes during the course of his lifetime. There is no question that what Jung did and said in 1933 and 1934 about Jews was naive, if not dreadful, and every time I read over Jung's statements about the racial differences between Jews, Aryans, and Chinese, I cringe. On the other hand, upon reading everything that Jung wrote about the nature of dictatorship and the personalities of Stalin, Mussolini, and Hitler, it is clear that Jung was always speaking as a psychologist. He was critically evaluating these dictators in the context of European countries, many of which were dictatorships. Therefore, Jung the psychologist was treating Nazi Germany as if it were a patient, pointing out the positive as well as the negative aspects. In his ironic style, he was provocative in everything he said. Taken literally, he sounded shocking. However, to me it is clear that after 1934 he was mocking the Germans, rather than praising them. By 1936 he saw that the phenomenon in Germany had become a mass movement. Jung did not like mass movements of any kind, as the individual was always lost in these collective situations. He grossly underestimated the power of Hitler and the Nazis and was continually surprised and amazed by how much Hitler could get away with. However, he saw Hitler as having been overtaken by the archetype of Wotan, no longer acting as a human individual. For instance, in 1938 he stated that Hitler speaks as voice for the German people and no longer for himself (Knickerbocker 1939). When I put together all my thoughts on Jung, I come up with the following conclusions. When Jung was with Freud, he was clearly pro-Semitic. After the break with Freud, he reverted to an endemic anti-Semitism which was common in Europe prior to the Holocaust.

He had a short flirtation with the Nazis in 1933 and 1934. After that he continued to work with them, but his statements were far more judicious and clinical. He had the opportunity to say something critical of the Nazis publicly, but he chose never to do that. That was a major omission, as he saw first hand what the Nazis were like. In 1944 he had his near fatal heart attack, during which he had a vision where he was part of a Jewish mystical wedding, where much joy was experienced. His attitude towards Judaism changed when he both discovered and experienced its mystical element. From that time on there was no problem for Jung with Jews. However, Jung continues to be labeled as an anti-Semite and is assumed to be guilty of that until proven innocent. His innocence is as hard to prove as his guilt. Jungians are always left with having to somehow defend Jung. Fifty years later it is still not possible for depth psychologists to get beyond the claim that Jung was anti-Semitic and to study his ideas instead.

9   Analytical psychology in Italy

EARLY HISTORY

From the beginning Jung's psychology found fertile ground in Northern Europe and the United States. In the Latin countries the influence of his work was slower in coming, with the exception of Italy. Why Italy was more receptive to Jung's ideas is open to conjecture. Many possible reasons may account for this, such as the roots of Greco-Roman culture, the medieval Renaissance, or possibly the Italian love of images. From Jung's perspective, Italian images were significant aspects of his psyche. From early on Jung's works were quickly translated into Italian, including his doctoral thesis in 1903 (Carotenuto 1977). In the 1930s the Italian edition of the *The Secret of the Golden Flower* deeply impressed Italian oriental scholars, who held powerful positions in Italy. One such scholar was Giuseppe Tucci, who was a close friend of Mussolini.

An important factor in the growth of analytical psychology in Italy was the political turbulence in Europe during the 1930s. The Italian history of analytical psychology again shows the effect of forced emigration of a German Jew from Nazi Germany. Ernst Bernhard, a psychiatrist, who had psychoanalysis with Otto Fenichel and Sandor Rado in Berlin, as well as with Jung in Zurich, was pivotal to the development of analytical psychology in Italy.

Ernst Bernhard (1896–1965)

Ernst Bernhard was born into a Jewish family in Berlin in 1896. His father was of Hungarian and his mother of Austrian origin. He studied medicine and intended to become a pediatrician. During World War I he became a Socialist–Zionist and encountered the writings of Martin Buber, which made a profound impression on him. Bernhard was the older first cousin of Max Zeller, a later founding member of the Los Angeles group, and they grew up together in Berlin. As the older of the two, Bernhard had a major influence on his cousin Max. Max followed in Bernhard's footsteps and had an analysis with Otto Fenichel. As a result of a spiritual crisis, Bernhard went to see Jung in Zurich. According to Aldo Carotenuto (1977), Jung and Bernhard had a difficult relationship. In 1935 Bernhard asked for asylum in England, where his friend and colleague from Berlin, Gerhard Adler, was living. The British Immigration Office referred Bernhard's application to a special commission which refused his request because of his interest in astrology. Bernhard sought out another hospitable country which turned out to be Italy. Ernst Bernhard and his wife Dora arrived in Rome in 1936 and located an apartment at Via Gregoriana 12 where they lived for the rest of their life, except for a time during the war when he was hidden from the Nazis.

Little is known about Bernhard's first few years in Italy. He became a friend of Eduardo Weiss, who was the first prominent psychoanalyst in Italy. Weiss had become a member of the International Psychoanalytic Association at age twenty-four in 1913 and was practicing in Rome. In the 1930s racial laws against Jews were instituted in Italy, and Weiss could no longer travel. Weiss relied heavily on Bernhard who was able to alleviate his despondency. In 1937 Bernhard gave a series of lectures to the Italian Psychoanalytic Society on "Dream Interpretation," which were later published in the Jungian journal *Rivista di psicologia analitica* (1971). Weiss and his wife Wanda left Italy for the United States in 1938. Wanda Weiss had analyzed with Bernhard and moved to Berkeley, California, where she practiced as a Jungian analyst, while Eduardo Weiss became a member of the Chicago Psychoanalytic Institute. This was an unusual arrangement and is probably the only known crossover between a Freudian and Jungian in that generation of analysts. As a consequence of the good personal relations between Weiss and Bernhard, the early Italian Freudians were on good terms with Bernhard.

Bernhard had to endure various vicissitudes in connection with racial persecution in Italy. In 1941 he was imprisoned in a concentration camp in Calabria. In the year before his imprisonment he made the acquaintance of Giuseppe Tucci, who was then president of the Italian Institute for Middle and Far Eastern Studies. Tucci was writing a book on the Indian mandala and had consulted with Bernhard. When he heard of Bernhard's imprisonment, Tucci took action to free him and described it as follows:

It was a great pleasure to know Professor Ernst Bernhard during the difficult time of his life in Rome. It was easy to accept his friendship in view of the fact that I was knowledgeable about psychology and Freud's theories and was writing a book on Indian mandala. The mandala can only be interpreted with the help of psychology and also parapsychology. Indians, especially in that part of their literature which deals with depth-problems, have anticipated many ideas of our current science of psychoanalysis. This was the subject of many of my frequent conversations with Bernhard who was always curious to acquire new knowledge and to deepen the meaning as well as evaluating possible applications. When new racial laws were introduced in Italy I could not tolerate that science had been violated and betrayed for such crude and stupid myths. I took advantage of my friendship with a few people who were not influenced by the new ideologies, and this intervention freed my friend Bernhard and several others.

(Carotenuto 1977: 46)

Bernhard was able to return to his home but was forced to live ensconced in one room until the day of the Allies' arrival in Rome.

Almost immediately after the liberation of Rome in 1944 Bernhard resumed his practice of analytical psychology. A well-known Jungian analyst and writer, Bianca Garufi, began working with him in analysis at that time. She described her first meeting with Bernhard and the beginning of her analysis in the following manner:

I came out of the experience of the resistance, I was a militant communist, I had a Marxist education. I told him that I came to see him in order to put order in my psyche, just as one goes to see the dentist to have one's teeth put in order. He willingly and with a smile accepted the task that I assigned to him, and in order to put me at ease he told me that during the War from 1915 to 1918 he had been involved in political activities in Germany as a socialist within his regiment. Since that time he had not changed his political and social point of view. Therefore, we were 'comrades' and from then on we addressed each other by first name. Obviously, I understood that I could not have worked with him on any other level than equality. I am grateful for this understanding (and the sacrifice it certainly required on his part).

(Carotenuto 1977:68)

After the war Bernhard began to attract both medical and non-medical students, and a number of important post-war cultural figures in Italy came to him for analysis. Between 1945 and 1955 he collaborated in a publishing project called "Psyche and Conscience," where papers on cultural subjects were presented from all points of view without discrimination. Bernhard continued to have excellent relations with the Freudians who returned to Italy from foreign lands after the war.

In 1958 the Bernhards attended the first International Congress for Analytical Psychology in Zurich and brought with them a number of their students. Ernst Bernhard became a member of the first executive committee of the IAAP, which had been formed in 1955, and he served until 1959. In 1961 the Bernhards were instrumental in forming the Associazione Italiana per lo Studio della Psicologia Analitica (AIPA). Ernst Bernhard was the acknowledged leader and supervised the training activities of the Association. In 1964 he suffered his first heart attack and died in 1965. After his death Dora Bernhard continued to practice at the same location for many years. She gradually moved away from the central activities of the AIPA and began to form her own circle with her analysands. She lived until the age of 102 and died in 1998.

Bernhard's name is not well known outside of Italy, because he did not publish due to writer's block. The only published materials are his seminars on "Dream Interpretation," first given in 1938. His private autobiographical journal was edited by Helene Erba Tissot and published in 1969 as *Mitobiografia* (Mytho-Biography). It is an autobiographical account of his spiritual quest. Bernhard was a deeply religious man, and his interest in religious questions was a life-long part of his individuation. His interest in astrology was also profound, and he continued to study and practice astrology throughout his life. In his *Mitobiografia* Bernhard states:

> Early on man experimented the live action of destiny in astrology – discredited today – in which he found above himself the internal images . . . astronomy only considers inorganic laws, while astrology is the biology of the stars which base themselves on inorganic law.

> (Carotenuto 1977:115)

Bernhard's study of astrology has paralleled Jung's own interest in the subject. His strong influence on analytical psychology has continued to the present, and a whole issue of the *Rivista di psicologia analitica* has recently been devoted to his memory.

EARLY PROFESSIONAL ASSOCIATION

It is typical for the first students in an area to have both their supervision and analyses with the founding members, which gives rise to
boundary violations. Italy was no exception since Ernst and Dora
Bernhard were the only analysts in Rome. On 26 May 1961 the first
planning meeting to form the AIPA took place at one of Bernhard's
residences on a lake in Bracciano. The meeting was attended by Dora
and Ernst Bernhard, Mirella Bonetti, Giuseppe Donadio, Enzo Lezzi,
Mario Moreno, Gianfranco Tedeschi, and Francesco Montanari. Ernst
Bernhard became the first president, Gianfranco Tedeschi was elected
as vice-president, Mario Moreno as secretary, and Dora Bernhard as
director of studies. This organization remained unchanged until Ernst
Bernhard's death in 1966. Bernhard personally certified all the students which led to problems later on, as Bernhard was known to trust
people who might not have merited it. The beginning of the training
program focused on clinical matters and always ended with a communal
meal, so that conviviality was a part of the early group's spirit.

Two founder-members of the Jungian group, Mario Moreno and
Gianfranco Tedeschi, were both medically trained psychiatrists holding university positions. Many of their students came to AIPA for
training in analytical psychology. Bernhard favored Tedeschi for his
academic standing, as he was holding the more senior professorship.
When Bernhard died, the line of succession was clear, and Tedeschi
was to become president of AIPA.

Split

Within months after Ernst Bernhard's death, a split occurred among
the twelve members of AIPA. Half the analysts, including Mario Trevi
and Mario Moreno, decided to leave AIPA and form their own association, the Centro Italiano di Psicologia Analitica (CIPA). All the
candidates except one remained within AIPA. *This was the first formal
split of a professional association within the IAAP and caused great
tremors within international Jungian circles.* The IAAP spent a great
deal of energy trying to prevent the split between the two groups.
Then-president of the IAAP, Jo Wheelwright, sent Adolf Guggenbühl-
Craig as an emissary to Italy, but a separation had already occurred.
At the time there were no great theoretical differences between the two
groups, and the conflict was purely on personal grounds.

The major figures in the split included Gianfranco Tedeschi in AIPA
and Mario Trevi and Mario Moreno in CIPA. Both Tedeschi and

Trevi were Jewish, as was Bernhard, and so they knew each other socially from the small Jewish community in Rome. Trevi had a degree in philosophy and had a culturally oriented approach to analysis in contrast to the clinical approach of the psychiatrist Tedeschi.

After a few years the persecutory anxieties abated, and relations between the two groups normalized. Editorial issues of mutual concern and the cooperation of organizing the IAAP Congress in Rome in 1977 helped to heal old wounds.

ASSOCIAZIONE ITALIANA PER LO STUDIO DELLA PSICOLOGIA ANALITICA

AIPA, as the original society, retained the candidates after the split and grew at a rapid rate. Satellite groups formed first in Milan, then Florence, and Naples. Over the years AIPA has developed a more pluralistic view towards Jung and analytical psychology. Within AIPA there is a wide divergence of opinion and practice, from classical Jung to those who are more conversant with object-relations theory. Currently there are approximately 150 analysts and 120 candidates within all of AIPA – the majority in Rome and Milan. As in many other European Jung societies, such as France and Switzerland, the future analyst is required to have two separate analyses. A personal analysis is done before the candidate applies for training; upon entering training, the candidate must undergo a second "training analysis," or "didactic analysis," which is done with a designated training analyst. The training requirements state that the didactic analysis has to last for 200 hours, and the didactic analyst has an evaluative function on the candidate in training.

Many prominent analysts are members of AIPA, including Bianca Garufi, a well-known poet, writer, and analyst; Paolo Aite, a leader in the Sandplay technique in Italy and former long-time president of AIPA; Marcello Pignatelli, the current editor of the *Rivista* and former member of the executive committee of IAAP; and Aldo Carotenuto before his resignation from AIPA in 1995. Carotenuto is a professor of psychology at the University of Rome and has written over twenty books in the field of analytical psychology. His major interests include Jung's influence on cultural and historical aspects of analytical psychology. In the early 1980s he obtained the correspondence between Sabina Spielrein and Jung which had been languishing in the basement of the Department of Psychology at the University of Geneva for about seventy years. Carotenuto published a small book, *A Secret*

Symmetry (1982), which includes the letters between Jung and Spielrein. The book caused a small sensation within the larger psychoanalytic community. There was much debate within the Jungian community as to whether the correspondence should have been published, and Carotenuto was widely criticized by first-generation Jungians. The overall effect has been the resurrection of Spielrein as an important figure, instead of just a footnote in the early history of psychoanalysis. Carotenuto's book on Spielrein brought him much acclaim, and since that time he has been a frequent lecturer at both psychoanalytic and analytical psychological meetings throughout the world. More recently the continuation of the Spielrein saga came to light, and it is a dramatic one; she became a prisoner in the Soviet Union and was murdered by the Nazis (Etkind 1998).

CENTRO ITALIANO DI PSICOLOGIA ANALITICA

CIPA, as the breakaway group, quickly established itself as an ener-getic and viable professional Jungian society. In the late 1960s Francesco Caracciolo, Mario Moreno, and Mario Trevi were the spiritual leaders of the group. Trevi, with his philosophical background, influenced the training deeply. He valued understanding on a philosophical level over dream interpretation. CIPA developed mostly in northern Italy and has its center in Milan. Its proximity to Zurich allowed many future analysts of CIPA to train in Zurich. CIPA has remained closer to the Zurich point of view and is committed to a study of the philosophical implications of Jung's theories. Membership in CIPA has been growing, and its size is now comparable to that of AIPA.

In 1974 a soon-to-be-prominent graduate from Zurich, Luigi Zoja, joined CIPA, soon became its president, and in 1983 was elected to the executive committee of the IAAP. As a person of integrity, with a gift for languages, his leadership qualities were immediately apparent. In 1989 he was elected as second vice-president of the IAAP and served in a vice-presidential capacity until 1998, when he became president of the IAAP. He is the first Italian to hold that position. Luigi Zoja lives and practices in Milan with his wife Eva Pattis, also a Jungian analyst who trained in Austria. Zoja published two books which have been translated into English, *Drugs, Addiction and Initiation* (1988) and *Growth and Guilt* (1995). Eva Pattis wrote a book on *Abortion* (1997).

Another prominent member of CIPA is Professor Umberto Galimberti, a student of Mario Trevi and a professor of philosophy at the University of Venice. He writes a twice-weekly column on subjects of culture, philosophy, and psychology for one of the major daily newspapers of Italy, and his writings are well known throughout Italy.

A major scandal sent tremors through CIPA in the early 1990s. An analyst named Paolo Bertoletti had colleagues, candidates, and patients buy shares in a financial cooperative for physicians, which was presumably linked to the official organization of physicians. In spite of official legal and state warranties, the administrative structure turned out to be corrupt, and all investors lost all their money. The newspapers covered the scandal in great detail. Bertoletti ended up serving time in jail and was evicted from CIPA. Interestingly, this affair served as a warning of corrupt connections between business and politics. Shortly thereafter it was discovered that such patterns of corruption ran through the entire Roman political system, and the Bertoletti affair was just the tip of the iceberg. The entire system of political parties was to be overthrown in the following years. As the scandal addressed much larger societal issues, the negative publicity has not affected the growth and development of CIPA as a professional society. In addition, the election of Luigi Zoja as the first Italian president of the IAAP has had a positive effect on CIPA and all Jungians in Italy.

In 1998 ten members of CIPA separated and formed their own group in protest against attempts to abolish the category of training analysts. From the beginning CIPA followed AIPA's model of having a separate category of training analysts, but recently the general membership of CIPA wanted to do away with this category. A majority of members are of the opinion that every analyst in good standing for a given number of years should be eligible to be a training analyst. The controversy was brought before the IAAP, and a "committee of enquiry" has met with all sides. At the time of writing no decision has been made.

PUBLISHING

The *Collected Works* of Jung were completely translated into Italian, beginning in 1966, by the publishing house Boringhieri. Aldo Carotenuto has been influential in the overall publishing of Jungian writings in Italy and was instrumental in having the *Collected Works* translated into Italian. The editor of the Italian translation was the Jungian analyst, Luigi Aurigemma, an Italian who lives in Paris and studied at the Jung Institute in Zurich. The *Collected Works* in Italian are a very impressive, high-quality edition. In addition to his own prolific writing, Carotenuto was the founding editor of the *Rivista di psicologia analitica*, a professional journal which has been published twice yearly by AIPA since 1970. After twenty-five years as editor he retired in 1995 and at the same time resigned from AIPA.

SANDPLAY

Dr Paolo Aite, a psychiatrist and past president of AIPA, has been utilizing Sandplay techniques for twenty-five years and has formed a small group to study and practice this method. Although heavily influenced by Dora Kalff, this group has developed an interest in the interpersonal context of work in the sand, in addition to the intrapsychic meaning of the images. Another group working with Sandplay utilizes the more familiar intrapsychic meaning of the images exclusively. There is an obvious tension between the two groups, but relations are cordial.

SUMMARY

Jung's works were translated into Italian shortly after the books were first written. When the Bernhards arrived in Rome in 1936 they found fertile soil for the development of analytical psychology. World War II interrupted the growth of the movement, but almost immediately after the war analytical psychology reemerged. Ernst Bernhard was the dominant figure in Italy, and upon his death in 1965 the "symbolic sons" quarreled as to who should be the rightful successor. The result was a formal split into two groups, which was the first official schism within the Jungian community. The two groups, AIPA and CIPA, have both continued to develop as national professional organizations on a parallel track. AIPA has become a more pluralistic professional group, whereas CIPA has continued to focus on the philosophy and psychology of Jung. Analytical psychology has found an important cultural and clinical niche within Italy, which was the first Latin country to warmly embrace the ideas of analytical psychology. The climate of political instability has not been lost on the Jungians in Italy, but in spite of tensions there is a sense of free but fractious communication among the various groups within the country. Analytical psychology is thriving in Italy.

10 Analytical psychology in France

EARLY HISTORY

Since Descartes in the sixteenth century, French culture has valued rationality and has been skeptical towards the non-rational. As a consequence, Jung's emphasis on the importance of the collective unconscious has not been easily accepted by the French. On the other hand, Jung was heavily influenced by French thought, mainly as a result of his contact with Theodore Flournoy in Geneva and the semester he spent in Paris with Pierre Janet in 1902. Janet was one of Jung's main teachers and his influence is evident throughout Jung's writings. It is also important to remember that even though Jung had already been *offered* a position in Munich, he chose instead to study in Paris. The French influence on Jung has been undervalued, and only recently the work of Sonu Shamdasani (1998c:115) and Eugene Taylor (1998:97) brought this connection to light.

Freud had already developed a strong psychoanalytical organization in France by the end of the 1920s (Alain deMijolla) and was able to exclude Jungians from all teaching positions within the universities. Jung's alleged connections to the Nazis during World War II did not improve his status in France. Accusations have continued until the present, although a more balanced view of Jung is now beginning to be presented in the news media and on television.

The first workshop in analytical psychology was founded in Paris in 1926 by Jean Bruneton, a Jungian analysand. It was called le Club du Gros Caillou (Club of the Big Stone), named after its meeting place. In terms of its structure the Club was modeled after the Analytical Psychology Club in Zurich. Elisabeth de Sury, who was an analyst in Basle and had trained with Jung, made frequent trips to Paris to give the group leadership. Among the early members were Ania Teillard, the graphologist, and Roland Cahen, later to be founders of the professional analytical psychology society. In 1932 Jung gave a seminar in Paris on "The Collective Unconscious," and a few years later Emma Jung presented her lecture on "The Animus" at the Club.

Le Club du Gros Caillou had international connections with the other clubs which were beginning to form in Europe and the United States. Representatives of the various clubs met at the yearly Eranos meetings in Ascona, Switzerland, and in 1939 they discussed the possibility of forming a confederation and planned a meeting to discuss the subject further in Paris for the spring of 1940. With the advent of World War II the plans had to be canceled. Analytical psychology remained dormant in France throughout the war and only slowly recovered thereafter. Le Club du Gros Caillou was not resurrected after the war.

In 1954 the Société C.G. Jung was formed and included among its members Carmen Affholder, Elie Humbert, Maurice Percheron, Ania Teillard, and Roland Cahen as president. In 1957 Cahen withdrew and Maurice Percheron, and later his wife, became presidents of the group. Subsequently it changed its name to Groupe d'études C.G. Jung de Paris. This group functioned much like Analytical Psychology Clubs in other cities; it was a membership organization which presented public lectures. It is still in existence today, functioning in a similar way, and is now complementary to the professional group, the Société française de psychologie analytique (SFPA).

FOUNDERS

Roland Cahen (1914–1998)

Roland Cahen, a French Jew, was one of the original members of Le Club du Gros Caillou. In the late 1930s he studied philosophy, with a special interest in Nietzsche, which brought him in contact with Jung. When the Nazis overran France in May 1940 he was a soldier on the Maginot Line, and then fled to Switzerland where he lived for the remainder of the war. He had an analysis with Jung and later with C.A. Meier. In 1943 Cahen published a book in Geneva, under the title of *L'homme à la découverte de son âme* which was a collection of Jung's writings translated into French for the first time. This book contributed greatly to the dissemination of Jung's thought in France. Under Jung's influence Cahen began his studies in medicine in Switzerland and completed them in Marseilles after the war. He returned to Paris where he worked as a psychiatrist at L'hôpital St Anne under the famous French psychiatrist, Professor Delay, and Cahen became the acknowledged leader in Jung's psychology. In his role as official translator of Jung's work into French, Cahen supervised the translation of more than twenty books, including Jung's autobiography. These translations have been widely criticized, as Cahen took many liberties and did not stay close enough to Jung's text.

At the time of the foundation of the Jung Institute in Zurich in 1948, C.A. Meier, as the Institute's president, asked the French group to participate and invited Cahen to become a patron. In 1954, under Cahen's tutelage, the Société C.G. Jung was formed in Paris. In 1957 he withdrew as president and the group was renamed the Groupe d'études C.G. Jung de Paris. Twelve years later in 1969 Cahen was a co-leader in the foundation of the Société française de psychologie analytique (SFPA), which became the Jungian professional society in France.

For many years he championed analytical psychology when there was very little public or private support. Through his long-standing friendship with Jacques Lacan, an influential figure in psychoanalysis in France and later internationally, Cahen provided a liaison between analytical psychology and psychoanalysis. In 1955 Cahen arranged for Lacan to meet with Jung, one of the first psychoanalytic dissidents, at a time when Lacan was becoming a dissident from psychoanalysis himself (Roudinesco 1997).

As the professional society began to grow, Cahen's influence within the society waned, and he became increasingly isolated. He died in March 1998 having been in good health until shortly before his final illness.

Elie Humbert (1925–1990)

The other pioneer founder of the French Jungian professional society was Elie Humbert, a Catholic priest from Normandy, who was at the *Couvent des Carmes* in Paris during the 1950s, where the well-known *Etudes carmélitaines* were published under the tutelage of Père Bruno. Père Bruno had chosen Humbert to be his successor at the convent. In 1957 Père Bruno arranged for Humbert to see Jung who quickly recognized Humbert's psychological sensitivities and agreed to accept him in analysis. Humbert was probably Jung's last regular analysand. When Jung's health began to fail in 1960, he transferred Humbert to Marie-Louise von Franz to complete the analysis. At the same time Humbert attended lectures and seminars at the Zurich Institute; however, he did not obtain a diploma. He met his future wife, Myrtha, in Switzerland, and they eventually married in 1977. Humbert had returned to Paris in 1965 and remained at the *Couvent des Carmes* for a short while before leaving the priesthood. He made contact with the emerging French

Jungian group and periodically returned to Zurich to continue his analysis with von Franz.

Elie Humbert co-founded the Société française de psychologie analytique (SFPA) along with Roland Cahen in 1969. When he was president of the professional society from 1974–1975, Humbert founded the *Cahiers de psychologie Jungienne*, now *Cahiers Jungiens de psychoanalyse*. He was the editor-in-chief of the *Cahiers* until his death in 1990.

A profound thinker, Humbert was the author of many articles and books on analytical psychology. One book, simply entitled *Jung* (Humbert 1988) has received wide acclaim for its brilliance, clarity, and depth as a study in analytical psychology. It is a highly original work, which Andrew Samuels described (on the jacket of the English edition) as "bringing them [Jung's ideas] close to human emotional experience and forcing the reader to confront its implications."

Humbert's views of analytical psychology changed over the years. In the early years he brought the classical Jungian approach from Zurich to Paris. Through his marriage he came in contact with leading psychoanalytic clinicians, both in the United States and in France. These encounters led him to develop more precise views on the clinical aspects of analytical psychology, simultaneously deepening his understanding of Jung and analytical psychology. Humbert's keen analytic and clinical sense led most SFPA members to seek him out as either analyst or supervisor. Humbert was influenced by Lacan's concept of "desire" and the psychoanalytic emphasis on infant development. He published many papers on different aspects of these issues in the *Cahiers* and in other professional journals.

Through his writings and lectures Humbert had a profound influence on French intellectual life, and he was invited to teach psychology at the University of Paris VII, a renowned bastion of Freudian thought.

In 1984 Humbert had surgery for a tumor of the kidney, supposedly benign. However, in 1986 a recurrence was discovered which proved to be malignant. From then until his death in 1990 he fought gallantly against the gradually encroaching effects of the cancer. He continued to see patients, friends, and colleagues. His spirit and mind remained clear, as his body slowly deteriorated. By the time of his death the SFPA had become a large professional group, with an adult and child training program, and satellite institutes in other major French cities. His influence in all these developments was crucial.

Elie Humbert's death was an enormous loss to the French Jungians for whom he was both the spiritual and secular leader. However, others were prepared to take over the responsibilities and responded well under adverse conditions.

SOCIÉTÉ FRANÇAISE DE PSYCHOLOGIE ANALYTIQUE

The 1960s brought a decade of intellectual and political upheaval in France, especially in Paris. The student uprisings which spread throughout Europe originated in that city. Lectures in Freudian psychoanalysis were well attended at the universities, and psychoanalytic literature attracted a wide reading audience. By contrast, analytical psychology had little influence in the culture and was still relatively undeveloped. In 1967 Hélène Téboul-Wiart, who had been analyzed by Roland Cahen and later by C.A. Meier, founded the Groupe de recherche de psychologie analytique, which was a first attempt at the formation of a professional Jungian analyst group in France. At about the same time Elie Humbert returned from Zurich. Slowly psychologists and psychiatrists were becoming interested in a formal training in analytical psychology.

In 1969 the increasing professional interest in analytical psychology resulted in the founding of the Société française de psychologie analytique (SFPA), a professional society to further the education and training of analytical psychologists. Roland Cahen was the first president of the society, and the founding members were André Arthus from Lyon, Luigi Aurigemma, a Zurich-trained Italian who was in charge of the Italian translations of Jung's works, Elie Humbert, Emile Rogé, Pierre Solié, whose books on "myth-analysis" attracted much popular acclaim, Hélène Téboul-Wiart, and Ania Teillard. The SFPA became officially recognized by the IAAP in 1971, and the C.G. Jung Institute of Paris was established in 1974 as part of the SFPA.

From small beginnings it has become a very active training institute, with a large number of candidates. The training consists of three distinct phases. Prior to admission the applicant is expected to have had a personal analysis of many years' duration. Upon admission the candidate undergoes interviews with five different training analysts and is assigned an analyst for a "didactic analysis," lasting from five to seven years. At the conclusion of this phase and after undergoing another series of interviews, a candidate is admitted to the "control phase," which lasts another five years, and becomes an "associate member" of the Society. As an "associate member," the candidate attends lectures and workshops of the Institute. At the end the candidate writes a thesis which is presented first to an *ad hoc* committee and then to the General Assembly, which votes on the final admission of the candidate to ordinary membership of the SFPA. Today the SFPA has approximately seventy ordinary members, sixty-five associate members, and about sixty candidates in the "didactic analysis" phase.

In the early 1970s, as the SFPA was developing, there existed the Baudouin Institute in Geneva which had been founded by Charles Baudouin. Baudouin had begun as a student of Freudian psychoanalysis and later had a Jungian analysis and became a student of Jung. The Baudouin Institute had both a Freudian and a Jungian tract. Baudouin's later writings were on Jung and topics on analytical psychology. Many of the graduates of the Jungian tract at the Baudouin Institute practiced as analysts in the area of Lyon and Grenoble and had to choose whether to remain with the Baudouin Institute or become members of the SFPA. Naturally tensions developed between these two institutes where they overlapped geographically. In recent years the influence of the Baudouin Institute has decreased, although it still has a lively presence in Geneva and in Belgium.

The growth of the SFPA has also brought changes within its internal institutions. In addition to the adult Jungian training, a specific training in the analysis of children and adolescents has been established. Erich Neumann's point of view has been espoused by Denyse Lyard who has written a book on the subject, *Les analyses d'enfants* (Lyard 1998). The French child analysts meet regularly for joint workshops with their counterparts in other European countries.

Since the death of Elie Humbert in 1990 the SFPA has continued to develop and find its place in the general psychotherapeutic milieu of France. Christian Gaillard has emerged as a leading figure in the SFPA. His book, entitled *Jung* (1995), is part of a well-known French series on famous personalities, and his recent publication, *Le Musée imaginaire de Carl Gustav Jung* (1998), combines his interest in art and psychology. Christian Gaillard is a professor at the École nationale supérieure des beaux-arts, a lecturer at several universities, former president of the SFPA, and a public discussant of analytical psychology in the public media. He has served on the executive committee of the IAAP and in 1998 was elected vice-president of the IAAP.

PUBLICATIONS

In 1974 the SFPA founded the *Cahiers de psychologie jungienne*. Since its inception it has been published three times a year, mainly with contributions from members of the SFPA and translations into French of important articles from abroad. The founding editor was Elie Humbert until 1990, followed by Geneviève Guy-Gillet until 1994. Since then the editorship has been shared among three individuals, Aimé Agnel, Christian Gaillard, and Marie-Laure Grivet-Shillito.

In 1987 the journal's name was changed to *Cahiers jungiens de psychoanalyse* which was due to a subtle change in philosophy in the SFPA. *Cahiers* had always been seen as a clinical journal and deeply engaged in debates about what constituted Jungian analysis. Recognizing that there were several developing strands of Jungian analysis, it was thought that the new name would more accurately reflect *Cahiers'* attitude. The new name of this primarily clinical journal mirrors the synthesis of Jungian and psychoanalytic concepts. Much of its high standard is due to the influence of Elie Humbert. His personality, books, and lectures were decisive for the change in name and attitude. However, *Cahiers* continues to express the views of classical Jung, Neumann, and Hillman, as well as those of contemporary psychoanalysis. *Cahiers* represents the SFPA, which encourages exchanges and interaction within all the trends of Jungian and psychoanalytical psychology. To this day Elie Humbert's influence and inspiration in the broad intellectual and psychological horizons is evident in *Cahiers*.

Translation of Jung's writings into French

The *Collected Works* of Jung have not been completely translated into French. Roland Cahen was given translation rights by Jung and later by the Jung estate, but the translations – by many people's accounts – have not been satisfactory. New translations are now being prepared under the editorship of Michel Cazenave, a philosopher, for Albin Michel Publishers, with the assistance of a team of translators, among them Christian Gaillard and his wife, Alix. The translation of Jung's correspondence has recently been completed. The remaining writings by Jung, such as the psychiatric and the word-association studies, are now in the process of being translated; thus the entire *Collected Works* will be available in French.

CURRENT STATUS

Relationship to psychoanalysis

Since the founding of the SFPA in 1969 analytical psychology has gained a solid foothold in France. Before that time psychoanalysis and the Lacanian school dominated depth psychology. Despite an increasing interest in the writings of Jung, analytical psychology still holds a minority position within the French psychoanalytical world, which has made it difficult for Jungians to obtain academic positions. On the other side, Lacan and neo-Freudian psychoanalysis have influenced the Jungian world greatly, which is best illustrated by the name change of the journal *Cahiers*.

Recent events demonstrate a shift in the relations between psycho-analyis and analytical psychology. In 1995 Dr Alain deMijolla was in the process of assembling a team to edit a new, comprehensive psy-choanalytic dictionary. Then-president of the IAAP, Thomas Kirsch, arranged to meet with deMijolla, and they agreed to include a Jungian section in the dictionary. The dictionary is scheduled to be published in French in the year 2000. The collaboration between the Jungians and Dr deMijolla on this project has been fruitful and has improved relations between psychoanalysis and analytical psychology.

A recurrent issue of concern for psychoanalysis in France has been the question of Jung's relationship to the Nazis during the 1930s. Elisabeth Roudinesco, a prominent French psychoanalytic historian, has recently published a well-researched article on the subject in *L'Infini* (1988), in which she asserts that the French Jungians, beginning with Roland Cahen, have attempted to overlook that period in Jung's life. Roudinesco did recognize that in 1995 an issue of *Cahiers* was devoted to the topic, and at the International Jungian Congress in Paris in 1989 a panel was presented where the subject was thoroughly discussed.

Relationship to the IAAP

The SFPA has become increasingly involved in the international world of analytical psychology. Although members of the French society had presented papers at international congresses since the early 1970s, a combination of language and cultural barriers kept the French ana-lysts somewhat separate. In the late 1970s Elie Humbert emerged as a prominent member of the French society in the international Jungian community with his paper on "Active Imagination" at the 1977 Rome Congress. As a representative of the French society to the executive committee of the IAAP he became a vital force in formulating IAAP policy. Denyse Lyard and Christian Gaillard have subsequently been representatives of the French society to the IAAP Executive Committee. In 1989 the SFPA hosted a very successful international congress in Paris. At the most recent congress in Florence in 1998, Christian Gaillard was elected to the office of vice-president of the IAAP and is the first French national to hold a position of leadership within the IAAP.

The SFPA has organized bilateral or multilateral workshops with English, Italian, Swiss, and Belgian colleagues. Thus, over the past twenty years the French society has emerged as one of the solid national professional societies with strong ties to the IAAP.

SUMMARY

The development of analytical psychology in France has been slow. A small enclave of students of Jung and analytical psychology met from 1926 until 1969, with an interruption during World War II. A professional society (SFPA) was formed in 1969 and became an official international professional group in 1971. From the very beginning analytical psychology has held a minority position within French depth psychology. Over the past twenty years the SFPA has become a vital group both professionally and intellectually. It has been able to hold together the different strands of analytical psychology and to reach out to different groups in Europe. Today the French society is one of the strongest groups within Europe, and it continues to evolve dynamically.

11 Analytical psychology in smaller European countries

AUSTRIA

There was no Jungian presence in Austria during the time of Freud. Nazi rule and World War II decimated psychoanalysis in Austria, and in the aftermath depth psychology of any sort was slow in developing. Victor Frankl was the leader of the school of *logotherapy*, which combined religious existentialist thought and psychoanalysis.

The first accredited Jungian to practice in Austria was Ellen Sheire, an American from the Midwest, who married an Austrian and lived and practiced in Vienna from 1975 through 1986. She was a graduate of the Jung Institute in Zurich. Many therapists from Vienna and Salzburg were interested in becoming recognized Jungian analysts in the IAAP. In Salzburg a circle of academic clinicians became interested in Jung's psychology in the mid-1960s, and they were supported by the late Freudian analyst and university professor, Igor A. Caruso. Two therapists from this early circle became founding members of the Austrian Association for Analytical Psychology (OEGAP). The husband of one of them had been lecturing on analytical psychology at Salzburg University since 1972 and was named by Aniela Jaffé as the person to contact when Austria was ready to form a professional Jungian group. Independently, Ellen Sheire contacted Hannes Dieckmann in Berlin, then-president of the IAAP, who agreed to make regular visits to Austria to give supervision to candidates and seminars. Some of the candidates traveled to Munich for analysis with Professor Pflüger, a Jungian analyst and close colleague of Wilhelm Bitter, whereas others went to Zurich for further supervision and training. By 1983 six candidates had the requisite number of hours of analysis, control, as well as sufficient seminar hours, and Dieckmann suggested that they form the Austrian Association for Analytical Psychology (OEGAP). In the same year, with Dieckmann's support, OEGAP was accepted as a group member of IAAP.

There was a short period when the Austrian Association seemed to be functioning properly. By 1990 critical differences concerning the nature of training surfaced between the group in Vienna and the one in Salzburg, and within months the disagreements were seen as insurmountable. Initially the Salzburg group had been envisioned as a local branch of the OEGAP where it could meet the existing demand for training. When the conflict could not be resolved, the group reconstituted itself as the Salzburger Gesellschaft für Tiefenpsychologie–C.G. Jung Institut. The analysts in Vienna continued their training, as they were the larger group and accredited by the IAAP. In the early 1990s the IAAP was asked to intervene in the conflict between the two groups, and it was hoped that some resolution of the conflict could be achieved. After much discussion between Salzburg and the IAAP, it was decided that the Salzburg group, which had steadily been building up its training program with help from analysts in Germany and Switzerland, should apply for IAAP membership as a separate group. At the international congress in 1998 the Salzburg Institute was admitted as a second group in Austria.

Analytical psychology in Austria has gone through a stormy period in the 1990s. The conflict has taken its toll on the membership. Of the six original members of the Austrian Association, only one remains, Reinhard Skolek. Three moved to other countries where they are now members of the respective societies in those countries. One member left the group completely, and another commutes between London and Vienna. Two are founders of the Salzburg group. Both groups also passed the accreditation process for training institutes under the new Austrian psychotherapy law of 1991, which kept both societies busy until 1996/1997.

Summary

Austria is an example of possible consequences when a group is brought along too quickly. It was not a good idea for one person, in this case Dieckmann, to play such a dominant role in the training of a group. The new analysts of 1983 would have benefited from a wider range of teachers and supervisors to broaden their experience. The candidates faced a very closed system during their training, and the proximity to each other did not help the individuals to grow. Accreditation as a member of an international organization was important, as Austria was then in the process of structuring its laws concerning psychotherapy. Over time the Austrian groups have become more stable, and they have developed collegial relations with their Freudian colleagues.

Thus, after a less than ideal beginning, the profession of analytical psychologist is now established on a firm grounding in Austria.

BELGIUM

Early history

Belgium, a commercial and political center, and now the "capital" of Europe, has had its own unique relationship to analytical psychology. The country of Belgium exists only because in 1830 France, England, and Germany wanted a small buffer state between them. Belgium has fitted that role perfectly and has survived hostilities in two world wars. The northern part of the country is Flemish (Flanders), and the southern part is Walloon. Flemish (Dutch) is spoken in the north and French in the south. In Brussels, the capital, both French and Flemish are spoken.

As Belgium is centrally located in Europe, persons interested in Jung's psychology had a number of choices for study. In the 1950s the first two analysts, Gilberte Aigrisse and Robert George, traveled to Geneva where they had analysis and training at the Baudouin Institute. The founder of this institute was Charles Baudouin, and his students formed satellite Baudouin Institutes in Lyon and Grenoble, which interfaced with the development of the French Jungian society in that area. Gilberte Aigrisse and Robert George became the founders of a Baudouin Institute in Brussels. At that time, the Baudouin Institute in Geneva was a prestigious and eclectic depth psychological center with a strong Jungian tract.

Charles Baudouin, by training a philosopher, was first a Freudian and later studied and had analysis with Jung and his students in Zurich. He coined the term *"psychagogie"* to describe his view of psychoanalysis and depth psychology. He was the author of nine books, which included *L'Oeuvre de Jung* (1963) and *Psychoanalyse de Victor Hugo* (1943), which is still in print. Baudouin's Institut International de Psychagogie et de Psychotherapie was founded in 1924 and developed programs for both the professional training of doctors and psychologists, as well as one for lay people. The Institute followed no particular psychoanalytic school and remained open to the different currents in psychology and the human sciences. Trainings in Freudian, Jungian, and Balint studies, as well as group psychotherapy, were all available in the 1970s. Baudouin died in the mid-1960s, but the Baudouin Institutes continued to have a strong presence through the 1970s. In 1972 the Institut International de Psychagogie et de Psychotherapie counted fifty-one members; of these, fourteen were French, ten were Swiss, and fourteen were Belgian nationals. Since that time, its influence has waned, and it no longer provides a conduit to becoming a Jungian analyst.

In 1973 nine members of the Baudouin Institute applied for individual membership in the IAAP. They had trained with Gilberte Aigrisse in Belgium and André Arthus and Alain Le Bars in France. In 1974 they were accepted as individual members in the IAAP. On 2 June 1975 Gilberte Aigrisse, Jacques Beaujean, Jef Dehing, Robert George, Jean Goffin, Michel Graulus, Lucie Jadot, Paul Lardinois, Jaques Masure, Gerd Rondia, and Jean-Marie Spriet founded the Société Belge de Psychologie Analytique (SBePA). From that time on, the nine founders had double membership – i.e., in the SBePA and the Baudouin Institute. The Baudouin Institute was sometimes referred to as the "la vieille charrette" (the old cart).

Relations between the Baudouin Institute and the SBePA deteriorated for several reasons:

1   Almost all the Jungian members of the Baudouin Institute were recognized by the IAAP, whereas the Freudian and Lacanian members were not accredited by their comparable international organizations.

2   The meetings of the Baudouin Institute took place mainly in Geneva and in France, and less often in Belgium, and the Belgians felt slighted.

3   In 1976 Alain Le Bars, one of the training analysts of the Baudouin Institute, took his own life. He had been one of its authoritative leaders, and his death took some of the life out of the Baudouin Institute.

4   Administrative upheavals, after the student riots of the 1960s in Europe, affected the Baudouin Institute.

5   André Arthus, a prominent Jungian in France, resigned from the presidency, and his successor, a "Freudian," proved unequal to the task. Many of the Belgian Jungians resigned from the Baudouin Institute in 1978, although some stayed in loyalty to Gilberte Aigrisse.

In 1977 the SBePA was accepted as a group member of the IAAP and the new society officially began to train analysts. In 1980 many Belgian members attended the IAAP Congress in San Francisco, and – surprisingly – the SBePA was elected to the IAAP executive committee. Jef Dehing resigned from the position of president of the SBePA so that he could become its representative to the IAAP executive committee. When the IAAP *Newsletter* was initiated, Jef Dehing became its first editor, a position he held with distinction until 1992. Under his editorship, the *Newsletter* grew in both size and quality, and by the end of his tenure, the *Newsletter* was a respected annual journal.

Split of the Société Belge de Psychologie Analytique

Over the following ten years the SBePA grew in numbers and influence. New candidates from Belgium and nearby Holland started to train at the SBePA. However, tensions were beginning to mount within the group around differences in the practice of analytical psychology. In 1993 the conflict came out into the open when then-president Michael Cautaerts wished to attend training committee meetings, but the committee members unanimously excluded him. Battle lines were drawn on both sides of the issue. The main issue appeared to be whether and how to formulate a code of ethics and what constituted ethical practice. Furthermore, when a candidate trained by participants of the future Belgian School was not accepted for membership into the SBePA, the division accelerated, and the differences between the two groups appeared insurmountable. Additional difficulties – and perhaps most important, as is usually the case in these matters – arose from personality conflicts. Leading members of both factions had extremely negative opinions of their counterparts on the other side.

The IAAP was contacted, and on 19 March 1994 then-vice-presidents Verena Kast and Luigi Zoja met with the two factions in Brussels. One side with thirteen members, led by Jef Dehing, decided to leave the SBePA and form its own professional group, named the Belgian School for Jungian Psychoanalysis. Before leaving, the members of this group wished to have the SBePA dissolved, because they believed that the organization could no longer function as a viable Jungian training institute. They failed in this attempt. The SBePA held to a Continental view, which placed less emphasis on a formal ethical code, whereas the School aligned itself more with the British and American positions, which called for a strong ethical code.

As the conflict proved to be insurmountable, the IAAP executive committee decided that two separate societies should be allowed to exist in Belgium. In 1995 a second Belgian group, the Belgian School for Jungian Psychoanalysis was accepted for membership in the IAAP.

Belgian School for Jungian Psychoanalysis

On 25 October 1994 the Belgian School for Jungian Psychoanalysis was formed, with its own statutes, by-laws, and ethical code. Most of its members were trained in French, having their roots in the Baudouin Institute in Geneva. However, five of the analysts were Dutch speaking, and currently two of them are training analysts. In addition, they have two analysts who live and practice in Holland. At present their membership is at sixteen, and they have ten candidates. Their training seminars are conducted both in Dutch and French, which presents this small group with much extra work.

In philosophy the Belgian School is heavily influenced by Wilfred Bion, Melanie Klein, and other British object-relations theorists. In reviewing their public lectures one notes the emphasis on Bion, in particular, as a leading influence in their work. Their clinical and theoretical position is much closer to that of the SAP in England than to Zurich. They appear to be attracting many people to their public seminars.

Belgian Society for Analytical Psychology (after 1995)

As the majority of the members stayed in the original group, it has continued its training program, which is in French only. However, the conflict with and eventual separation of the new group proved extremely painful, leaving deep wounds on its members.

In a discussion with its president, Dr Alex Luyckx, he stated that the current position of the Belgian Society is "more flexible, not so rigid in its rules." The Belgian Society is more apt to make exceptions in training, if it is seen that an individual is creative. A friendly connection exists between a branch of the Baudouin Institute and the SBePA in Brussels. They often share the expenses of bringing a lecturer to both Institutes. The Belgian Society has continued to maintain a more classical orientation to analytical psychology.

Summary

The founding of analytical psychology in Belgium is unique in that the group traces its beginnings to the Baudouin Institute in Geneva. The only other society with connections to the Baudouin Institute is in France. At the time the Belgian founders were seeking Jungian analysis, Charles Baudouin was the main Jungian exponent in the French culture. In 1977 the Belgians had enough members to become an accredited training society within the IAAP. The evolution of the group seemed to proceed without any difficulties until there was a major conflict in 1993 which split the original society into two factions and created a second group, the Belgian School for Jungian Psychoanalysis. Although a personality conflict intensified the controversy, the main issue revolved around ethics and boundaries in the analytic setting. There are definite theoretical differences between the two groups: the SBePA is more classically oriented, whereas the School has an affinity for the British object-relations school. However, both sides state that the theoretical differences are not a problem. The wounds between the societies are still fresh, and only now are members of the two groups beginning to speak to one another.

NETHERLANDS

In contrast to its neighbor, Belgium, the Netherlands has not been able to organize a Jungian professional group. When Jung was president of the International Medical Society for Psychotherapy in the 1930s, he had frequent contact with Dutch psychotherapists. At the time he encouraged them to form a chapter in the International Medical Society for Psychotherapy, and they followed through. However, he did not encourage the formation of a specifically Jungian chapter.

In the post-war era individuals have trained to become analytical psychologists in Holland. Probably the most visible Jungian in Holland has been Robert Bosnak, Dutch born and raised, who trained at the Jung Institute in Zurich. He moved to Boston in 1978 and has been practicing there ever since. However, he is a world traveler, has led frequent workshops in the Netherlands, and even had a meeting with Queen Beatrix. Another active Jungian analyst is Patricia de Hoogh-Rowntree, an English woman who trained at the BAP and married a Dutchman. She was very active in the 1990s, trying to organize training in the Netherlands. In fact, she organized training for Holland's independent candidates with all four Jungian groups in London on several occasions. Recently her husband died of a heart attack, and she returned to England.

Sonny Herman trained at the SAP and has been in the Netherlands for approximately twenty years. He is a rabbi and specializes in analysis with survivors of World War II camps. André de Koning trained with the Belgian society before the split and hosted the first meeting of the founding members of what became the Dutch Society for Analytical Psychology. The founding members were Sonny Herman, Giuliana

Sachetti de Tudo, Patricia de Hoogh-Rowntree, Frank Turner, and André de Koning. No constitution was formally drawn up, and the group remains an unofficial one. Before moving to Perth, Australia in 1993 de Koning was actively supervising Jungian-oriented therapists. At the time of writing there are nine accredited analysts in the Netherlands. Some have Zurich training, others trained with either of the two Belgian groups, or via the individual membership route. Currently there are six individuals in training. No matter how small the group is, there is already a split primarily between the individuals who have trained via the individual member venue and those who have been trained in officially certified programs. This division might slow the process of forming a national group which could apply for membership in the IAAP. All the analysts and training candidates are fully aware that a split is not conducive to the development of analytical psychology in Holland and will slow down the process of becoming a non-training group recognized by the IAAP.

SPAIN

Analytical psychology developed recently in Spain. The long reign of Generalissimo Franco did not encourage an exchange of communication between Spain and the rest of Europe. In Barcelona there was one woman who found her way to Jungian psychology, and largely through her efforts a professional society was eventually established. Rosemary Douglas's story is a rather dramatic one.

Rosemary Douglas was born into a family of English origin and grew up on a large ranch in Patagonia on the Argentinean–Chilean border. In 1938 she was sent to England to continue her university studies. There she met her future husband, a Spaniard, who was also studying in England. They returned to Spain during the Spanish Civil War, and she told stories about some close calls with death which she experienced. Rosemary and her husband settled in Barcelona, where she became interested in Jung's psychology. During Word War II and afterwards she would regularly take the train from Barcelona to Zurich where she had a long analysis with Professor C.A. Meier. She practiced as a psychotherapist informally in Barcelona, and in 1980 applied for individual membership to the IAAP. She was accepted and became the single IAAP-accredited analyst in Spain. By the 1980s many Spaniards developed an interest in Jung and began to train with Rosemary Douglas. They had their training analysis with her and then went either to France or Switzerland for supervisory work. By the early

1990s several psychologists had fulfilled the requirements for individual membership, and their group, Sociedad Española de Psicologia Analitica, was accepted for membership in the IAAP in 1992. It is a small group of around ten members, and most of them live in Barcelona. Rosemary Douglas died in 1994, but she lived to see her dream fulfilled with the admittance of the Spanish Jungian society into the IAAP.

IRELAND

Many Irish have gone either to London or Zurich for Jungian analytic training, but they have generally not returned to Ireland, giving rise to the notion of forming an Irish Jung Society made up of IAAP members of Irish extraction who no longer live in Ireland.

In 1996 Patricia Skar, an American and Zurich graduate, and Rita McCarthy, a graduate of the AJA in London, took the initiative to form a professional association, now called the Irish Analytical Psychology Association (IAPA). The inaugural meeting took place on 20 September 1997 in Dublin, with over sixty people attending a public lecture.

Currently the IAPA has thirteen full members, five student members, and thirty-four associate members. Full members fall into two subcategories: "Analyst Member" which means member of the IAAP, and "Analytical Psychotherapist Member" which includes those who have had analysis and supervision with an IAAP or IAPA member. "Associate Members" are those professionals who have an interest in analytical psychology, but who have not had analysis or supervision with a Jungian.

The IAPA has an active public seminar program, bringing in many speakers from abroad, as well as giving an introductory course in Jungian psychology. Both programs have been enthusiastically received.

At present there are four individual members of the IAAP residing and practicing in Ireland. At the international congress in 1998 the IAPA was officially accepted as a "Developing Group" within the IAAP.

SCANDINAVIA

Over the years many individual Scandinavians have been interested in Jung's psychology. When Jung was president of the International Medical Society for Psychotherapy in the 1930s, he had extensive contact with Swedish and Danish psychotherapists in order to help them become group members of that organization. However, there was no organized interest in analytical psychology in those days.

When the Jung Institute in Zurich was founded in 1948, a number of Swedish students trained there and received their diplomas. However, because of the high taxes in Sweden, most of them did not wish to return to Sweden but instead remained in Switzerland and started analytic practices. Many kept their ties to their home country and made efforts to start a program in analytical psychology in Sweden. Lay interest groups around Jung and analytical psychology have sprung up in many of the major cities of Sweden, but without a resident analyst these programs could not develop. Currently there are three individual members of the IAAP who practice in Sweden, but they have not formed a group. They do act as advisors to the lay groups which have formed. Analysts from Switzerland and other European countries are frequently invited as guest lecturers. Many of Jung's works have been translated into Swedish, and are widely read judging by sales volumes.

There have been individual Norwegian and Finnish students at the Jung Institute in Zurich, but there is no organized professional group presence in Norway or Finland.

DENMARK

Of all the Scandinavian countries, the greatest interest in analytical psychology has developed in Denmark. It has had a difficult and circuitous history.

In the early days of the Jung Institute in Zurich, a psychiatrist, Ruth Poort, studied there without finishing her diploma. She returned to Denmark where she established a practice and also wrote about Jungian psychology in a popular vein. Outside of her books, she had no further influence on analytical psychology in Denmark.

Another student at the Jung Institute in Zurich, Eigil Nyborg, graduated in 1956 and had a profound effect on what eventually happened to analytical psychology in Denmark. He was born in 1916 and had a degree in law. His primary analyses were with Marie-Louise von Franz and C.A. Meier, and his dissertation on Hans Christian Andersen was later published in a book. He returned to Copenhagen where he opened a private practice of analytical psychology.

Over the years Nyborg informally began to give seminars on dream interpretation and fairy tales, and at the same time do supervision with interested students. These activities constituted an informal training, which led to the formation of a Jung Institute in 1980. Nyborg received permission from the Jung family to use the family name, and the Jung Institute in Copenhagen seemed destined for success. Aase Maaløe, a student of Marie-Louise von Franz, Ole Vedfelt, Pia Skogemann, and Eigil Nyborg were the prominent members of that first Jung Institute in Copenhagen. The public lectures were well attended and many new students became interested in Jungian training.

The first split

Nyborg was clearly the one in control, as almost all of the other members of the Institute had been or were in analysis with him at the time. In 1984 two issues surfaced which caused a split within the Institute. First, in order to try and maintain his control over the group he discouraged Ole Vedfelt and Pia Skogemann from their pursuit of becoming individual members of the IAAP. Nyborg also discouraged Skogemann from publishing her first book. Second, Nyborg became sexually involved with one of the students in the training group, which caused a rift among the members and resulted in Nyborg's expulsion from the Institute of which he was the founder.

Outwardly the Institute continued to function normally, but inwardly it was a time of reevaluation and reassessment. The Institute continued to take in new students until 1986, but then a decision was made to suspend new admissions. At the time no one realized that it would be another twelve years before students would again be accepted.

Skogemann and Vedfelt did apply for individual membership in the IAAP in 1986, and they were provisionally accepted. Two other Danes, Kirsten Rasmussen and Peer Hultberg, left Denmark and studied in Zurich. Hultberg received his diploma from the Zurich Institute, and Rasmussen became an individual member of the IAAP without a diploma. Hultberg has practiced in Hamburg, Germany, and periodically gives lectures in Copenhagen, whereas Rasmussen returned to practice in Denmark, but has now retired.

The second split

As all the candidates and members at the Jung Institute in Copenhagen knew each other well, it was difficult to obtain supervision and/or analysis in Denmark. The executive committee of the IAAP recommended that every candidate find supervision and analysis outside Denmark. In response, a plan was devised by Hannes Dieckmann and

Andrew Samuels whereby students would go to London twice a year for a week to have seminars and supervision with members of all four Jungian groups in England. Samuels was appointed to administer this program, which was no small undertaking. The students accepted the plan eagerly, as they wanted the international recognition which such a program would provide. The older "analysts," who had been trained by Nyborg and had no international recognition, did not support the program, and this produced a split between the older members and the students who wanted to be accredited by the IAAP. At this juncture in 1988 Skogemann resigned from the board of the Institute, although she continued to teach a continuous case seminar for several years.

The London program continued for four years, with the result that many candidates from Denmark were ready to apply for individual membership in the IAAP. In 1991, as part of the evaluation process, then-president and vice-president of the IAAP, Thomas Kirsch and Verena Kast, went to Denmark to interview the students in the London program. At the same time they talked to the older "analyst" members who did not want the international accreditation. Kast and Kirsch worked out a compromise solution so that after the Danish group would be accepted for membership by the IAAP, the "older members" would be "grandfathered" into the group. In 1992 the individual members and a new group from Denmark were admitted for membership in the IAAP. It appeared that the Danish problem had finally been resolved.

The third split

After all the candidates who participated in the London program had been certified by the IAAP, conflict developed between the psychologists and the non-clinically trained people. They could not agree on a central issue of training, and the pent-up frustrations and wounds from the years of conflict finally surfaced. Two members of the IAAP executive committee, Eli Weisstub and Luigia Poli, were able to mediate an agreement in 1993 which satisfied all the members.

The fourth split

Finally, in the spring of 1994 it was possible to establish the Danish Society for Analytical Psychology. Some people still stayed outside the professional group, but by then there was a stable group of analysts who wanted to work and train. Pia Skogemann became the director of studies of the newly reborn Jung Institute of Denmark, and in 1997 the Institute accepted its first new students in twelve years.

Ole Vedfelt, another early individual IAAP member, separated from the Jung Institute and has gone on, together with his wife, to form his own institute.

Current status

An open society, "Friends of C.G. Jung," has formed in Copenhagen, with a "sister" organization in Arhus, Jutland, where public lectures and workshops are presented. In May 1998 the first international conference on analytical psychology was held in Denmark, arranged by the Friends of C.G. Jung. The conference was a big success, and one of the major newspapers of Copenhagen wrote a long piece on the history of analytical psychology in Denmark. This conference seemed finally to pull together all the various strands which made up analytical psychology in Denmark, and the Danish Jungians were ready to move on to the next phase of their development.

On a more mundane level the Danes, like most other Europeans, are working out what it will mean to be a psychotherapist or analyst in the era of a new united Europe. The Danish Jungians have become more friendly with the psychoanalytically oriented therapists in Denmark, and many of them have become members of the Danish Society for Psychoanalytic Therapy. This umbrella group plans to offer postgraduate training for psychiatrists and psychologists in different forms of psychotherapy and analysis, and it will eventually include analytical psychology. The first manifestation of this effort was a two-day workshop in November 1999 on "What works in Psychotherapy?" Representatives from all the groups participated in this workshop.

The Danish Society for Analytical Psychology is now functioning as a stable group. There are seminars by the Danish members, as well as regular guest lecturers from abroad. The candidates are in a special two-year accelerated program to compensate for the long delay in accepting new students.

It appears that analytical psychology in Denmark has stabilized, and that academic studies and training in Jungian-oriented psychotherapy can now take place.

12 Analytical psychology in Israel

EARLY HISTORY

The development of Jung's ideas in Palestine, a mandate of the United Kingdom which – in 1948 – became Israel, is an important piece of the overall history of analytical psychology. In the early 1930s the rise of Nazism in Germany, combined with the growth of the Zionist movement, influenced many German Jews to emigrate to Palestine. James Kirsch arrived in Tel Aviv in 1933, and he encouraged all his family, friends, and Jewish patients to leave Germany as well. One of them was a recently widowed patient, Hilde Silber, who followed him to Tel Aviv. James opened a practice there; Hilde was not an analyst at that time. In the 1930s the conditions in Palestine were difficult. The country had not yet been built up, sanitation was poor, desert conditions existed for water, and the battles between Arabs and Jews were fierce. It was not an easy transition for Jews coming from developed Europe. Those who had a strong Zionist ideology were able to overcome the hardships of living in Palestine and make a new life there. Others, including James Kirsch, whose commitment to Zionism waned, did not want to stay. In 1935 he and Hilde migrated to England, and finally to Los Angeles, California in 1940. Two other Berlin Jews, Erich and Julia Neumann, who had arrived in Palestine in 1934, remained and became the founders of the Israel Association of Analytical Psychology. There has been an uninterrupted Jungian presence in Israel from 1933 until today, which gives an interesting perspective to the anti-Semitic charges leveled against Jung in the 1930s. Erich Neumann was not only the leader of the Israel Jungians, he played an important role in the history of analytical psychology, and many considered him to be Jung's most creative student.

Erich Neumann (1905–1960)

Erich Neumann was born in 1905 and grew up in Berlin, Germany. He met Julia, his wife to be, at age fifteen, but they spent several years apart before they married when both were in their early twenties. According to their daughter, Rali, they had a life-long harmonious marriage (personal communication, 1998).

After World War I, as a student, Neumann was deeply interested in questions of philosophy, psychology, the Jewish identity, poetry, and art. Neumann's first creative work was a long novel entitled *Der Anfang* (The Beginning). His early writings include a commentary on Franz Kafka, then a relatively unknown author. Another pole of his creativity was Judaism. According to Gerhard Adler, Neumann had his deepest roots in the Jewish heritage without being in any way orthodox. He was most drawn to the mystical side of Judaism and in this was influenced by Hasidism. He strongly related to the renewal of Jewish life in Palestine, and his emigration to Palestine in 1934 followed naturally. He and Julia felt at home in the Palestine of the 1930s and never regretted having left the centers of European learning. Their four-room apartment in Tel Aviv became the center for both their personal family as well as their professional lives. They saw patients, held weekly seminars, and carried on their private life within the confines of this small apartment. A son, Micha, became a psychiatrist, president of the Israel Psychiatric Society, and a Freudian psychoanalyst, whereas the daughter, Rali, studied psychology in Switzerland and has had a psychotherapeutic practice with a Jungian orientation in Jerusalem for many years. She never underwent formal Jungian training.

Erich Neumann's academic training began with a doctorate in philosophy in 1927. His dissertation was on a Jewish mystical philosopher of the late eighteenth century. When his interests gravitated towards psychology, he returned to university to obtain a medical training which he finished in 1933. After receiving his medical degree both Neumanns spent a year in Zurich in analysis: Erich with Jung and Julia with Toni Wolff. It was through his analysis with Jung that Erich Neumann was able to translate his many interests into the practical work of analysis. Julia Neumann had previously studied psychochirology (hand analysis) with Julius Spier, and she continued to practice it in addition to doing analysis.

A life-long correspondence between Neumann and Jung provides a glimpse into their relationship (Neumann 1991:273–289). In the early letters from the 1930s Neumann was imploring Jung to become more interested and knowledgeable about Judaism rather than studying

Eastern religious and philosophical systems. Jung, on his part, was validating Neumann's move to Palestine wondering how it was for a Jew to have his own earth under his feet. Neumann wished that Jung would become more concerned about the plight of the Jews in Europe, whereas Jung continued his studies in alchemy and related fields rather than attuning himself to the world events around him. Reading excerpts from their correspondence one senses Neumann's disappointment in Jung's stance: there is not the sense that Jung expressed anti-Semitism in his responses, but rather a lack of real interest in the political events of the times. In spite of this major disappointment Neumann continued to develop his ideas within a Jungian framework and for the remainder of his life considered Jung to be his primary mentor, teacher, and friend.

Meanwhile in Tel Aviv Neumann began to hold a series of weekly seminars on a variety of subjects, Jewish mysticism, mythology, and analytical psychology. A group of eight to ten child therapists began to supervise with Neumann on a fortnightly basis. They came from great distances to be in analysis with either Erich or Julia and to attend his supervisory conferences. These case conferences for child therapists lasted for over ten years, and the discussions formed the basis for his book *The Child*, published posthumously in 1973. As Neumann never saw children as patients, the question was often asked as to where he had obtained his knowledge about children. He developed his theories during the many years of case conferences with child therapists, and many of these child therapists later became members of the Israel Association of Analytical Psychology.

Erich Neumann did not return to Europe until 1947 when he and his wife spent a summer holiday with the Adlers in Ascona. There Erich Neumann was introduced to Olga Froebe-Kapteyn, the founder of the yearly Eranos conference. This meeting started a fruitful collaboration between the two, and Neumann continued to lecture at the Eranos conference each year until his death in 1960. His Eranos lectures showed the development of his thoughts. The first lecture in 1949 was called "Mystical Man" (*Eranos* 6:375–415). Other lectures which Neumann presented at Eranos include, "On the Moon and Matriarchal Consciousness," and "The Psyche and the Transformation of Reality Planes."

During the war years Neumann had a chance to write, and his studies were later published as a book entitled *Depth Psychology and a New Ethic* (1969). Neumann discusses the impact which the idea of psychological wholeness has on the idea of traditional and conventional ethics. Self-realization imposes a new morality on the individual who takes into account the unconscious. This book caused quite a stir because it implied an individual morality not covered by collective ideals. In 1949 Neumann's classic in analytical psychology, *The Origins and History of Consciousness*, was published in German. In this book there is a bold new scheme to illustrate the phases in the development of human consciousness by the interpretation of basic mythologems. In Jung's introduction he praises the book and states, "It begins just where I, too, if I were granted a second lease on life, would start to gather up the *disjecta membra* of my own writings, to sift out all those 'beginnings without continuations' and knead them into a whole" (Neumann 1954b:xiii).

Subsequently Neumann focused his writing on the psychology of the feminine. He published another classic text on *The Great Mother* in 1955 and wrote a commentary on the tale of *Amor and Psyche* in 1956. In this text he utilized images from the Archive for Research in Archetypal Symbolism at Eranos to illustrate his theme. His strong aesthetic interests culminated in his writing a number of essays on artists and musicians gathered in *Art and the Creative Unconscious*, and *The Archetypal World of Henry Moore*, both published in 1959.

Every summer the Neumanns visited Zurich and Ascona for the Eranos conferences. Many of Jung's students in Zurich were jealous of the time which Jung gave to Neumann each summer, implying that he did not deserve so much attention. Neumann's interpretations of the *Amor and Psyche* story were questioned by Marie-Louise von Franz. Neumann interpreted the story as part of a woman's development, whereas von Franz interpreted it from the point of view of the anima of a man. Neumann and many Zurich analysts were locked in a heated debate about similar issues. Although Jung did not completely agree with Neumann's interpretations, he encouraged him to follow his own path, not wanting to stifle Neumann's creativity. Neumann was made a patron of the Jung Institute in Zurich in the early 1950s.

Neumann presented a significant paper at the first international congress in 1958, titled "The Genetic Aspect for Analytical Psychology" (Adler 1959). He made a bridge between the personalistic genetic view and the transpersonal archetypal aspects of the psyche. At the time it was a radical departure for most analytical psychologists who were not influenced by Fordham and the SAP. In contradistinction to Fordham, Neumann based his theory of personality development in terms of different archetypal themes and did not directly borrow from psychoanalysis. Owing to the leadership of the Neumanns, Israel became a charter group member of the IAAP in 1958.

Erich Neumann died on 5 November 1960 from a rapidly fulminating rare kidney cancer. His wife, Julia, died in 1985 at age eighty-two when she was run over by a car when walking across the street.

Neumann's work was clearly in the tradition of Jung in extending and refining Jung's archetypal theory. Today the pendulum has swung away from historical research of archetypal symbolism among Jungians, and he is not as widely read as in earlier years. However, there are analysts in most larger Jungian societies who even today study Neumann's work carefully. He had a significant influence on the world of analytical psychology, and is considered one of the seminal figures after Jung.

THE ISRAEL ASSOCIATION OF ANALYTICAL PSYCHOLOGY

Although both Erich and Julia Neumann were analyzing and Erich gave a weekly seminar for many years, it was only at the conclusion of World War II that a Jungian group began to form. In the late 1940s a group of child therapists began to meet every two weeks with Erich Neumann to discuss their cases. One of the original therapists of this group, Geula Gat, has described the "intense and creative atmosphere" of the group in an unpublished paper entitled, "In Remembrance of Erich Neumann" (1980). Neumann would present his work in progress to the group, and the group in turn was awed by his creativity, dynamism, and breadth of knowledge. Thus, by the end of the 1950s a cohesive group of child therapists with a Jungian orientation had formed in Israel.

Slowly psychologists and medical doctors became interested in doing Jungian work with adults. At the time of the first international congress in Zurich in 1958 the initial group of analysts practicing with adults, consisting of four women and Erich Neumann as the only man, was included as a charter member in the IAAP. Although one of the smaller groups, Israel has generally been elected to the executive committee of the IAAP. Perhaps this has come about for sentimental reasons, but the Israel group has always had an unusually large impact on the international Jungian community. The child analysts were not part of the founding group and stayed separate for a few years until they were accepted as members of the Israel society.

Jung's reputation in Israel after the war was not good, because of his association with the Nazis during the 1930s. Many analysts in Israel espoused Jung's ideas and theories, but had little sympathy for Jung the man, and were more identified with Neumann.

Over the years Israel has attracted Jews from other parts of the world, and this has meant subtle changes for the Jungian community.

Several of the new immigrants made significant contributions to analytical psychology both within Israel and internationally. A brief description of some of a number of important Jungians in Israel follows.

Geula Gat

Geula Gat was a member of the original child analysis supervision group with Erich Neumann. She was born a Christian in Prussian Germany who, as a teenager, was strongly anti-Nazi, and she and a Jewish girlfriend went to Palestine. She has never left. For the past fifty years Geula Gat has been working with children in the Galilee, the most northern part of Israel, and has been living at the same kibbutz, Ayeleth-Hashachar, for most of that time. This kibbutz is located close to the Golan Heights, so prior to 1967 it was one of those kibbutzim which was constantly being shelled by the Syrians. She was widowed with two small children whom she raised on the kibbutz. Every week she would take the long bus ride to Tel Aviv to have analysis with Julia Neumann and supervision with Erich Neumann, and she learned to work with the dreams and drawings of children, and also how to talk with the parents. She never became strongly attracted to Sandplay work, and the methods and theories of Michael Fordham seemed "too abstract" to her (personal communication). Instead, she and the other child analysts developed a way of working with dreams and the unconscious which was unique to this group. They adopted Neumann's developmental model which follows the emergence of the self, mother, and father archetypes. Her work has been recognized, and Geula Gat has received numerous awards for her fifty years of work with children in northern Israel.

Dvorah Kutzinski

Dvorah Kutzinski followed another path to Israel. She was born into an academic family in Prague and during the Nazi occupation ended up spending four of her teenage years in Auschwitz. Having survived this ordeal, she emigrated to Palestine in 1946. She had difficulty finding herself until, through an acquaintance, she was introduced to Erich Neumann in 1948. Then began a long analysis with Erich and later with Julia. She described Erich Neumann as an "extremely optimistic man" (personal communication, 25 October 1998), and found his encouragement and support absolutely vital. After obtaining a degree in psychology, Kutzinski became one of the founding members of the

Israel Society of Analytical Psychology in 1958. She believes that Jung had a European anti-Semitism, typical of his time, but she does not believe that this detracts from her being very Jungian to the core. Along with her mentor and friend, Erich Neumann, she believes that Jung made a big mistake during the 1930s and, according to her, Neumann tried on many occasions to warn Jung not to write about race and nationalism during that time (personal communication, 1998). Professionally, Kutzinski was president of the Israel Association and served as a member of the executive committee of the IAAP. To this day she continues to practice in Tel Aviv and is a vibrant, direct, no-nonsense woman.

Gustav Dreifuss

"Gusti," as he is known to his friends, arrived in Israel from Switzerland in 1959. He graduated from the Zurich Institute in 1958 and in his student days had a few hours of analysis with Erich Neumann during the summers. After graduation Gustav and his wife, Lela, moved to Haifa, where he has been practicing for the past forty years. He has had a strong interest in working with Holocaust survivors as well as interpreting stories from the Old Testament. He has published many articles on these subjects in the *Journal of Analytical Psychology* and elsewhere. In addition, he has served as consultant and advisor on many international Jungian publications and is one of the best-known members of the second generation of Jungian analysts.

Rivkah Schaerf-Kluger and Yechezkel Kluger

Rivkah Schaerf was born in Switzerland in 1907 and was torn between wanting to emigrate to Palestine before World War II or completing her studies. She obtained a Ph.D. in religious studies, and her thesis "Die Gestalt des Satans im Alten Testament" (The Figure of Satan in the Old Testament) made a great impression on Jung. He decided to have it published as part of one of his own works, *Symbolik des Geistes* in 1948. Having her work published in a book of Jung's brought Rivkah immediate prominence as one of the leading figures around Jung. When the Los Angeles Institute invited analysts from Zurich in 1950, she was the first one to be chosen. As a very bright, intellectual woman, she became a leading lecturer at the Jung Institute in Zurich.

Yechezkel Kluger was a New York Jew who was an optometrist in Los Angeles and had entered Jungian analysis. Through his analysis he decided to study in Zurich in order to become an analytical psychologist.

He graduated from the Zurich Institute in 1955, and by then Yechezkel and Rivkah had fallen in love and decided to marry and return to Los Angeles. In Los Angeles Yechezkel received his Ph.D. in psychology from Claremont College. From 1955 until 1969 both Rivkah and Yechezkel practiced as Jungian analysts in Los Angeles and were integral parts of the Society of Jungian Analysts of Southern California.

In 1969 the Klugers moved to Haifa, a move they had both planned for many years. They continued to practice in Israel for the remainder of their respective days. In the late 1970s Rivkah developed the onset of Alzheimer's disease. Her once brilliant mind became just a shell of its former self. She died in Haifa in 1987. Meanwhile, Yechezkel edited her unfinished work on the Gilgamesh epic which was published in 1991. Yechezkel continued to practice in Haifa and was an important international figure until his death in 1996.

William Alex

William Alex was a New Yorker who had trained as an osteopathic physician. As a result of his analysis he decided to study at the Jung Institute in Zurich. He was one of the very first students at the Institute when its doors opened in 1948. Upon graduation he returned to southern California where in time he became president of the Los Angeles Jung Institute. In 1962 he and his family moved to San Francisco where he became an active member, teacher, and eventually president of the San Francisco Institute. In 1975 he decided to move to Jerusalem. For the following fifteen years he was an active member of the Israel Association, but then he had the yearning to return to San Francisco. However, having given up all his credentials to practice in California, he was no longer able to do so. His health deteriorated and he died in 1993.

Eli Weisstub

Eli Weisstub came from an Eastern European family who had settled in Winnipeg, Canada. He eventually came to the San Francisco area for psychiatric training, and went through the training program of the San Francisco Jung Institute, graduating in 1978. Shortly thereafter he moved to Jerusalem where he has been teaching and practicing ever since. He has been president of the Israel Association of Analytical Psychology for many years, and has guided it through many controversies. In 1989 he was elected second vice-president of the IAAP and reelected twice. In 1998 he decided to disengage from the Jungian international political arena, and he has returned to teaching, analyzing, and his writings.

Development of the Israel Association of Analytical Psychology

Dreifuss's arrival in Israel in 1959 brought the beginning of the influence of the Zurich point of view into the Israeli training. In the early 1960s the child and adult analysts came together to form one society, and all the members of the Israel Association of Analytical Psychology became members of the IAAP. With the Klugers' arrival in 1969, the influence of Zurich on the training program was increased markedly. There was a slight tension between those who favored Neumann over Jung versus those who favored Jung over Neumann. In 1975 William Alex brought in another aspect because of his experience of three different training programs. Weisstub had academic experience in California and made a connection to the academic world in Israel. The Association was still relatively small, as there were under thirty members divided between Jerusalem, Tel Aviv, Haifa, and some kibbutzim. However, the Israel Association was slowly growing.

At the international congress in San Francisco in 1980, Israel offered to host the following congress in Jerusalem. It had been assumed that the 1983 congress would be in Berlin, but when Jerusalem was proposed, the German group deferred. In March of 1983 the Ninth International Congress was held in Jerusalem. It was smaller than some of the others because of the explosive Middle Eastern political situation, and some members stayed away to protest Israeli politics. The congress was significant in that the subject of Jung, Nazism, and Germany was first brought into the open. Informally a group of Germans, Israelis, and other Jews entered into a dialogue about the underlying tension, but the meeting was not part of the official program. The result of the informal discussions led to the issue becoming part of the formal program in later congresses. At the following two congresses formal panels on the subject of Jung, Nazism, and anti-Semitism were included in the program. This airing of the shadow has been essential, and Jerusalem was the right place to have this dialogue begin.

CURRENT STATUS

In the 1990s the Israel Association has grown to approximately thirty analysts and eighteen candidates. An important change has been the fact that there is now a desire to have courses on Jung taught at many of the major universities. Some of the newly certified analysts, such as Esti Weisstub at the prestigious Hadassah Hospital, have full-time academic positions. As a corollary new candidates for training are coming from the universities in a way which did not occur earlier.

As many of those who worked directly with Neumann have either retired or died, his influence in the overall training has lessened, although it is still considerable. The influence of object-relations theory is not significant, so that the training continues to be a combination of Jung, Neumann, and clinical subjects. In the early days of the training the seminars were held mainly in German. Today the seminars are held primarily in Hebrew, and it is expected that all candidates be able to speak Hebrew.

Israel is such a small country that most of the professionals know each other. This includes the relationship between analytical psychologists and psychoanalysts. As Micha Neumann has been an important figure both in Israeli psychiatric and psychoanalytic circles, he has sometimes been a bridge between the two. Since the death of his mother in 1985 he has been actively working on the correspondence between his father and Jung. The entire correspondence has been accepted for publication in German, but at the time of writing there are still contractual problems to finalize.

There is an interest among some Jungian analysts in Sandplay work. One analyst, Rina Porat, who is also a member of the International Society for Sandplay Therapists, practices and teaches Sandplay, and others are interested.

Analysis in Israel is paid for privately, and medical insurance covers very little of the cost. A further issue is that 50 percent of the payment to the analyst goes toward taxes and social security. Thus, the analyst in Israel has a more difficult time financially than in most European countries or in the United States.

SUMMARY

It is significant that analytical psychology has had an uninterrupted presence in Israel since 1933. Initially the conditions were rather primitive as settlers, mainly from European countries, arrived and transformed the arid land. World War II brought survivors of the Holocaust to Israel in large numbers. Subsequent migrations from Africa, other Middle Eastern countries, and the Soviet Union, in addition to the Arab–Israeli wars, have changed the atmosphere of the country even

13 Analytical psychology in Australia and New Zealand

Analytical psychology in Australia and New Zealand developed later than comparable professional associations in Europe and the United States. Distances and expense of travel from other countries, and internally, were prohibitive until recently. Australia itself is approximately the size of the continental United States, and population centers are located mainly on the eastern seaboard, with the exception of Perth on the west coast and Alice Springs in the interior. The long distances, both within and to the outside world, have precluded intensive person-to-person contact with colleagues, slowing down the development of professional affiliations. Analysts settling in New Zealand and Australia practiced in relative isolation after obtaining their training in England or Switzerland.

The first person from New Zealand to have contact with Jung and analytical psychology was Grete Reiche Christeller. Born into a Jewish mercantile family in Berlin in 1895, she moved to Switzerland in the 1930s to study massage and have analysis with Jung. From there she moved to Genoa, Italy, where a friend suggested that she move with her two children to New Zealand. In 1939 she arrived in Auckland and worked as a Jungian-oriented psychotherapist there and in Christchurch until her death in 1964. She never had any official status as a Jungian, but she qualifies as the first Jungian in New Zealand.

A similar story is that of Kathe Silber Nothmann of Melbourne, Australia. She was also born into a Jewish business family in Berlin, where she had a Jungian analysis. She was a dear friend of Max Zeller, and her twin brother was the first husband of Hilde Kirsch. Kathe strongly influenced Max and Hilde to begin Jungian analysis in Berlin. When the Nazis came to power in Germany, she emigrated to Melbourne, where she practiced Jungian-oriented psychotherapy and graphology for over thirty years. She never had any official status within the Jungian community.

An official Jungian presence began in 1977 with five analysts. Three of them were graduates of the Jung Institute in Zurich, Donald Broadribb, Patrick Jansen, and Janice Daw Koh; Anne Noonan had trained with the AIPA in Italy, and Rix Weaver had gone to Zurich for analysis in 1955 and was made an individual member of the IAAP in 1974. The executive committee of the IAAP encouraged the group to form an association covering all of Australia and New Zealand. They made that recommendation without the benefit of a site visit and without realizing the enormous distances involved. From Perth in Western Australia to Christchurch is over five thousand miles! They had even thought of including Professor Kawai from Japan, too!

In 1977 this new group of analysts was accepted into the IAAP, and it was named the Australian and New Zealand Association of Analytical Psychology, or ANZAAP. The name presented a legal problem in Australia, and it was changed to the Australian and New Zealand Society of Jungian Analysts (ANZSJA). Within two years Dorothea Wraith (née Norman-Jones), a New Zealand psychiatrist trained in London, and Leon Petchkovsky, a Russian-Polish-Jewish émigré living in Australia, who is a psychiatrist trained in England, became members. For many years the small group tried to meet once a year, but there were not enough analysts to start a training program. Three of the original five resigned for personal reasons, but slowly new members came into the region. Two individuals were able to obtain accreditation as analysts in New Zealand and Australia, partly through training at ANZSJA and earlier training at other institutes.

One early member of ANZSJA deserves special mention, and that is Dr Paul Lie, of Chinese descent born in Java, who studied medicine and psychology in Holland. In the 1950s he traveled to Zurich and attended Jung's seminars and met Jung informally. He returned to Indonesia, but was forced to emigrate for political reasons; in Sydney he associated with the public sector of Gladesville Psychiatric Hospital, and the St John of God Private Psychiatric Hospital. He became a member of ANZSJA, where his grandfatherly wisdom lent a certain dignity to the proceedings. Shortly before his death in 1997 he returned to Indonesia.

In 1988 then-president of the IAAP, Hannes Dieckmann, suggested that vice-president Thomas Kirsch visit Australia and New Zealand to view the situation first-hand. He and his analyst wife, Jean Kirsch, visited the major areas where analytical psychologists practiced. The first stop on their trip was Perth, where the C.G. Jung Institute of Western Australia had existed for over two decades. Rix Weaver had formed the Institute for professionals and lay people interested in analytical psychology. Several professionals had gone to Zurich for partial training and had become accredited through ANZSJA. In 1988 Rix Weaver was in her late eighties and was the *grande dame* of analytical psychology in Australia. She had been drawn to Jung's work through her own interest in the Aborigines of Australia, which led her to seek Jungian analysis in Zurich. She was the author of the *The Wise Old Woman*, which had an international circulation, and other books on analytical psychology which were published only in Australia. As a frequent contributor to radio and television, she was well recognized in Australia for her interest in Jung's psychology.

For Tom Kirsch's visit, Sydney was designated as the central meeting place for all the analysts of Australia and New Zealand. The analysts who came from different parts of Australia and from New Zealand represented among themselves Jungian viewpoints from England, Switzerland, Italy, the United States, and ANZSJA. A tension existed between the Zurich-oriented and the developmentally oriented analysts, and it was unclear whether there was enough cohesiveness to undertake an organized training program. There were also some other analysts, both from the developmental and the symbolic side, who had never joined ANZSJA because they did not feel comfortable with it as it was then constituted. There were approximately thirty therapists and individuals in related disciplines who were eager for a Jungian training program to begin, but the ANZSJA analysts were reluctant to take on the responsibility. A training program along the model of the IRS in North America was encouraged by Jean and Tom Kirsch, but ANZSJA lacked the cohesiveness to make such a program work.

The last stop of Jean and Tom Kirsch's visit was in Wellington, New Zealand, where training had begun in 1984. Dorothy Wraith (née Norman-Jones) and Dale Dodd, an American clinical psychologist, had designed a syllabus and curriculum, and held seminars for seven prospective trainees. Of the original group, Peter Reid, a social worker and psychotherapist, and Wilson Daniel, a psychologist and therapist, born in New Zealand but who had lived in the United States for many years and had begun his analysis there, became the first candidates to complete training under ANZSJA. An active C.G. Jung Society was already in existence in Wellington and another one in Auckland.

From 1988 to 1998 many changes took place within ANZSJA. New members joined from Belgium and England, in addition to many Australians and New Zealanders returning from training at the Zurich Institute. As of March 1999 there are twenty-one analyst members, and twenty-eight candidates at various stages in their training. Regional training groups exist in Sydney, Melbourne, Perth, and Wellington. A critical mass of analysts has been reached, so that a more effective professional association is possible and training is taking place.

A significant development is the academic connection which ANZSJA has made with La Trobe University in Melbourne and Western Sydney University. A master's degree program in analytical psychology is now possible at La Trobe, and the combined efforts of David Tacey, a Jungian academic psychologist at La Trobe, and Jungian analysts Anne Brown and Peter Fullerton are coordinating the program. As a result students interested in analytical psychology will be able to combine their academic and clinical interests into a single training.

Another notable undertaking has been the work of Craig San Roque and Leon Petchkovsky with aboriginal tribes in and around Alice Springs. Substance abuse and cultural breakdown have been immense problems for the indigenous peoples of Central Australia. San Roque has drawn upon Jung's view of myth and ritual to address the serious substance abuse which afflicts many of today's aboriginal peoples.

One matter that continues to undermine ANZSJA, in Australia particularly, is that some graduates from the Zurich Institute still do not wish to become members, protesting that ANZSJA should not be training, as they do not have enough qualified analysts. Rivalry between locally trained analysts and Zurich-trained analysts exists in many places in the world. The conflict is probably greater in Australia, because it is still such a small Jungian community. Zurich graduates, who made great sacrifices to receive their Zurich training, often believe that those who stayed at home did not have the deep immersion in Jung's psychology which the Zurich graduates believe is necessary. This topic has been discussed in an article titled, "IAAP and Jungian Identity," by Thomas Kirsch (1995). The question of who carries the proper Jungian spirit can arouse very deep emotional responses on both sides.

ANZSJA members, with their great diversity, represent a microcosm of the larger world of analytical psychology. In many parts of the world, Jungians have not been able to have constructive dialogue around subjects, such as the interpretation of the transference in analysis, analytical psychology and object-relations theory mixture, the role of classical dream interpretation, and active imagination. The smallness of the ANZSJA group, the great distances between Jungian centers, and the relative newness of the organization, have produced a surprising and refreshing openness to one another's point of view. Having developed later, ANZSJA has a chance to learn from the conflicts which have wreaked havoc on other Jungian groups around the world. There appears to be a consolidation and stabilization of organizational and training processes, and some of the emergent issues are:

1   stabilizing and refining a clinical approach which is consistent with and responds to the culture of the region;
2   engagement with some of the political and cultural matters which are an expression of the cultural unconscious, including multicultural issues, recognition of the traumatic origins of new families from trouble spots of the globe, and the development of the intercultural relationship with indigenous Aborigines, especially concerned with substance abuse, cultural vitality, issues of land and psyche;
3   development in communication technology necessary in far-flung places;
4   relations between ecology/psyche/environment;
5   the ongoing development of relationships with academic institutions such as La Trobe University and the University of Western Sydney, where students can obtain both an academic background and a clinical approach which will further their careers in becoming analysts.

How ANZSJA will evolve on all these fronts will be most interesting to watch. At this point there is a mutual respect among all the members which bodes well for the future.

14 Analytical psychology in Latin America

Decades ago different schools of psychoanalysis were established in Chile, Argentina, Brazil, Mexico, Venezuela, and other Latin countries, but the development of analytical psychology in all of South and Central America has been slow and uneven. Possible explanations are many, but one factor may be the number of European Jewish refugees who fled to this region during the 1930s, carrying with them Freud's legacy. From these origins, a Kleinian establishment developed in Buenos Aires, followers of Erich Fromm went to Cuernavaca, Mexico, and psychoanalysis has played an important role in the cultural life of the Latin American continent. Another inhibiting influence has been the political instability of the region.

Currently, however, analytical psychology is experiencing a period of rapid growth. Many countries of the Latin American region have developed "Friends of Jung" type organizations where Jungian books are read, and lectures and workshops on Jungian themes are presented. In 1998 the first Latin American Conference for Analytical Psychology was held in Uruguay, and in the year 2000 the second Latin American Conference will be held in Rio de Janeiro. In 1999 the *Journal of Analytical Psychology* Conference was held in Merida, Mexico, and many Latin Americans participated. At the international level, Spanish will be added as an official language of future IAAP congresses.

Acknowledging that at the moment the development of analytical psychology in Latin America is in dynamic transition, the focus will be on three countries i.e., Brazil and Venezuela in South America, and Mexico in Central America, to examine the history of analytical psychology in the region.

BRAZIL

Institutional history

The first person to practice Jungian analysis in Brazil was Léon Bonaventure, a Belgian and former priest, who came to São Paulo around 1968. His experiences at the seminary in Belgium led him to seek a Jungian analysis and training in Zurich. Although he had not finished the training in Zurich when he decided to start a new life in Brazil, he was able to practice there as a Jungian analyst in the absence of any other Jungians. Subsequently, he became an individual member of the IAAP. At about the same time Carlos Byington, a medical doctor, graduated from the Zurich Jung Institute and began to practice in Rio de Janeiro and São Paulo. Each analyst attracted his own group of analysands and students.

By 1977 their respective groups had grown to a size where the organization of a professional society was possible. Adolf Guggenbühl-Craig, then-president of the IAAP, made an official visit to Brazil to evaluate the progress of analytical psychology. Bonaventure's notion was that a professional group would be loosely organized, permissive, and open to non-medical and non-psychologically trained people. Byington, on the other hand, envisioned a professional organization which would only accept medical doctors and psychologists. After much discussion within the IAAP executive committee, Byington's group, the Sociedade Brasileira de Psicologia Analitica (SBrPA), was accepted as a member in the IAAP. Bonaventure and Byington went their separate ways, and Bonaventure has continued to practice as an individual member of the IAAP until the present.

Byington became the acknowledged intellectual and political leader, revising Jung's ideas into his own language, and publishing many books on analytical psychology. The group has continued to flourish, and at present there are over sixty members in São Paulo and Rio de Janeiro. The training is structured so that a group of trainees is accepted every four years, and they are all expected to finish their training at the same time. When one group graduates, another group is selected, and the process repeats itself. A quarterly journal, named *Jungiana*, is published by the Society with both clinical and cultural contributions. The SBrPA is the oldest and most established Jungian training in Brazil. The founding members of the SBrPA are getting on in years and are withdrawing from leadership positions. Younger members have been heavily influenced by object-relations theory, and others have been open to the writings of James Hillman. Currently, the SBrPA is becoming more receptive to new ideas in the field of analytical psychology.

In the early 1990s a few members became disillusioned with the attitudes and policies of the SBrPA. Two founding members of the Society, Glauco Ulson and Walter Boechat, decided to form their own group, the Associaçao Junguiana do Brasil, São Paulo (AJB) to counteract what they felt were the rigid policies of the SBrPA. For over a year no accord could be reached between the two groups. In August 1993 then-president of the IAAP, Thomas Kirsch, visited Brazil and met with the two groups individually and jointly. The concern of the SBrPA was that the other group would accept unqualified candidates, which would provide an easier path to becoming a Jungian analyst. A compromise was reached whereby members of the IAAP executive committee would participate in the final evaluations of the AJB candidates; this way the evaluation of candidates would be more objective. The AJB became an official IAAP group in 1998. At this time the AJB has fifteen members and many new candidates. As soon as the AJB has six members, each with five years of analytic experience, it will no longer require help with the evaluations from the IAAP.

Analytical psychology in Brazil: non-institutional

Nise de Silveira

Dr Nise de Silveira was the only woman in a class of 157 men in the School of Medicine in Salvador, Bahia. She began her career as a psychiatrist in a large public institution. She quickly realized that schizophrenics do not lose their affective life, and that one must contact them in their intact psychological areas. She began with the ideas of Spinoza but quickly came to Freud and Jung. When she saw the images painted by schizophrenic patients, she became convinced of the validity of the archetypes. In 1954 she wrote to Jung, asking his opinion about a series of circular paintings, and he wrote back on the meaning of mandala symbolism. Based upon her work with these schizophrenic patients, she proposed a treatment based upon the curative effects of working with the archetypal images. In 1952 she created the Museum of Images of the Unconscious, which today has over 3,300 pieces. One of the pictures was included in *Word and Image*, by Aniela Jaffé (1979). Nise de Silveira published the first book about Jung in Brazil, as well as another book, portraying images from the unconscious. She has had a Jung study group for years, and many future analysts have been introduced to Jung through her. She has never become an official analyst, but today, in her nineties, she continues to see patients and to give seminars and workshops.

Pethö Sandor (1916–1992)

Pethö Sandor was a Hungarian gynecologist who came to Brazil in 1949. A highly intuitive and introverted man, he taught at the Catholic University in São Paulo, where he made private translations of Jung's "Vision Seminars," and led discussions on the *Collected Works* of Jung. At the time they were not yet translated into Portuguese. He developed his own theory of "Subtle Touch Therapy," a kind of psychosomatic treatment. Though not accepted by the "theoretical" Jungians, he continued to work independently in his own individual way.

Individual analysts in Brazil

The professional climate in Brazil has been relatively closed to non-clinically trained Jungian analysts. Roberto Gambini, a trained anthropologist, graduated from the Zurich Institute in 1981 and returned to his native Brazil. He was admitted to the SBrPA as an exception, but after a year he resigned and has been practicing as an individual analyst in São Paulo ever since. In 1995 he reemerged from relative isolation and has been a popular lecturer. His wife, Fatima, trained with Dora Kalff in Zurich, and is considered the foremost Sandplay therapist in Brazil. She did not receive formal training at the Zurich Institute.

Another analyst who has been on her own is Myriam Gomes de Freitas, a neurologist, who graduated from the Jung Institute in Zurich. She lives and practices in Rio Grande de Sul, far away from the metropolitan centers of São Paulo and Rio de Janeiro. She has made contact with a "Friends of Jung" group in Buenos Aires, which is closer to where she lives. She has no contact with either of the Brazilian groups.

Summary

Brazil is a country with enormous potential and tremendous problems, and the Jungians mirror the culture of the country. There are no state licensing laws, so that therapists can call themselves whatever they like. The result is that there are literally thousands of therapists who consider themselves "Jungian," although they do not belong to any official group. They may have had some analysis, are generally self-educated, have attended some workshops, and may be part of a study group. As is to be expected, their quality is uneven. Some are very good and may even teach at the university level. Then there are the two official Jungian groups with a recent history of intense conflict, which is now in the process of healing. Besides, there are individual Jungian analysts who have never joined either group, but who carry on with their analytic work. We cannot forget Dr Nise de Silveira who continues to do her work with severely disturbed patients and leads a study group on Jung. Despite many conflicts, Jungian psychology appears to be thriving in Brazil at this time.

VENEZUELA

Venezuela is an oil-rich country which has a history of democracy in a hemisphere where dictatorships have been the rule. Analytical psychology found fertile soil in this tropical country. As in many other South American countries, Catholic priests and nuns were the first to teach Jung's psychology.

A professional interest in Jung's psychology began with Dr Fernando Risquez, a psychiatrist who has been teaching at the Military Hospital in Caracas since the 1960s. Generations of students have heard his lectures on Jung and analytical psychology, and many of them have become Jungian analysts. In 1950 Risquez spent a year in Jungian analysis in London, and in the early 1960s he went to Zurich where he analyzed with Dr Franz Riklin, who became his mentor. Risquez returned to Caracas to become one of the leading psychiatrists of Venezuela. In 1983 he was made an individual member of the IAAP. Although strongly drawn to Jung, Risquez does not like the label "Jungian." He remains an active and vigorous teacher today.

The person with the strongest international presence from Venezuela is Rafael López-Pedraza. Born in Cuba, he emigrated to Caracas in the 1950s where he came in contact with Fernando Risquez. In the 1960s Rafael spent several years in Zurich, taking courses at the Institute, working with James Hillman on the journal *Spring*, and having analysis. He returned to Caracas in the early 1970s where he has had a clinical practice ever since. In 1980 he was made an individual member of the IAAP, at the recommendation of Adolf Guggenbühl-Craig and James Hillman, and became Venezuela's first accredited analyst. Rafael López-Pedraza's books, *Hermes and His Children* (1989) and *Cultural Anxiety* (1990), have been widely read within the Jungian world, and he has lectured extensively in the United States and Europe. His interest in art has led him to lecture and write on Picasso and Anselm Kiefer, and he has participated in many Jungian workshops on art and psychology. He has been a strong proponent that the Venezuelan analysts should form a training group slowly, because he has seen the power shadow of training.

Several other Venezuelans graduated from the Jung Institute in Zurich and returned to practice in Caracas. Many qualified professionals from within Venezuela have had the necessary analysis and supervision to qualify for individual membership in the IAAP. In November 1994 then-president of the IAAP, Thomas Kirsch, together with Betty Meador, interviewed all the applicants and recommended five people for individual membership in the IAAP. They were accepted in 1995, which brought the total number of accredited analysts in Venezuela to ten. In 1998 the Venezuelan Society of Jungian Analysts was admitted for membership as a non-training society of the IAAP.

Some individual members were not satisfied with the reluctance of other analysts to begin training, so under the guidance of Fernando Risquez and Luis Sanz they have formed their own "School," separate from the Venezuelan Society. At the present time they have fourteen candidates who are enrolled in their course in depth psychology. This has produced a definite tension between the now official Venezuelan Society and the "School," which does not have IAAP recognition. How this conflict will be resolved is unclear at this moment.

MEXICO

Mexico is a country with a rich cultural history where archetypal images and rituals have never been far below the surface of the collective consciousness. The ancient Mayan and Aztec civilizations are a living presence in contemporary society. The capital, Mexico City, with a population of twenty million, has become one of the main cultural centers of the Americas and has developed a lively interest in analytical psychology.

The first person to begin a Jungian group was Maria Abac-Klemm, a Mexican who graduated from the Jung Institute in Zurich in the 1980s. For many years she split her time between Zurich and Mexico City, but since the end of the 1980s she has lived full time in Mexico City. She organized a number of study groups, depending upon the level of the students, and had many of them in analysis. As she was the only analyst there, it became increasingly difficult to separate the professional and personal issues. Attempts were made to bring in analysts from the United States for lectures and supervision, but the infrequent visits of analysts did not suffice.

In 1990 Abac-Klemm contacted Thomas Kirsch, then-president of the IAAP, and asked him to come to Mexico City to interview her different groups. He tried to organize another series of lectures by analysts from the United States, but the Mexican group broke up before a curriculum could be finalized. Several Mexican therapists interested in becoming Jungian analysts were willing to travel to the United States for analysis and supervision. In addition, American analysts traveled independently to Mexico City to lecture and supervise, establishing regular contact between the Mexican therapists and American Jungians.

In 1995 Patricia Michan was accredited as an individual member by the IAAP. At the same time it was decided to begin a two-year course, similar in nature to what had been done in Eastern Europe, where visiting analysts spend a weekend with the students in seminars and supervision. A weekly seminar by Patricia Michan was an important part of the overall program. An academic committee was formed, including Thomas Kirsch, Kennon McKee, Murray Stein, James Wyly, and Beverley Zabriskie, in addition to Patricia Michan. It was clear that this program was not to be construed as an IAAP training program, but rather it trained therapists to work in a Jungian fashion. The first group has completed the course, and a second group is in process.

Three other Mexican women therapists were accredited by the IAAP in 1998, and others are in the process of applying for membership. In a few years there will be enough analysts to form a Mexican group, but it remains to be seen whether all those accredited will be able to work together to form a single group. Conflict among the individual analysts already exists, which raises a doubt about the eventual formation of a single society.

Individual Jungians have been able to make contact with psychoanalysts, and together they have organized two well-attended conferences where both psychoanalysts and analytical psychologists have spoken on the same themes.

As the psychotherapy laws in Mexico are not strictly enforced, the situation has allowed for many unofficial Jungian groups to form. This has been confusing to therapists wishing a Jungian training, as it has often not been possible to ascertain the legitimacy of organizations putting on programs. Visiting Jungian analysts are often not aware of these problems until they arrive in Mexico.

URUGUAY

Three individuals from Uruguay have become IAAP-accredited analysts by obtaining their training through the SBrPA in Brazil. One of them, Dr Mario Saiz, is the director of the Analytical Psychology

School of the Catholic University of Uruguay and president of the C.G. Jung Foundation of Uruguay. The program at the university is serious, and lecturers from abroad have strengthened the program. In 1998 the first Latin American Conference on Analytical Psychology was held on an island off the coast of Uruguay.

SUMMARY

The last decade has seen an enormous growth of interest in analytical psychology in all of Latin America. This chapter has included only those countries where official IAAP members reside. There are serious study groups in Argentina, Ecuador, Chile, and Colombia, in addition to the countries already described. Latin American analysts are travelling to these other countries to help disseminate information on analytical psychology. Increasingly, non-Latin American Jungians are lending support, and the increased involvement of all analysts bodes well for the future development of analytical psychology in the region. The addition of Spanish as an official language at international congresses is symptomatic of the growth of interest in analytical psychology in Latin America.

15 Analytical psychology in South Africa

Two figures were central to the development of analytical psychology in South Africa: Sir Laurens van der Post and Dr Vera Bührmann.

Jung met van der Post, the South African author, film-maker, and storyteller, after World War II when Mrs van der Post became interested in Jung's psychology. Sir Laurens never analyzed with Jung, but they became close friends; he championed Jung's thought for the remainder of his life until his death in London in 1996 at the age of ninety.

The other central figure, Vera Bührmann, was a child psychiatrist from South Africa who trained at the Society of Analytical Psychology in London in the early 1950s and then returned to her native country. Her major supervisor during training was D.W. Winnicott. Dr Bührmann, who died in 1998 at the age of eighty-eight, was an extraordinary individual who supervised most of the present-day analysts of Cape Town, and worked with indigenous people. Her quiet passion for both activities was enormous. Without using psychological language she treated sufferers of "possession," a common term for psychological illness, helping them to feel at home with themselves again (Roloff 1999).

In 1975 Dr Bührmann conceived the idea of a Jungian training center in Cape Town. For many years she had seen psychologists and psychiatrists go abroad for further training, seldom to return. Her dream of a training center was further nourished when academic psychologists Renos Papadopoulos and Graham Saayman, along with Ian Player, director of the Wilderness Leadership School, became involved in teaching Jung's psychology. However, there was no possibility of developing a training institute with only one IAAP-certified analyst. Years of persuasion and negotiation with the IAAP led to an official visit by then-president, Hannes Dieckmann, and in 1987 the Cape of Good Hope Centre for Jungian Studies was inaugurated.

Immediately, the first group of training candidates was selected to begin seminars and supervision. A second group was admitted to training shortly thereafter, increasing the number to thirteen candidates in analytic training. However, the group still had only one analyst. Sir Laurens van der Post then arranged for Julian David, a Zurich-trained analyst living in England, to spend five years in Cape Town doing analysis with its candidates. He arrived in January 1989, establishing a highly unusual situation in which all the candidates were in analysis with him, while in supervision with Vera Bührmann. To normalize the training they instituted the practice of inviting analysts from abroad for three-week periods to present seminars and provide additional supervision.

Another unusual aspect of this training program is its link to nature. The Wilderness Leadership School takes trainees and visiting lecturers into the bush. Walking for five days among lions, rhino, buffalo, buck, and cheetah, sleeping outdoors, and listening to the sounds of wild nature have helped candidates connect to their "bush souls." Jung had voyaged to Central Africa in 1925 to study the dreams and myths of several indigenous tribes and returned with enduring impressions, perhaps some of which helped crystallize his hypothesis of the collective unconscious. Certainly, that is the effect the bush experience has upon the visiting scholar, when the concept takes on immediate meaning.

In 1990 property was donated to the Centre which became home to its administration, public lectures, training seminars, and its library. The latter was established through a bequest from the Frank McMillan Foundation of Texas, arranged by Sir Laurens van der Post. At the opening ceremonies of the Centre in 1991 Sir Laurens planted a ginkgo tree in the garden.

In 1992 then-president of the IAAP, Thomas Kirsch, interviewed all the candidates to assess their readiness for individual membership in the IAAP. Eight candidates were deemed suitable and were accepted for membership in 1992. In the same year three additional Jungian analysts arrived from abroad, swelling the number of the South African group to thirteen.

The Southern African Association of Jungian Analysts (SAAJA) was constitutionally formed in 1993. Four additional individual members from South Africa were accepted for membership in the IAAP in 1995, and the SAAJA was admitted as a group with official training status.

Outside of Cape Town there are small "Friends of Jung" groups in Johannesburg and Durban. An American graduate from the Zurich Jung Institute has settled in Johannesburg, and some of the Cape

Town analysts visit there occasionally. A satellite training program may soon develop in Johannesburg.

This is just a bare outline of what has taken place in South Africa, where Jungian history has been a small part of the much larger political picture. One cannot avoid the looming racial and political issues, which seep into every facet of life; Jungian analysts have not been immune to them. Controversies exist within the Jungian community as to how to respond to these complex social issues. Meanwhile the training program thrives with many highly qualified candidates. Though geographically removed, they are very much connected to the world of analytical psychology. The combined legacies of Vera Bührmann and Sir Laurens van der Post have been well rewarded.

16 Analytical psychology in Russia and Eastern European countries

EARLY HISTORY: RUSSIA

The early twentieth century was a time when the craving of Russian intellectuals for world culture found a natural outlet in extended stays in the West, linking some of the most creative Russian personalities with leading intellectuals in Europe, including Freud and Jung. This fact has tended to be forgotten as communism and the Soviet State have been so dominant for such a significant portion of this century, a time which has seen the development of depth psychology. Freud, writing in 1912, said: "In Russia there seems to be a veritable epidemic of psychoanalysis" (Etkind 1998:6). Many Russians came to Freud for psychoanalysis, and, prior to the Revolution in 1917, St Petersburg and Moscow were leading psychoanalytic centers. The early revolutionary leaders continued to value psychoanalysis, but with the emergence of Stalin as a leader in the mid-1920s psychoanalysis was systematically wiped out.

The first Russian who became interested in Jung's psychology was Sabina Spielrein, the daughter of a Russian Jewish merchant from Rostov-on-Dom, who was brought to the Burghölzli Psychiatric Clinic in Zurich as a patient in 1904. She was Jung's first patient to be treated in a psychoanalytic manner (Carotenuto 1982; Kerr 1993). After a ten-month in-patient stay in the Burghölzli, Jung continued to treat her as an out-patient; she began medical studies and graduated from the University of Zurich. She had a powerful transference towards Jung, fantasizing a child by him named Siegfried, and reciprocally he had strong positive feelings towards her. Jung wrote to Freud about his transference difficulties in the treatment. The Freud–Jung correspondence contains over forty references to her. Freud initially took Jung's side, but as their relationship deteriorated, his allegiance shifted towards Spielrein. After her graduation from medical school in Zurich in 1909, she moved to Vienna where she became a psychoanalyst and member of the Vienna Psychoanalytic Society. Although a psycho-analyst, Spielrein was one of very few people who continued to correspond with both Freud and Jung after their split. At the conclusion of World War I Freud suggested to Spielrein that she return to Russia, where she could be part of the newly emerging psychoanalytic movement. Under Stalin the psychoanalytic movement was erased, and after 1931 she had no further contact with the West. She was killed by the Nazis in Rostov in 1941 when they invaded Russia (Etkind 1998).

There were other Russian doctors and psychiatrists, such as Max Eitingon, who worked at the Burghölzli during the tenure of Jung, but they all followed Freud, and so do not figure in the further history of analytical psychology.

Emilii Medtner (1872–1936)

A Russian who made an impact on analytical psychology was Emilii Medtner, a Russian Symbolist, who has received far too little attention from Jungians. He was referred to Jung for analysis by Eugen Bleuler in 1914, and he continued his analysis throughout most of World War I. He attended the first meeting of the Analytical Psychology Club in Zurich in 1916 and was the librarian of the Club for many years. We are indebted to the research of Magnus Ljunggren, a Swedish scholar, who has written a biography of this significant Russian Symbolist entitled *The Russian Mephisto*, for the following information. This material has particular significance because we have so little information about Jung during the period of 1913–1918, and of his "confrontation with the unconscious." Medtner was in analysis with Jung during that period of time and traveled with him to Château d'Oex in 1917, where Jung was the commandant of the British prisoners of war and where Medtner had daily analytic sessions with Jung.

Emilii, or Emil in German, came from a family of German origin living in Russia. One of his brothers was Nicolai Medtner, a child prodigy at the piano, who later became a well-known composer. Nicolai Medtner was a contemporary of Scriabin, Rachmaninov, and Stravinsky. Both brothers were in love with the same woman, and they lived in a *ménage à trois* for many years. Interestingly enough, the symptom which brought Emilii Medtner to analytic treatment was that he could not listen to music. He saw Jung's writings as the answer to the sickness of the soul overcoming Russia. Through his friendship with Edith Rockefeller McCormick, he was able to persuade her to finance the translations and publications of Jung's works into Russian. This three-volume set was completed in 1929 in Zurich, and a few copies made it to Soviet Russia. When the Soviet Union collapsed in 1989, copies of Medtner's translations surfaced again.

Medtner remained part of the inner circle around Jung during the 1920s, and he did some analysis as well as giving lectures at the Analytical Psychology Club. With the rise of fascism he became fascinated with both Mussolini and Hitler and began to move away from Jung. However, in 1935 he was the editor of the *Festschrift* for Jung's sixtieth birthday entitled *Die Kulturelle Bedeutung der Komplexen Psychologie* (Medtner 1935). He died shortly thereafter in a psychiatric hospital in Germany.

ANALYTICAL PSYCHOLOGY IN POST-COMMUNIST RUSSIA

Under the dictatorship of Stalin and the leaders following him, open interest in analytical psychology was not possible. In the late 1980s the political climate began to thaw. Two Americans, Robert Bosnak and Laura Dodson, independently made contact with people interested in nuclear disarmament and analytical psychology inside the Soviet Union. Dodson was interested in bringing families from both countries together, whereas Bosnak approached the Russian leader, Gorbachev, directly. When the Berlin Wall fell in 1989, both Bosnak and Dodson had numerous connections within the Soviet Union.

In January 1990 the first post-communist Russian who expressed an interest in analytical psychology, Valery Zelensky, was invited to England as a guest of the Russian Orthodox Church. He was greeted with great enthusiasm and fanfare in London. As a clinical psychologist who specialized in the group treatment of alcoholics, he had been a dissident under communism and had read much of Jung. In 1990 he was interested in translating and publishing Jung and Jungian authors in Russian. Subsequent to his visit to England, the major American Jungian Institutes and the IAAP arranged for him to visit New York, Chicago, San Francisco, and Los Angeles later that year, where mutual exchanges took place.

The breaking down of barriers between the Soviet Union and the West brought a flood of inquiries, and the executive committee of the IAAP decided that it was time to send an emissary to Moscow and Leningrad to evaluate the situation. In May 1991 then-IAAP president, Thomas Kirsch, and his wife Jean, made a two-week trip to Russia to meet selected persons. The first priority was to see whether Jung's works could be translated into Russian. Other important objectives were to assess the state of psychotherapy and analysis in general and, if depth psychological psychotherapists existed, whether it was possible to arrange for Jungian seminars in either or both of these cities.

PUBLISHING

In 1991 the publishing industry in the Soviet Union was chaotic. There were many old-style communist publishing houses which were losing their influence because of a lack of state support, and smaller publishing houses began to emerge. There were mimeographed and pirated translations of some of Jung's major works, and copies of Medtner's translations of Jung, long out of print in Zurich, were also found. Jung's works were always hidden behind some other books, in case of KGB searches. The disarray in the publishing field caused the IAAP president to follow many leads which led nowhere. On the last day of his stay in Moscow Thomas Kirsch was introduced to Vitale Savenkov, an intellectual with a Ph.D. in philosophy and the owner of Interbook, a small publishing house. Interbook was already in the process of publishing a collection of Jung's papers from the 1930s with the intention of publishing other works of Jung. Finally, an appropriate publishing house had been found! Before leaving for the Soviet Union, Kirsch had procured a grant from the van Waveren Foundation to subsidize the translation and publication of the *Collected Works* of Jung in Russian. Negotiations began in Moscow, were continued the following week in Leningrad, and a meeting to sign the contract was to take place at the annual Moscow Book Fair in September of that same year. Bob Hinshaw, Jungian book publisher in Switzerland, and Thomas Kirsch were to represent the IAAP. In August the communist coup took place, Gorbachev was ousted, and hard-line communists were again in control for two days, before Boris Yeltsin came to the rescue. In that short time-frame the book fair was canceled; however, it was decided to proceed with the signing of the contract in Moscow. The terms of the contract stated that two books of the *Collected Works* would be published each year, and that half would be paid for by the van Waveren Foundation and half by Renaissance, the new name for Interbook. In addition, each translation was to be vetted by accredited Jungian analysts who were fluent in Russian. The first book published by Renaissance was volume 15, *The Spirit in Man, Art, and Literature*. As a result of the political turmoil inside the new Russia, the publication of translations of additional volumes was suspended. Other translations were completed, but attempts to find different publishers failed. Over the years, unofficial translations of many of the *Collected Works* have appeared, but their quality is uneven.

In addition to the publication of Jung's works, efforts have been made to publish other Jungian authors. Zelensky, whose primary interest has been in book publishing, has undertaken the translation of several of Andrew Samuels' books, including the *Critical Dictionary of Jungian Analysis* (Samuels *et al.* 1986); but all these projects have taken years longer than anticipated. At present many other Jungian authors are being translated into Russian.

STATUS OF PSYCHOTHERAPY AND JUNGIAN ANALYSIS IN RUSSIA

No official individual psychotherapy or analysis existed in the Soviet Union from 1925 until the collapse of communism in 1989. Anyone practicing individual psychotherapy had to do it secretly, and no one had the opportunity to receive a proper therapeutic or training analysis. However, there were some individuals who were attracted to Eastern thought and set themselves up as therapists and analysts; they were able to influence many young people who congregated around them. The most significant of these groups was named the Association of Practical Psychology, which has chapters in Moscow, Leningrad, and other major cities.

Moscow

In 1991 Renos Papadopoulos made contact with the Association of Practical Psychology in Moscow, where approximately fifty members practiced individual psychotherapy, all under forty years of age. Generally speaking, they espoused a broadly psychoanalytic orientation. There were no separate schools of analysis as in the West. Western therapists of many different persuasions started to give seminars for the Association, making the first real contact with Russian therapists.

Papadopoulos organized a two-year basic curriculum in analytical psychology for this group. He assembled a team of Jungian analysts from England and the United States, and in the fall of 1991 these analysts began to give weekend workshops and/or lectures and listened to case presentations. The visiting analysts paid their own transportation, but while in Russia the Association took care of their expenses. This introductory program worked reasonably well, and each Russian participant received a certificate of completion at the end of two years.

Many of the participants wanted further training in analytical psychology, especially analysis, but the costs were prohibitive. In 1995 Angela Connolly, a psychiatrist from Scotland, who had married an Italian journalist and trained in CIPA, moved to Moscow with her husband on assignment for four years. Angela became the first Jungian analyst in Russia, and many Russians were able to have an analysis with her. In 1997 then-president of the IAAP, Verena Kast, asked Alice Merz of the Jung Institute in Zurich to organize another two-year program in Russia with analysts from Zurich. Eight analysts and twenty-two Russian colleagues are currently participating in this program, and it has proven to be meaningful for the analysts from Switzerland and the Russian therapists. Besides the seminars, there are two case supervision groups.

The first analytically oriented psychotherapist in the post-communist world was Sergei Agrachev, a fiery, red-haired, humorous, and brilliant psychologist. It was predominantly his energy which brought this first group of therapists together. Although drawn to psychoanalysis, he had a deep understanding of analytical psychology and paved the way for subsequent Jungian influence in the Association of Practical Psychology. In January 1998 Sergei died suddenly and prematurely at age forty-five from heart disease. It was a tragic loss for depth psychology in Moscow.

St Petersburg (Leningrad)

St Petersburg is the Russian city with the closest link to Europe. In the beginning of the eighteenth century Peter the Great made St Petersburg the capital of Russia and brought in Italian architects to accentuate its European flavor. Many of the pre-communist Russian adherents of psychoanalysis came from St Petersburg, and it is also the home of the Bechterev Institute, the most famous research and psychiatric treatment center in Russia; it is the institution where Pavlov did his experiments.

After the demise of the Soviet Union, an interest in psychoanalytic thinking emerged in St Petersburg. Mikhail Reshetnikov, a former military psychiatrist, became the leader of an institute where all forms of psychoanalysis, including analytical psychology, were taught. After several name changes this institute is now known as the East European Institute of Psychoanalysis. Over the years several individual Jungian analysts from London have taught there, receiving partial support from the IAAP. In 1998 a structured curriculum was set up by Jan Wiener and Catherine Crowther, two SAP London-trained analysts. They brought together analysts from the four London Jungian groups who are teaching analytical psychology on twelve weekends between 1998 and 2000. This venture has brought members of all four London groups together to serve a common aim. Thirty-four Russian students are enrolled in the course, and the majority are third- or fourth-year trainees and graduates of the Institute. Each weekend is a mixture of formal presentations, small group discussions, and case presentations. The training has had to remain rather on the theoretical side, as analysis and individual supervision are still not possible. At the end of the course the participants will receive a certificate of completion from the IAAP. Reshetnikov and the Institute are eager to be accepted on an international level, but so far that has not been possible.

SUMMARY

Russia is slowly emerging psychologically from the long period of communism which did not allow depth psychology to exist. Recently, the Russian Government decreed that psychoanalysis is now again officially recognized, and there is a growing interest in the field. Courses in analytical psychology are now available in Russia's two main cities, supported by the IAAP and taught by IAAP members. Visiting Jungian analysts find the Russians psychologically minded and natural symbolic thinkers. The Russians are conscious of having missed out on about seventy years of Western thought, which includes most of the developments in depth psychology. On the other hand, Russians have always been avid readers and are eager to assimilate the knowledge and experience of analytical thought. In many other ways they share a cultural heritage which should permit them to bridge the gap. Jungian analysts traveling to Russia have uniformly been deeply moved by the experience of relating to their Russian colleagues.

EASTERN EUROPE

The history of analytical psychology in Eastern Europe is intimately intertwined with World War II and the rise of communism. There was little interest in Jung's psychology prior to 1939, and after 1945 communism inhibited any latent curiosity that might have developed. As the Soviet Union gradually lost its hold over the people of the region, individuals interested in analytical psychology began to surface. The interest switched from a trickle to a flood by the time the Berlin Wall fell in 1989. People in all the Eastern European countries requested books, information on analytical psychology, grants to study in the West, and visits of analytical psychologists to their respective countries to present seminars and workshops. It was deeply moving to learn how enterprising individuals had smuggled in Jung's books, or found them on the Internet. No analysis had been available in any of the Eastern European countries, as long as travel to the West was practically impossible. A brief description follows of the circumstances arising in each of these countries as a result of the political, economic, and cultural turmoil.

HUNGARY

Hungary has had a long and almost continuous relationship to psychoanalysis. Several of the most significant early psychoanalysts came from Budapest, including Melanie Klein, Sandor Ferenczi, Michael Balint and others. The city of Budapest is geographically near Vienna, and as they were both part of the Austro-Hungarian Empire, they had a long history of exchange. World War II and the takeover by the communists brought many changes. Psychoanalysis was able to survive through most of the Nazi period and was tolerated during the communist years. Thus, there has been a continuity to psychoanalysis in Hungary which does not exist in the other Eastern European countries.

The first Hungarian interested in Jung was a protestant minister, Endre Gyökössy, whose wife was Swiss. Gyökössy had studied in Basle, Switzerland and heard Jung lecture many times. He read Jung avidly, and after the war small study groups met at his apartment on a regular basis; but to call the meetings "Jungian" would have resulted in difficulties with the authorities. Nevertheless, he was influential in intellectual circles and after the 1956 revolution had an easier time as a Jungian. He died in 1998.

Since the 1970s there has been a Jungian Association connected with Hungarian psychiatry and psychology. The leader of this group is Ferenc Sülé, a psychiatrist who works on a psychiatric ward for patients with religious problems. Sülé first became interested in Jung's psychology through Gyökössy. The Jungian Association has about a hundred members, who meet on a regular basis. They include psychiatrists, psychologists, ministers, and social workers. None of the members has had any analysis, including Sülé. The Association has a training program which includes five "training analysts." In 1992 Ferenc Sülé published a book entitled *Jungian Psychology Nowadays*, which gives information on different aspects of Jungian thought.

Two émigré Hungarian analysts, who trained at the Jung Institute in Zurich, Judith Luif from Zurich and Ferenc Sasdi from Berne, have independently made regular visits to Budapest over a period of years. Individuals in Hungary have been in analysis with them, but none of them have gone to Zurich to complete their analytic training. The two have discontinued the exhaustive practice of regular visits to Hungary. The connection between these analysts and Dr Sülé's group was not close.

In the past ten years over twenty of Jung's books have been translated into Hungarian. Also, the Pro Helvetia Foundation sponsored an exhibition on Jung, honoring him on the hundredth anniversary of his birth, which has traveled to all parts of Hungary as part of a cultural exchange with Switzerland. It was very well received and drew large crowds. There are a number of Hungarians who have had an unofficial training in analytical psychology. It still has not been possible to transcend the economic and cultural barriers which the legacy of communism has left to the country, but analytical psychology has definitely made itself known in Hungary.

LITHUANIA

When the Eastern European countries opened to the West, individuals in Lithuania were among the first to express an interest in analytical psychology. Tom Kapacinskas from Chicago, whose family came from Lithuania, made contact with a group of interested individuals. He made several trips to Vilnius, the capital, to deliver lectures and workshops. They named themselves the "Lithuanian Society of C.G. Jung's Analytical Psychology." In 1992, Grazina Gudaite, a psychology professor from Vilnius, was one of the first Eastern European participants invited to an IAAP congress. Two years later she spent her sabbatical year studying at the Chicago Jung Institute, where she had analysis and supervision, in addition to taking academic courses. She has continued her training through the Internet, and was one of the first individuals from the former Soviet bloc to have Jungian analysis and supervision.

In 1996 the Lithuanians asked Robert Strubel, a Zurich analyst, to arrange a course for interested psychotherapists in Vilnius. He organized a program for Zurich analysts to teach and supervise in Lithuania for a week and give a public lecture. In addition, longer summer seminars gave the participants an intense academic course in analytical psychology, with experiential work using art and other media complementing the theoretical work. At the end of 1998 the candidates took an examination, writing a paper on a subject in analytical psychology of their choice. According to the teachers, the papers were of a high quality, and each candidate received a certificate affirming that they had passed a theoretical examination. While this certificate did not entitle the candidate to practice as a Jungian analyst, completion of this certificate program was quite an achievement for these candidates. There continues to be a growing interest in analytical psychology in Lithuania, both among psychology professionals and the lay public.

POLAND

There has been an interest in analytical psychology shown by academicians and therapists in Warsaw. In the mid-1990s the Polish Jungian Club was formed for people seriously interested in further study. They have a publication, called *Either–Or: A Journal of Jungian Inspirations*. Many European analysts have given workshops and lectures in Warsaw and other cities over the years. Patricia de Hoogh-Rowntree from England had been visiting Poland regularly on her own for almost ten years, giving lectures and workshops. In 1997 Patricia took over the responsibility of organizing a study program for the Polish psychologists and psychiatrists and is receiving financial support from the IAAP to begin a more structured course for psychologists and psychiatrists who wish more intensive study of analytical psychology. Many other analysts have expressed an interest in helping her with the teaching, and a number of German analysts in Berlin have offered to help the Poles obtain analysis and supervision. With analysis and supervision there would be the possibility of some of these candidates being eligible for individual membership in the IAAP. The Polish Jungian Club is also in the process of changing its name to the C.G. Jung Institute, which is a reflection of the ongoing process of their changing identity.

CZECH REPUBLIC

The Czech Republic has developed a study group in analytical psychology, centered in the cities of Brno and Prague. Brno has the larger group at present, but both centers have an active program. Many Zurich analysts have been traveling regularly to the Czech Republic, giving seminars and workshops. In addition, individual psychotherapists from the Czech Republic have been going to Zurich for analysis and supervision, so that it will not be long before there will be accredited individual members of the IAAP in the Czech Republic. Also, the group includes translators, and ten of Jung's works now can be read in the Czech language.

BULGARIA

Soon after the fall of the Berlin Wall, information reached the IAAP that there was a small group of academicians and therapists who had formed a study group in Sofia, Bulgaria. When the first group of individuals from former Eastern bloc countries was invited to the International Congress in Chicago in 1992, Krassimira Baytchinska, an academic psychologist from Sofia, was among them. She had secretly been studying Jung and analytical psychology for many years, and finally was able to follow her interest openly.

There is not the same level of contact between Bulgaria and the West as with some of the other Eastern European countries, but an important liaison has been established between Bulgaria and San Francisco. Teodora Petrova, a young psychologist and dance therapist from the study group in Sofia, has become the second foreign student in the International Student Analytical Psychology Pilot Program of the San Francisco Jung Institute. She participates in the training program of the Institute, including analysis and supervision, and is benefiting greatly from her experience. When she finishes the two-year program in San Francisco she will return to Sofia, where her Jungian experience will stand her in good stead.

GEORGIA

Since the break-up of the Soviet Union, Georgia, a small country of six million people, has undergone a most painful civil war. Two-thirds of the population are Georgian and the rest are Armenians, Russians, and Azerbaijanis. There are over eighty different ethnic groups. In the capital, Tbilisi, the one and only psychotherapy center in the country was established. One of its founders, Marina Chatiashvili, has been teaching analytical psychology and has developed a small study group around her. Astri Hognestad, a Zurich-trained Norwegian analyst, met her in 1991 and has made several trips to Tbilisi teaching basic concepts of analytical psychology. Dr Chatiashvili attended the IAAP congress in Zurich in 1995, and others from her group have wished to obtain further Jungian training in the West.

YUGOSLAVIA

A small group of people interested in analytical psychology has formed in Belgrade, Serbia. Psychiatrists and psychologists, as well as interested lay members have formed a Jungian group. Several members of this group have attended IAAP International Congresses. One member of the IAAP, Renos Papadopoulos, received his doctorate in psychology in Belgrade, and he has been active in helping this group along. Furthermore, he has worked through the United Nations with victims and refugees from all sides of the conflicts in Bosnia and Kosovo. It has been extremely painful work, and no other Jungian analyst has engaged in this type of activity.

SUMMARY

The political and historical events of this past century have inhibited the growth of depth psychology, including analytical psychology, in the entire region. The only country in the region to have had continuity in depth psychology was Hungary, which somehow managed to keep psychoanalysis alive. As a result, those interested in analytical psychology in Hungary were able to carry on in their own limited fashion. Since the fall of the Soviet Union, all the countries which made up the former Eastern bloc have enthusiastically been drawn to depth psychology, including analytical psychology. In every country of the region there is some activity related to Jung's psychology. In many countries an academic course in analytical psychology over a two-year period is being offered. The big problem to date is that it is difficult for interested people in these countries to obtain a Jungian analysis. As strides are made to overcome obstacles, individuals from many, if not all of these countries will be able to become individual members of the IAAP. When that happens, a formal Jungian group may become possible. To accommodate individual practitioners from these countries, a new form of membership in the IAAP has been designated. A group from a country achieves associate membership as a "Developing Group," and thus becomes eligible to receive financial aid from the IAAP. Much of the IAAP's resources are going into furthering these developing groups, many of which are in Eastern Europe. In every one of these countries an interest in analytical psychology is growing.

17 Emerging groups in Asia

Jung was drawn to the religions, philosophies, and psychologies of the Far East, especially those of ancient China and Japan. In turn, Jung's writings have been well received in modern Japan, Korea, and now in China. However, there has been relatively little contact between Asian psychologists and Jungian analysis, compared to what has occurred in the West. This is beginning to change, as students from Japan and other Asian countries matriculate at the Jung Institute in Zurich, increasing the number of Asian Jungian analysts in the years to come. At the present time there are IAAP members only in Japan and Korea, and this chapter chronicles the developments in those countries, and more recently in China.

JAPAN

As part of Jung's interest in the Far East, he was acquainted with the writings of D.T. Suzuki, the man most responsible for introducing Japanese Zen Buddhism to the West. In 1939 Jung wrote an introduction to Suzuki's *Introduction to Zen Buddhism*, when it was published in German (Jung *CW* 11:538–557). Suzuki was also a speaker at the yearly Eranos Conference in Ascona, Switzerland. No professional Jungian outgrowth occurred from this contact.

The individual who introduced Jung to Japan was Hayao Kawai. In 1957 he received a Fulbright scholarship to study the Rorschach test in Los Angeles. There he met Bruno Klopfer, who was teaching the Rorschach and was also a Jungian analyst. Klopfer encouraged the student Kawai to enter into a Jungian analysis, and shortly thereafter he received a scholarship to matriculate at the Jung Institute in Zurich. Upon receiving his diploma from the Zurich Institute in 1965 he returned to Kyoto, Japan, where he began an academic career in psychology.

Over the years he has written books on analytical psychology, fairy tales and myths, and Sandplay; his achievements are too numerous to name. His book, an introduction to analytical psychology (in Japanese), continues to sell well after twenty years in print. He introduced Sandplay therapy to Japan and frequently invited Dora Kalff to give workshops. Sandplay is now a well-known form of therapy in Japan. Following in Hayao Kawai's footsteps, many Japanese students of analytical psychology have gone to the Zurich Institute for training.

Today there are fifteen members of the IAAP teaching and practicing in Japan. The analysts meet quarterly on an informal basis to discuss cases as well as the future of analytical psychology in Japan. Among them are eight medical doctors and seven analysts who teach at the university level. There has been a reluctance to form a professional group because of fears that issues of power and control would surface. However, Professor Kawai thinks that within the next few years there will be a Japanese professional society (personal interview, 7 October 1996).

In addition to the individual analysts there exists a Japanese Jung Club which has 1,600 members. The Club publishes a journal entitled *Psyche* which comes out four times per year. The president of the Club is Kazuhiko Higuchi, a theologian and Jungian analyst who studied for a year and half at the Zurich Institute. He and Kawai have worked together to help analytical psychology develop in Japan.

In the past few European or American analysts have visited Japan, but this is beginning to change. The Japanese analysts have wanted to remain more self-contained until they are ready to form a professional society.

Jungian psychology is well known in Japan and, according to Kazuhiko Higuchi (1996), it is the most dominant group in clinical psychology in Japan. On the other hand, among the medical doctors Freudian psychoanalysis is more established (personal interview with Hayao Kawai, 7 October 1996). There is a tension between medical doctors and clinical psychologists, of the kind which exists in many countries. It has taken the Japanese many years to accept the idea of individual analysis. Kawai reports that in the early days he used to accept food or other goods in exchange for analytical work. For this reason most analysts needed an academic or institutional position to support themselves. Today the culture is changing, and it is possible to have a private practice in Jungian analysis.

KOREA

Perhaps it will come as a surprise to many that there has been an active Jungian group in South Korea since the mid-1960s. In 1962 a young psychiatrist, Bhou-Yong Rhi, traveled to Zurich for analysis with Marie-Louise von Franz and began training at the Jung Institute. Upon receiving his diploma in 1966 he returned to Seoul, Korea, where he became the chief of psychiatry at Seoul National University, the most prestigious hospital in Korea. He retired in 1997 after a distinguished career, writing several books, organizing a Korean Association for Analytical Psychology, receiving many international awards, and after sojourns as a visiting professor at numerous prestigious American and European universities.

A second Korean psychiatrist, Dr Zuk-Nae Lee, also graduated from the Zurich Jung Institute in the late 1960s. He remained in Zurich to undergo a second training analysis in *Daseinanalyse*, the existential analytic school co-founded by Medard Boss and Ludwig Binswanger. Then Zuk-Nae Lee returned to Korea where he became a professor of psychiatry at the Kyungpook University School of Medicine. Two other psychiatrists, Oh Su Han and Chul Lee, spent three years at the Jung Institute in Zurich and passed the first examination there, at which point family and financial pressures necessitated their return to Korea. Professor Oh Su Han became an individual IAAP member in 1994, but Professor Chul Lee has postponed completion of requirements for individual membership because of busy academic and teaching duties.

The Korean Society for Analytical Psychology comprises about fifty members. Many are professional psychiatrists and psychologists, and others are scholars in related fields. They meet on a regular basis and, in addition, once a year have a national meeting to present formal papers. There is also a journal which is published twice yearly with English abstracts. Through the efforts of the Korean Society many of Jung's books have been translated into Korean. It is still difficult to maintain a private practice of analysis in Korea, and so the Jungian analysts either have an academic or institutional post.

Then-president of the IAAP, Thomas Kirsch, was invited by the Korean Society for Analytical Psychology to visit their group in 1994, which resulted in a strong connection between Jean and Thomas Kirsch and their Korean hosts. When the International Student Analytical Psychology Pilot Program was inaugurated in 1996 by the San Francisco Jung Institute, a Korean psychiatrist, Dong-Hyuck Suh, was selected as the first foreign scholar. The experience was very positive on both sides, and it appears that in the future there will be more frequent contact between San Francisco Jungians and Korean Jungians. Up to now the Korean Jungians have been relatively isolated in a manner similar to the Japanese. In both countries this pattern appears to be changing.

Summary

Analytical psychology has been known in Korea for over thirty years. The founder, Professor Bhou Yong-Rhi, has held an important academic post within Korean psychiatry, and many of his students have become involved in analytical psychology. An active professional Korean Society for Analytical Psychology presents lectures and publishes a journal. As most of the professional members are psychiatrists, they have undergone the same influences which the field of psychiatry has undergone in many Western countries; i.e., the enormous growth of the biological side of psychiatry over and against the psychodynamic one. Psychiatric training in Korea has become predominantly biologically oriented. Therefore, there has been a lessening of interest in analytical psychology among the young psychiatric residents. In spite of recent developments, analytical psychology has a firm foundation in Korea.

CHINA

Of all the Asian countries, the psychology, philosophy, and religion in China were of greatest interest to Jung. Through his friendship with the noted Sinologist Richard Wilhelm in the 1920s, Jung became fascinated by Chinese alchemy and Taoism. In 1929 he published a psychological commentary on *The Secret of the Golden Flower*, an ancient Chinese alchemical text. This was Jung's introduction to alchemy, a topic of major interest for the rest of his life.

China, even before communism, had only a minimal contact with depth psychology, and no contact at all with analytical psychology. By the 1990s, China began to relax its restriction on the exchange of information.

An event occurred which led Murray Stein, then-honorary secretary of the IAAP, to suggest that a visit to China would be useful. Professor Heyong Shen, a psychology professor from Guangzhou, was in the United States on a Fulbright scholarship, and he was most interested in analytical psychology. When visiting Stein, Shen suggested that representatives from the IAAP visit China to have an exchange on Jung's psychology. The organization of such a venture was not easy, but with the aid of Yehua Zhu-Levine, a Chinese woman living in Los Angeles, arrangements were made to visit major hospitals, Guangzhou University and Bejing University. Then-president Thomas Kirsch and Murray Stein visited Beijing and Guangzhou in August 1994 and gave lectures on basic analytical psychology, as well as on the relationship between Taoism and analytical psychology. These talks were well received, but – more importantly – it was clear that there was a strong interest in Jung's psychology among the hospital staffs, the psychologists, and the academicians.

Professor Shen returned to the United States on another Fulbright scholarship, and at that time inquired into the possibility of obtaining further Jungian training in the United States. The International Student Program of the San Francisco Institute appealed to him, and negotiations are still ongoing.

When Professor Shen returned to China after his second Fulbright, he began to organize a joint IAAP analytical psychology conference, titled First International Conference of Jungian Psychology and Chinese Culture, which was held at Guangzhou University in December 1998. The following Jungian analysts represented the IAAP: John Beebe, David Rosen, Stan Marlan, and Ruth Ledergerber. Twenty Chinese scholars joined the Jungian analysts for five days of fruitful exchange. The many connections between Taoism and analytical psychology were explored. It is hoped that this conference represents the first of many conferences to be held in the future.

Another result of the initial visit of Stein and Kirsch in China was the translation of several Jungian books. Ms Li Yihong, a Chinese scholar and friend of Yehua Zhu-Levine, had a deep interest in the work of Jung and Neumann. With financial help from the IAAP and the van Waveren Foundation, she translated a group of books entitled *Mandala Series* into Chinese. As the translation rights for Jung's books were prohibitively expensive, other Jungian authors were chosen. Ms Li Yihong had many other Jungian translations planned when she died from cancer in 1998. There are other book publishing projects in the planning stages, but nothing else is confirmed.

The contact between analytical psychology and China is important even though there are no IAAP analysts there at this time. Jung was deeply influenced by ancient Chinese wisdom. There has been a long-standing affinity between analytical psychology and Taoist philosophy.

18 The International Association for Analytical Psychology

Jung had a decidedly ambivalent relationship towards organizations. At the beginning of his professional career he displayed an extraverted role in the politics of psychoanalysis. His leadership qualities were recognized by many of the early members, and Freud anointed him as the "crown prince" in 1908. He was elected the first president of the newly founded International Psychoanalytic Association (IPA) in 1909, a position he held for four years until the breakdown of his relationship with Freud. Freud had Jung removed from the presidency, even though Jung won 60 percent of the delegates' votes at the psychoanalytic congress in Munich in September 1913. The only other time he became active in professional organizations was during the 1930s, when he reluctantly took on the presidency of the International Medical Society for Psychotherapy. Otherwise, on account of his introverted nature, he avoided organizational matters as much as possible.

Analytical psychology as a discipline developed out of Jung's own inner experience. The only Jungian organizations which existed prior to the formation of the Institute in Zurich were the Analytical Psychology Clubs in some of the major cities of Europe and the United States. Even there Jung kept his distance and was never closely involved with the administration of any of the Clubs, including the one in Zurich, but he did lend support by giving lectures and seminars. The first attempt at some kind of internationalization of analytical psychology occurred just prior to World War II, when representatives of all the existent Clubs had arranged a meeting in Paris in the spring of 1940 to discuss a confederation of the Clubs. The advent of the war curtailed their efforts.

After World War II the Jung Institute in Zurich was founded, and small professional societies formed in London, New York, San Francisco, Los Angeles, and Israel. Therapists began to claim that they had been trained by Jung; there was no way of knowing whether a person had a one-hour discussion with Jung, or indeed had a deep analysis with him. There was no official Jungian body to determine whether an individual was a generally accepted Jungian or someone misrepresenting a connection to Jung.

In 1955 Jung celebrated his eightieth birthday, and some of his Zurich followers urged him to consider the formation of an international professional organization (C.A. Meier, personal communication, 1992). Thus, the International Association for Analytical Psychology (IAAP) was founded in Switzerland in 1955 and was structured according to Swiss law.

At its inception the aims of the IAAP were to (1) promote analytical psychology, (2) accredit professional groups, and individual members where no group existed, and (3) hold congresses on a regular basis. The organizational structure called for a president, two vice-presidents, a treasurer, and an honorary secretary to function together with representatives from elected societies as an executive committee. Each member group is entitled to one delegate for every ten members, and societies with less than ten members send a single delegate to the Delegates Meeting. Delegates meet at the international congress to vote on proposals submitted by the executive committee. The charter groups of the IAAP included Switzerland, England (SAP), New York, San Francisco, Los Angeles, Israel, and the Association of Graduate Analytical Psychologists of the C.G. Jung Institute Zurich, known as AGAP.

In order to accredit analysts, minimum standards of training are stipulated in the constitution. The major criteria included 250 hours of personal analysis with an IAAP-accredited Jungian analyst, fifty hours of personal supervisory work on analytic cases, and at a minimum an academic degree at master's level or its equivalent. These minimum standards were to be used as a guideline for new and developing societies. In areas where no professional group existed, individuals could submit a written application, outlining their Jungian training and analysis, and the application would either be accepted or rejected by the executive committee and the delegates. Over the years the requirements for both group and individual membership have changed and become more stringent.

The circumstances of the Association of Graduate Analytical Psychologists of the C.G. Jung Institute Zurich (AGAP) must be explained because it was, and still is, an anomaly. The Zurich Institute, having existed prior to the IAAP, has no geographical boundaries. All other groups cover a defined geographical area, whether it be a city, state, or country. The Jung Institute in Zurich is an international center, and its graduates become AGAP members and can practice anywhere in the world. Zurich graduates have played a dual role after leaving the Institute. Many times they have become founders of a new professional group in their new area of residence. In other instances graduates moved to places where a professional society existed already but they did not join it. Often such individuals represent a contrasting point of view to the existing society, which can produce a conflict and question who truly represents analytical psychology. AGAP graduates often sense that they have the "deeper" knowledge of analytical psychology, having trained in Zurich. Much rivalry and envy ensues in these situations, which have been documented (Kirsch 1995).

The first international congress was held in August 1958. One hundred and twenty members attended, and only analysts were allowed in the lecture hall at the ETH. If and when friends and spouses of speakers attempted to enter the hall, the rules were strictly enforced. Jung was present at the opening night reception as well as the banquet. One day the entire congress took a boat trip on the Lake of Zurich and passed by Jung's house, where he waved to the participants. Many of the first-generation analysts gave lectures at this congress, and the tenor of the papers followed Jung's thought closely. The papers were published as *Current Trends in Analytical Psychology*, edited by Gerhard Adler. A report on the congress appeared in *Time Magazine* (25 August 1958) and showed a picture of Jung with Heinz Westmann of New York; the text underneath the picture stated, "Naturally, analysts will have to be analyzed more and more." The *Time Magazine* article also discussed the political issues of that first congress, stating that there were two factions: "1) an orthodox group in favor of strict adherence to Jung's doctrines . . . , and 2) a progressive element in favor of a widened approach to man's problems, including the importance of childhood experiences . . . " The article continued: "Jung refused to commit himself publicly . . . , he favored the more progressive wing, feared that his movement would die if it became too introverted and parochial." So, the tension between the archetypal and developmental schools was already in the air at this first congress and, interestingly enough, *Time Magazine* reported Jung favoring the developmental school.

The first president of the IAAP was Robert Moody, a psychiatrist and member of SAP in London. He died during his presidency, and Franz Riklin, the vice-president from Zurich, took over and assumed the IAAP presidency.

The second international congress also took place in Zurich in August of 1962, four years after the first one. Jung had died in the interim, and the topic of the congress was "The Archetype." At this congress the tension between the London and Zurich groups, already present at the first congress, surfaced. Murray Jackson, at the time a newly trained London analyst, presented a paper entitled "The Nature of Symbols," and Esther Harding was the discussant. Harding, in her comments, chastised Jackson severely for his lack of understanding of Jung's meaning of the term "symbol," and further stated that he completely misunderstood the concept of "archetype." At the conclusion of her talk, students from the Zurich Institute clapped wildly and stamped their feet in approval. This was the beginning of the split between the developmental school of London, headed by Michael Fordham, and the Zurich school, which most other members of the IAAP followed. Fordham and the London analysts were clearly in the minority. As editor of the *Journal of Analytical Psychology*, Fordham promoted the London point of view with a steady stream of articles demonstrating their way of working. For the following decade the atmosphere made it unlikely that any non-developmental articles would be published.

In the elections at the Delegates Meeting, Franz Riklin was opposed by Gerhard Adler but was reelected president of the IAAP. A decision was made to hold international congresses every three years from then on, a pattern which is still in effect. Italy and the Südwestdeutsche Gesellschaft became group members of the IAAP at the second congress.

In 1965 the third congress was again held in Switzerland, but this time in Montreux on the Lake of Geneva. Franz Riklin ran for reelection as president and was opposed by Gerhard Adler and Jo Wheelwright in the only contested election for the presidency in IAAP history. On the first two ballots, the vote was fairly evenly split between Riklin and Adler because the delegates did not want to vote for Wheelwright, due to the fear that an American president would want to hold the next congress in the United States. In the mid-1960s travel costs from Europe to America were prohibitive, and few Europeans had traveled to the United States. Finally, Wheelwright was able to reassure the delegates that he would keep the congresses in Europe, and on the third ballot he was elected president of the IAAP. During his tenure Wheelwright introduced the American system, which allows a president to serve only two three-year terms. From 1965 until 1995 a pattern was followed where the first vice-president moved up to become president, and the second vice-president became first vice-president. With this ladder system elections became predictable and only the position of the new second vice-president was contested.

The fourth congress in 1968 again took place in Zurich, although by that time there was strong protest from the Swiss group against having to take on the responsibility of organizing yet another international meeting. Wheelwright was reelected to a second term as president. The IAAP membership had begun to grow, and congresses became less intimate affairs. For the first time spouses were permitted to attend, but against the will of a number of senior female analysts. Attendance had increased to between two hundred and three hundred. In 1968 Germany as a national group was accepted as a member of the IAAP, and the Südwestdeutsche Gesellschaft became a satellite institute within the German group.

In 1971 the first international congress was held outside of Switzerland at the Royal College of Physicians in London and was hosted by the SAP. It was a successful event and shifted the absolute center of gravity away from Zurich. Gerhard Adler assumed the presidency, and Adolf Guggenbühl-Craig became first vice-president. In the election for the second vice-president post, Hannes Dieckmann won by a single vote over Thomas Kirsch.

The 1974 congress again took place in London, this time at the School of Pharmacy, during a worldwide recession, which affected attendance. In retrospect it was also evident that it was too much of a burden on the same group to organize two congresses in a row, and the Swiss were duly recognized for having done it four times. In the interim times had changed and the IAAP had grown to a membership of almost one thousand.

The first six international congresses illustrated the dominant national trends within the IAAP. The Swiss and British contingents were the major national groups, both theoretically and politically. They continually vied for control of the organization, with the Swiss generally winning out. There was no national group from North America, only professional associations from New York, Los Angeles, and San Francisco, with diluted power within the IAAP. It was definitely a Eurocentric organization which was apprehensive of too much American influence. The question was: what would happen to Jungian psychology if it lost its European roots? Jo Wheelwright was sensitive to this issue when he assumed the presidency. Another issue was the languages used in the congresses. English and German translations were assured, but French and Italian were rotated as the third language in the simultaneous translations. Both the Italians and French experienced themselves as less important in the hierarchy of the IAAP.

In 1977 the Swiss–British domination of the IAAP was beginning to shift. The two Italian Jungian groups had offered to host the congress in Rome. Symbolically, this was an important venue, because the Italian Jungians had split into two groups a decade earlier, but relations between the two groups had improved sufficiently to enable them to sponsor the congress jointly. Planning the congress together further helped to heal the split. It was the first time that a Jungian congress was held in a Latin country, and the participants experienced the extraverted warmth of the hosts and their country. The congresses in Switzerland and England had been excellent, but a more formal atmosphere had prevailed. As had been the custom, most of the speakers at the Rome congress were well-known, first-generation analysts, who were getting on in years. No one realized at the time that this would be the last time a great number of them would lecture at an international congress.

On the political side, professional groups from Brazil, Australia and New Zealand (ANZSJA), Belgium, New England (USA), AJA (UK) were admitted into the IAAP. Adolf Guggenbühl-Craig assumed the presidency, James Hillman became the honorary secretary, Hannes Dieckmann moved up to first vice-president, and Thomas Kirsch was elected as the new second vice-president. Guggenbühl-Craig's choice of Hillman as his honorary secretary set a new course by choosing someone of equal stature as the honorary secretary, rather than a younger analyst to be a junior member of the team. By doing so, the president had a true colleague to discuss complicated issues, and many presidents have followed the example. The role of the honorary secretary is one that has not been clearly defined.

In 1980 the first international congress to be held outside of Europe took place in San Francisco, and only speakers who had never lectured at a congress before were selected. Many new voices were heard, among them John Beebe, Geneviève Guy-Gillet, Russ Lockhart, Sonja Marjasch, Andrew Samuels, and others. Another innovation was that all the congress participants were invited, on a random basis, to a small dinner at the homes of local analysts or candidates. The dinners throughout the Bay area were logistically difficult to arrange, but proved to be a huge social success. They brought together people who might otherwise not have had a chance to meet. At every subsequent congress a comparable experience has been included in the program.

In a further attempt to encourage communication among the membership, the IAAP allocated funds for the publication of an annual *Newsletter* in English. From modest beginnings it has become an important means of communication among the members. News from the different societies, new books published in analytical psychology, as well as interviews and articles are a part of the *Newsletter*. Jef Dehing of Belgium was the first editor for twelve years, with Renos Papadopoulos taking over the editorial responsibility in 1992. Starting in the year 2000 Jan Marlan of Pittsburgh will become the new editor. At the 1980 congress it was decided that both Italian and French would be included as official languages of the congress in the future. James Hillman resigned as honorary secretary, and Niel Micklem replaced him.

All indications were that the 1983 congress would be held in Berlin, but at the last moment the Israeli Society requested that the congress be held in Jerusalem. The German group politely stepped aside, and the venue became Jerusalem. Because of the hot summer weather, the date of the congress was changed to March. The timing of the congress was such that it occurred shortly after the first Israeli occupation of southern Lebanon. Tension in the region was high, and attendance at the congress was smaller than on previous occasions, but it was a more intimate one. The setting of Jerusalem brought up many political and religious issues, and many informal discussions took place between Germans, Israelis, Jews, and the other participants. For the first time, Jung's connection to the Nazis during the 1930s was openly and informally discussed. Unfortunately, then-president Adolf Guggenbühl-Craig had to undergo emergency coronary by-pass surgery and could not attend the congress. Hannes Dieckmann was elected president, Thomas Kirsch, first vice-president, and Bianca Garufi from Italy became the second vice-president.

In 1986 an international congress was finally held in West Berlin, hosted by the large German Society. Symbolically, it was very important to have an international Jungian congress on German soil. The Freudians had faced the same issue a few years before. In 1977 the German Psychoanalytical Association offered to host the next congress in Berlin, but the IPA refused the invitation because, for too many of the émigré psychoanalysts, Berlin still symbolized associations with the Nazi regime. Although the German Psychoanalytical Association had been readmitted after the war, the issue between the German psychoanalysts and the rest of the IPA had to be confronted. Only after much discussion and deliberation did the IPA hold their congress in Hamburg in 1983, but not in Berlin.

In 1986 it was the Jungians' turn to face their relationship to Germany. At this congress there was no program which specifically dealt with the German–Nazi–Jungian connection, but the mere fact of having the congress in West Berlin made people confront the issues. In the Delegates Meeting the by-laws were changed to include the position of an additional second-vice-president position in order to stimulate more competition for office. Verena Kast was elected to the new position, and all the other officers were reelected.

The following congress was held in Paris at the UNESCO building in August 1989. Eight hundred participants attended, and many excellent papers and workshops were presented. Two afternoon panel discussions, titled "Jung and Anti-Semitism," were well attended and evoked great interest among the participants. It was a breakthrough to have Jungians at their own congress discussing Jung's shadow in relationship to Jews and to Nazi Germany as part of the official program.

The election results were as follows: Thomas Kirsch was elected president, Verena Kast became first vice-president, and Luigi Zoja from Italy and Eli Weisstub from Israel were elected second vice-presidents. Bianca Garufi had resigned her position in between congresses, because she did not wish to ever become president.

Toward the end of the congress international news made headlines as East Germans were allowed to cross the border into Hungary without visas. No one knew that this would be the beginning of the fall of the Iron Curtain and would liberate the Eastern bloc countries from Soviet domination. During the following three years the IAAP received numerous requests for information about analytical psychology and Jung from former Eastern bloc countries. The executive committee of the IAAP encouraged the president to visit the Soviet Union and Hungary and to meet with representatives in other Eastern European countries. During that term in office much of the president's time was taken up establishing contacts in these countries. The first order of business was to arrange translation and publication of Jung's *Collected Works* in Russian, the common language which most people in the Eastern bloc had learned under Soviet rule. With the help of the van Waveren Foundation, the IAAP signed a contract to finance the publication of the *Collected Works* in Russian. However, the political instability of the early post-communist governments undermined the completion of this ambitious task, and only volume 15 was published in Russian. Other volumes were translated but never officially published. Other unofficial translations have surfaced in the meantime, but none sponsored by the IAAP.

In 1992 the international congress took place in Chicago. Five Eastern Europeans, including two psychologists from Moscow, one from Lithuania, one from Bulgaria, and a fifth from Hungary, were invited guests of the IAAP. They received a warm welcome from the congress participants, and connections to former Soviet bloc and Asian countries have continued to grow in succeeding years.

In 1995 the congress returned to Zurich for the first time since 1968. Numerous people from Eastern Europe were invited, and there was even a participant from mainland China. The IAAP had definitely become a worldwide organization. In the IAAP elections, Verena Kast was elected president, Luigi Zoja became first vice-president, and

Murray Stein and Eli Weisstub were elected second vice-presidents. Bob Hinshaw became the honorary secretary.

During the following three years the executive committee worked on changing the structure of the IAAP and proposed the following:

1   Representatives from the large societies had continually been members of the executive committee and seemed to control the activities of the IAAP. Limiting the number of consecutive terms a society could serve on the executive committee was proposed.
2   The two-term presidency was deemed too long and was to be shortened to one.
3   The first vice-president was now to become the president elect.

These by-law changes were accepted at the recent congress in Florence in 1998. The effect was that smaller societies were elected to send a representative to the executive committee, including ANZSJA and South Africa. To set a new trend, Verena Kast retired after one term, and Luigi Zoja became the next president of the IAAP. South Africa and Venezuela were admitted as new group members.

In addition to the political changes admission requirements for new groups and for individuals have been modified. The major changes in training requirements for groups are the following: the minimum number of people to form a new group is now six; formerly, there was no prescribed number, but the usual was four or five. Before, if a group was accepted it could immediately begin to train. In many instances groups had already begun training prior to acceptance by the IAAP. Now acceptance as a group is separate from becoming a training group. In order to become a training institute a group must have ten members, and six of them must have been practicing for five years or more. Furthermore, the requirement for supervisory hours has been increased to a minimum of one hundred. A recent in-house survey of training institutes has demonstrated that all training programs require far above the minimum for both analysis and supervision. This was expected, because the pattern is to increase numbers of hours of analysis and supervision whenever a candidate does not perform as expected, and this happens in all training programs.

The requirements for individual membership have also changed considerably. It is no longer sufficient for an applicant simply to submit an application and have it evaluated by the executive committee. When the IAAP was small, this method worked, as most applicants were known to some members of the executive committee; now it is no longer adequate. Currently the individual has to write up a case report and present it to two analysts designated by the executive committee. This is followed by an oral examination of the individual's knowledge of basic analytical psychology.

At the time of the foundation of the IAAP, membership was around one hundred, and by 1999 it had risen to over 2,300. There are now thirty-four separate training institutes around the world, and new ones are in the process of being formed. Professional associations, except those in the United States, are mostly national in character, and their members reside anywhere in the country. There may be satellite institutes, like in France or Germany, but they are a part of the national group. ANZSJA is a special case and includes both Australia and New Zealand. The United States societies are all in localized geographical areas, except for the IRS which has a quasi-national agenda. It is a major reason for the conflict between the IRS and some of the other local American training programs. The United States has not been able to form a national group, because no society has been willing to relinquish its autonomy to a national body. The confederation known as CASJA is not a legal entity and cannot make binding decisions.

The work of the IAAP has increased markedly since its founding. Conflict between groups and individuals, evaluation of new groups and individuals, reaching out to new areas of development such as Russia and Asia, organizing congresses, publishing congress proceedings and an annual *Newsletter*, as well as a membership list, and other assorted duties, make for a large workload for the leaders of the IAAP. Since 1983 the officers have been paid a small honorarium in addition to travel expenses, which gives some recognition for the work involved, but is truly an honorarium and not a salary. Politically, the Association has broadened from its Northern European roots to encompass the rest of Europe, the Americas, and parts of Asia and Africa. The areas of greatest growth at the present time are in Latin America, where there appears to be a great interest in analytical psychology. Spanish will become the fifth official language of the IAAP.

Different countries and nationalities have been dominant in the history of the IAAP. At first the main foci of power were the Swiss and the British, and the first six congresses took place either in Switzerland or England. The Americans and Germans became more influential beginning in the 1970s, and one sensed a shift away from the Swiss–British axis. The Italians made their presence known starting with the Rome Congress in 1977, and Elie Humbert in France was able to bring recognition to the French group. Thus, a Western European–American axis dominated the IAAP for about twenty years. By the mid-1990s many new societies had begun to form outside of Europe and the United States. These new groups from South America, Australia, and South Africa had to be included in the changing power structure of the IAAP. This made necessary the many constitutional changes which were approved in 1998.

The IAAP, with its many functions, has played an increasingly prominent role in the growth of analytical psychology. Through IAAP membership all professional Jungians are accredited and have their identities in the world as Jungian analysts.

19 The history of Sandplay

Any history of analytical psychology would not be complete without a discussion of the technique of Sandplay. Sandplay is a specialized form of non-verbal therapy which utilizes a tray of very specific dimensions (28.5 × 19.5 inches with a depth of 3 inches, standing at a height of 30 inches), the inside of which is painted blue to give the impression of either water or sky. Usually there are two trays provided, one for wet and the other for dry sand. The tray, as described by its founder, Dora Maria Kalff, constitutes a "free and protected space" where no judgment is made on the quality of the picture. The client, either child or adult, chooses figures from open shelves which he/she then places in the sand to make a picture. The method is a specialized form of active imagination and was encouraged by Jung, who himself went through a period of playing in the sand along the shores of the Lake of Zurich during his "confrontation with the unconscious" (1913). The role of the analyst is to be a participant observer in the process, but interpretation is not central to the method; rather, the direct experience of the symbols is the most important aspect of the therapy. For some it is a way of evoking archetypal material, which frees the patient to do verbal analytic work. For other patients who may be trapped in verbal content, it is an auxiliary method to access inner imagery more directly. One question has been whether the analyst should also be the Sandplay therapist. Whatever mix of therapies or therapists one wishes to choose, the experience in the sand has been shown to have healing effects upon the psyche. Sandplay has also been used in school systems, family therapy, and experimental situations other than therapeutic ones. However, that takes us beyond the scope of this book. The method has grown immensely in popularity both within the Jungian community and outside. In 1985 Dora Kalff founded the International Society for Sandplay Therapists (ISST) to provide training and certification in Sandplay, and its members include many Jungian analysts, but also many others who are not trained analysts. Archives of the case histories can be found in Zollikon, Switzerland, and at the library of the C.G. Jung Institute of San Francisco.

The history of Sandplay can be found in the book, *Sandplay, Past, Present, and Future*, by R. Mitchell and Harriet Friedman. Margaret Lowenfeld in London was the creator of a technique in a sand tray called "World Technique." She had conceived the idea from H.G. Wells' book *Floor Games*, published in 1912, where a boy plays with his father in the sand. Margaret Lowenfeld took this idea and applied the technique in her work with children, where it seemed to help all kinds of children in psychological distress. During the 1930s her work did not receive the recognition that it should have, because the conflict between Melanie Klein and Anna Freud overshadowed everything else taking place in the London therapy milieu. However, her work was known, and she had contact with Michael Fordham, the prominent Jungian child analyst.

At this point the story moves to Switzerland where Dora Kalff, a Swiss married to a Dutchman, became acquainted with the "World Technique." During the war she and her son, Peter, were introduced to Gret Baumann-Jung, the daughter of C.G. Jung, who recognized Dora Kalff's natural abilities with children. Gret Jung-Baumann brought Dora Kalff and Jung together, and he encouraged her work with children. She began her studies at the Jung Institute in Zurich in 1949 where she was a student for six years. In 1954 she met Margaret Lowenfeld, who was lecturing at the Jung Institute, and decided to study with her in London. This was encouraged by Emma Jung and arranged by Michael Fordham. From this experience Dora Kalff adapted the "World Technique" of Lowenfeld to a Jungian-oriented therapy where the symbols of the unconscious became the focus of the work. Dora Kalff did not have an academic degree so she was not allowed to graduate from the Jung Institute in Zurich. This forced her to do her work outside the Institute, and most of her teaching and lecturing were done outside official Jungian organizations. In due time she was elected to be a member of the Swiss Society, and also became a member of the International Association for Analytical Psychology.

Dora Kalff's lack of formal certification never dampened her enthusiasm, nor did it represent an obstacle. She embodied the Great Mother, and managed to go wherever she wanted. Her work was quickly taken up in Japan, in India, and in the United States. Through her interest in Buddhism she befriended the Dalai Lama, and her work always bridged the East–West divide. Professor Kawai, a noted Jungian analyst in

Japan, became a strong proponent of her work which has gained popularity among Japanese therapists.

Dora Kalff had a close personal relationship with Hilde Kirsch who
encouraged her to come to Los Angeles and give seminars on her
Sandplay work. In the decade of the 1960s she would spend several
weeks a year in Los Angeles as the guest of Hilde Kirsch, teaching, giving
consultations to candidates, and seeing individuals for short-term
Sandplay therapy. Harriet Friedman in Los Angeles benefited from
Dora Kalff's frequent visits and has become a prominent exponent of
Sandplay technique. While in California, Dora Kalff made frequent
visits to San Francisco where a strong interest in Sandplay work was also
developing. Most senior women analysts in San Francisco, including
Renee Brand, Kay Bradway, Bertha Mason, and Elizabeth Osterman,
found the Sandplay work useful in their analytical practices. In New
York Estelle Weinrib studied with Dora Kalff, and by the end of the
1960s a network of therapists and analysts using Sandplay had developed
throughout the American Jungian community. Dora Kalff continued
her annual visits to the United States to give seminars and workshops.
At the point when lay people who were not therapists or Jungian analysts became interested in her work, it became necessary to establish
standards, and the ISST was formed to provide a method of certification.

The technique of Sandplay had been developed to work with children,
and the model used Jung's classical archetypal theory. The "work in
the sand," as it is often referred to, ran counter to Fordham's developmental model for child analysis. Although Fordham was instrumental
in bringing Dora Kalff to London to study with Margaret Lowenfeld
in the 1950s, he was not an enthusiastic supporter of Sandplay therapy
with children. He felt that it encouraged an impersonal aspect to child
therapy, and he maintained that the child needed a more interactive
approach with the therapist. Thus, he personally gave up using Sandplay
with children, and the same conflict which happened in adult analysis
happened in work with children. There is the familiar ideological
conflict between the archetypal and the developmental approaches to
therapy.

Dora Kalff died in 1990. By that time her work was well established
in many parts of the world. Currently Sandplay is used equally with
children and adults. Most of the senior people practicing Sandplay are
Jungian analysts, but most of the members of the ISST are not. The
technique has gained great popularity and continues to attract many
people to its use.

20 Observations and conclusions

The aim of each chapter is to relate how analytical psychology developed in different areas, not interrupting the story to make comparisons. Now I shall generalize and draw conclusions based on my historical research and discuss possible consequences on the future of analytical psychology and Jungians.

ORIGINS OF ANALYTICAL PSYCHOLOGY

Wherever and whenever analytical psychology has been inaugurated and developed into a Jungian society or institute, certain psychological characteristics of the founders can be noted.

Psychological type

The founders of each group tended to be introverted. The only extraverts, by their own accounts, were Peter Baynes in London, and Jo Wheelwright in San Francisco, who also happened to be medical doctors. These factors may explain why in those two locales there was some relationship to Freudian psychoanalysis, whereas in other places it was minimal to non-existent. Jung's psychology offered the potential of new meaning for the introvert who was otherwise surrounded by extraverted values. At that time not many other paths were open to introverts; they often were made to feel "odd" for their preferred introversion. Today, growing knowledge about Asian philosophies and religions, with their emphasis on meditative practices, has changed societal values.

Relationship to spiritual values

In the early part of the twentieth century, a belief in science, materialism, and the order of rationalism held sway. Two world wars and the advent of the Atomic Age have forced us to realize that human nature is not solely rational. Reliance on the rationality of mankind alone will not change our collective behavior and attitudes. Failure to recognize the non-rational leads to spiritual hunger, and Jung's ideas spoke directly to this lack. Furthermore, most of the founders were individuals who could not accept the collective standards of their day. They were seekers, looking for something beyond these norms. Many people who had had a religious experience read and studied Jung in their search for a meaningful spiritual attitude.

Relationship to Freud and classical psychoanalysis

Many founders of analytical psychology had looked to Freud and his psychoanalysis before coming to Jung. Not satisfied there, with Jung they found what had been lacking and/or what they had been seeking. In the early days of depth psychology feelings between Freudians and Jungians were extremely explosive. Like taking sides in a divorce, with rare exceptions, one could not be for both. For a Jungian, a prior Freudian psychoanalytic experience was valued, yet it was usually seen as personalistic, reductive, and limited. Almost all founders would say that until they had read and been analyzed by a Jungian, their lives had not been changed essentially. The exceptions to this strong anti-Freudian sentiment were found in San Francisco and London, where the early Jungians and Freudians were on collegial terms. Even there, where good personal relations existed, on the institutional level the Jungians continued to be ignored or criticized by the Freudian establishment and its followers.

Why were relations between Freudians and Jungians more cordial in San Francisco and London? I would suggest three possible reasons for the better connections there: psychological types; the nature of the founders' transferences to Jung; and the fact that the founders were medical doctors. In both London and San Francisco, the extraverted Baynes and Wheelwright could relate to Freudians and make them feel comfortable with Jungians, if not with Jung's theory. Most of the founders had an extremely strong positive transference to Jung, seeing him as a charismatic figure. Furthermore, many of the non-Swiss analysts in analysis with Jung had their analyses interrupted by World War II. By the end of the war in 1945, Jung had essentially retired from practice due to ill health. Thus, the majority of first generation analysts had abrupt endings to their analyses, which tended to augment the already present idealization of Jung. Michael Fordham, who had been rejected for analysis by Jung, had a strongly ambivalent relationship towards Jung, an ambivalence that was imbedded in the development of the Society of Analytical Psychology in England, with its early inclusion of Melanie Klein's theories. Joseph Henderson, on the other hand, had terminated his analysis with Jung naturally before the outset of the war, and had returned to the United States. It has been my impression that he resolved his transference to Jung better than most others of his generation.

In other Jungian groups, a powerful idealization of Jung and analytical psychology existed. For many, only someone who had analyzed with Jung was considered "worthy" as an analyst, and everything that Jung said or wrote was considered "gospel." There was a certain specialness and entitlement common to all Jungian groups in the beginning, and they took on an air of superiority and exclusivity. This made it difficult for a new person to enter, and I know of many examples where individuals interested in analytical psychology found it hard to join the group. However, the combination of feeling superior on the one hand, and feeling ostracized on the other, made bonding within each group strong and close.

Representative types of individuals among the founders

Although generalizations can be dangerous, especially in analytical psychology, there are several representative types of individuals who became the founders of groups in analytical psychology.

German-Jewish men

One of the most striking observations of this study of Jungians was to discover the great number of German-Jewish people who were involved in the founding of Jungian analytic societies in diverse parts of the world. This finding is so striking that it requires special attention.

To review the situation briefly, in the late 1920s in Berlin there existed a group of young Jewish men in their twenties who were caught up in the chaotic post-World War I Weimar Republic in Germany. Most of them were just one generation away from the orthodox Judaism of Eastern Europe. Many of them had had some Freudian analysis and found it unsatisfactory. In part, they were on a spiritual quest for something to take the place of their traditional, but no longer meaningful, Jewish religious values. Jung's psychology presented them with an individual solution to this spiritual dilemma. In alphabetical order they include Gerhard Adler, Ernst Bernhard, Werner Engel, James Kirsch, Erich Neumann, and Heinz Westmann. Max Zeller came to Jung a bit later in the early 1930s. Many of them had begun their analyses with Kaethe Buegler, and later went to Zurich to continue in analysis with Jung.

When the Nazis came into power in 1933, over time the men fled to other countries. In their new countries they all became intimately involved in the founding of analytical psychology groups, Adler in London, Bernhard in Rome, Engel in New York, Kirsch in Tel Aviv and Los Angeles, Neumann in Tel Aviv, Westmann in London and New York, Zeller in Los Angeles. What is so striking is that they all had contact with Jung during the 1930s (except Zeller), when Jung was involved with the International Medical Society for Psychotherapy and supposedly enmeshed with the Nazis. Many of them questioned Jung's behavior towards the Nazis, but none of them felt any personal anti-Semitism and continued to support him wholeheartedly.

Each of these men played a significant role in the development of analytical psychology in their respective community. They were deeply interested in spiritual and religious matters, and as they began to write and lecture, carried the spirit of the *numinosum* and the "God-image within." They came to interpret Judaism from a Jungian point of view, which further deepened their sense of a Jewish identity.

By singling out the Berlin Jews I do not wish to underplay the role many other Jewish people played in the beginnings of analytical psychology. Many of the Jewish spouses of the above-mentioned Berlin Jews were instrumental in the founding of analytical psychology groups, such as Julia Neumann and Hilde Kirsch. Other early Jewish Jungians were Rivkah Schaerf in Zurich and Israel, Erna Rosenbaum and Fred Plaut in London. Hella Adler, although not Jewish, was supportive of her husband, Gerhard.

Jung's relationship to Jewish people was very complex. The irony was that as Jung was being criticized for his ideas and writings on Jews and his involvement with the Nazis, this group of young Jewish men from Berlin were planting the seeds of analytical psychology in disparate parts of the world. These men were studying Jewish texts, especially in relationship to Kabbalah. This most interesting history of Jung's early German-Jewish followers gives new meaning, and perhaps can offer a fresh perspective, to Jewish analysts in particular, who might find some resolution to their conflict about Jung and his alleged anti-Semitism. What my study of early Jungian history has clearly demonstrated is that Jung trained a first generation of German-Jewish analysts – mostly from Berlin – who were to become the founders of Jungian groups all over the world. This Jungian German-Jewish exodus began a world-wide movement that affirmed the reality of the spirit in the Europeans' newly discovered world of the unconscious. The ultimate irony surrounding the question of whether Jung was anti-Semitic is that he personally engendered a generation of Jews, born and raised in Germany who carried a religious spirit into the world of psychoanalysis, while Freud, himself a Jew, as were many of his followers, denigrated the value of the spirit as an illusion and a defense.

Single women

Many of the Jungian groups, such as those in Spain, South Africa, Australia, New Zealand, New York, Chicago, and the IRS in the United States, have been founded by professional women. In the post-war period it was not as common as today for a woman to achieve professional authority. Forming an analytical group is a lonely undertaking and pioneers tend to stand alone. Almost all the women were psychologists or medical doctors. In most cases the women chose not to marry and had no children, but as they were engaged in life's pursuits, they put a great deal of energy into their work. They include Vera Bührmann in South Africa, Rosemary Douglas in Spain, Dorothea Norman-Jones in New Zealand, June Singer in Chicago, and Rix Weaver in Australia. The New York pattern is somewhat different in that several single women – Eleanor Bertine, Esther Harding, and Kristine Mann – developed and led the group.

Male doctors and psychologists

Male medical doctors and psychologists made up the majority of founders. In some cases the men were both doctors and Jewish, so the two categories overlapped. Even when a man was at the head of the group, the majority of early professionals were women. The single exception among the larger societies was San Francisco, where the early professional association consisted predominantly of male medical doctors. This was such an exception that some members from the other societies commented on it; San Francisco was "too medical" and not "Jungian" enough. The make-up of the San Francisco Institute has changed markedly since those early days and now resembles other Jungian societies more closely; it has achieved gender balance, and medical doctors no longer predominate.

JUNGIANS IN RELATIONSHIP TO OTHER DEPTH PSYCHOLOGIES

When Jung withdrew from the International Psychoanalytic Association in 1913, Freud made sure that no one from his circle maintained contact with Jung, who was the strongest dissident from Freudian psychoanalysis up to that point. In fact, one could argue that no other individual who ever left Freud's circle was as thoroughly rejected as Jung. Analytical psychology became a marginalized minority in the few places it existed. From the time of the split, the animosity between Jungians and Freudians was extreme. I call them Freudians and Jungians because the direct disciples of both men carried the feud forward.

Jung himself became quite famous, but in professional circles he was always considered an outsider, Freud's arch-dissident. For a young professional psychiatrist or psychologist to enter Jungian training was always a big risk, because collective attitudes were set against this path. Many young professionals were told that they were throwing away a perfectly good career in order to become a Jungian analyst. On the other hand, the individuals who chose to become Jungians generally did not concern themselves with collective opinion, most first-generation Jungians being introverts. As a result, the small Jungian groups which formed around the Analytical Psychology Clubs were more interested in inner growth than in fostering relationships to the wider professional community or, for that matter, most aspects of the local culture. In most cities where Jungians practiced, they were not known to the other mental health professionals in the community. London and San Francisco were always the exceptions.

To train as an analytical psychologist was considered marginal by professional and academic establishments until around 1970. The counter-culture revolution, changing values from a narrow scientism to more holistic ones, renewed interest in spiritual matters East and West, and brought about a change in consciousness in which Jung was a prominent figure. Books and lectures on analytical psychology, and applications to training institutes, increased at a rapid rate. The changes that I am describing took place all over the United States and Canada, as well as in all parts of Western Europe. The exact way in which this transformation occurred varied from country to country, but the overall effect was the same. All the older institutes were inundated with applicants for training, and new institutes formed across the United States and Western Europe. To become a Jungian analyst was now a legitimate, and ultimately even legitimizing, professional choice. Analytical psychology had become an established discipline in its own right.

Meanwhile psychoanalysis was undergoing many changes, too. Object-relations theorists had an enormous impact in Great Britain; Kohut's self-psychology radically transformed psychoanalytic theory and practice in the United States; and the theory of inter-subjectivity also gained prominence in America. These were approaches which were in accord with many of analytical psychology's basic tenets, and so a gradual *rapprochement* began to occur.

In earlier times, Jungian analysts had to create a model of analysis based upon their own experience of analysis, since Jung's had not given much consideration to the practical details of conducting an analysis, and Freud's technical papers were too confining for most Jungians. Therefore, many Jungian analysts welcomed these developments in psychoanalysis, which provided new clinical insights and methods that were helpful in their work. This also allowed analytical psychologists and psychoanalysts to find common ground, to dialogue on an individual basis, and later to hold joint conferences. *The Journal of Analytical Psychology* has been a leader in bringing psychoanalysts and analytical psychologists together in Sebasco, Maine in 1996 and 1997, and in Merida, Mexico in 1999.

An interesting phenomenon has occurred throughout the Jungian world: whereas in the beginning most of the early Jungian analysts had moved from Freud to Jung, today some are moving in the opposite direction. Many Jungians in need of further therapy will now seek out some variation of a psychoanalytic approach. In part, this has to do with finding a therapist outside the Jungian circle to circumvent transference/countertransference complications, but it also has to do with the fact that a psychoanalytic approach sometimes can be more helpful with personal developmental issues. In turn, Freudian-trained individuals seeking a broader analysis with archetypal and mythological amplifications have turned privately to Jungians for that experience.

ETHICS

Ethical issues in analytical psychology are an extremely delicate subject. At the formation of most Jungian institutes, professional ethics were rarely noted. Jung made his own distinction between morality and ethics. In part, he saw morality in terms of the individual ego in *relationship* to the unconscious (Jung *CW* 10). To ignore the dialectic between ego and the Self was an immoral act, because he believed one had a moral obligation to attend the unconscious contents revealed. Individuation was seen as being at the heart of personal morality. Ethics, on the other hand, were precepts coming from outside the individual. During the 1960s, major institutes – New York, San Francisco, Los Angeles, and Zurich – began to have professional problems with ethical implications. Until that time most institutes did not have an ethical code, and if they did, it was of a general nature. Analysts who were clinically trained were expected to follow their respective professional codes of conduct; but other non-clinically trained analysts had no formal ethical code.

Most ethical issues have arisen out of sexual transgression between analyst and patient, although in Italy there were issues regarding money. As analysts, we know that, to work, analysis requires a confidential and intimate relationship. Jung wrote in "Psychology of the Transference" that this intimate union (the *coniunctio*) necessarily be expressed in symbolic terms only; this is significant given the frankly erotic nature of the images which Jung used in this essay, which he published late in life. It reflected his most mature thoughts on the subject of transference. However, what Jung wrote in this essay was not consonant with his prior behavior. He had had a forty-year relationship with Toni Wolff, an ex-patient. Jung has frequently been presented as a "womanizer" and there have been undocumented rumors of sexual relations with other patients, but none have ever been proven. Jung's emphasis on the dialectical, interactive relationship between analysand and patient led him and many of his followers to express more directly their countertransferential thoughts and feelings towards their patients, which in turn led to a greater liability to act out in the therapeutic relationship.

Sexual acting out in analysis was not confined to the Jungians alone. Falzeder (1998:127) has charted the lines of development in psychoanalysis with respect to who analyzed with whom. Furthermore, he notes where a sexual relationship was involved in the analysis. So, in the early days of both psychoanalysis and analytical psychology, sexual liaisons were not uncommon. Among Jungians, sexuality between analyst and patient/and or candidate led to major eruptions in the institutes where these incidents occurred. Sexual acting out was not tolerated once its damage to the patient was fully recognized. Furthermore, the American collective was no longer tolerating this kind of behavior from any kind of therapist. In the 1970s both the American Psychological Association and the American Psychiatric Association came out strongly against patient–therapist sex. So, both from within and outside institutes, social, interpersonal, and intrapsychic pressures mounted for a change in the consciousness of the Jungian analyst. Strict guidelines for conduct between analyst and patient were developed by many of the major American Jungian institutes. Since there was no national Jungian organization, some institutes, like the New England one, chose to believe that an outer code was not necessary, rather seeing it as the responsibility of the analyst himself/herself to face this matter. Yet, after many years of discussion, the New England Institute adopted a code of ethics for its members in 1997.

European Jungian institutes in general have had a more *laissez-faire* attitude towards the sexual issue. It is the general belief that the problem should not be legislated, that the issue of sex and therapy is the responsibility of the individual analyst. One must be trusted to monitor his/her own professional ethical behavior through the individuation process. Thus, the European institutes have been generally slower in developing a comprehensive ethical code. The United Kingdom's position is much closer to that of the American one, although the Independent Group is closely aligned to the Zurich position, which is much less structured. Israel's position is close to that of the American one. As of this writing, all institutes have developed at least a general statement about practicing in an ethical manner.

In 1992 the IAAP adopted an amendment to its constitution requiring all members to practice in an ethical manner. The wording was deliberately ambiguous in order to gain approval by the majority of institutes, with the expectation that each would develop a code of ethics depending upon its prevailing philosophy. Henceforth, any new group applying for membership into the IAAP must have an ethics code as part of its constitution.

As a result, Jungian analysts around the world are more aware of the negative effects of acting upon the transference/countertransference dynamic. Today, there is a strong ethic against sex between analyst and patient. When the analyst does not hold the boundaries in analysis, the issue is taken very seriously by the professional community.

JUNG, THE NAZIS, AND ANTI-SEMITISM

The question of Jung's relationships to the Nazis and to Jewish people has been discussed in many different places in this book, and is a *leitmotif* in the history of Germany. From my research it is clear that early on the events in Nazi Germany captured Jung's attention. He has described this as a clinical interest, with Germany as the patient. No matter how he portrayed his attention, it seems he was pulled into the orbit of the Nazis, and was not aware of the ramifications of his association with them. However, it is also a big relief to have found definitive evidence that Jung pulled away from this association by 1935, perhaps as early as 1934, having apparently gained insight into their underlying agenda; he was personally anti-Nazi from that point on. This is corroborated by the anecdotal evidence I personally gathered from many Jewish people who knew him during the 1930s.

Successive generations of Jungian analysts and analysands have wrestled with the question of Jung's complex relations to Germany, Nazism and Jews. Many Jewish and non-Jewish analysts have asked themselves whether their gravitation toward Jung has been in some way related to latent anti-Semitism. For Jewish analysts, has it been a way to assimilate and renounce their Jewish origins? Or, alternatively, is it a way to find their deeper Jewish identity? I have heard similar questions being raised by non-Jewish analysts as well. Jung's relationship to early Nazism, his split with Freud, and his relationship to Jewish people have been among the most perplexing and disturbing issues for Jungians and non-Jungians alike. The fact that over the past two decades Jungians themselves have tackled this has helped to bridge the divide between Jungians and other schools of psychotherapy. Earlier generations of Jungians simply defended Jung unequivocally. At the time of writing (1999), the continuing controversy around this remains an obstacle to Jung's greater acceptance worldwide.

THEORETICAL DIFFERENCES

I have traced the history of every Jungian training center, each of which began with a person or persons who had analyzed with Jung and/or one of his assistants. All the pioneers brought with them the ideal of a psychology closely akin to Jung's own. This is an important point which needs to be emphasized. Even in London, which is so identified with developmental issues and object-relations theory today, the early group was classically oriented and followed Jung's own ways closely. Every Jungian institute developed its own style, depending upon the individual characteristics of its founders, the local culture under which it grew, including the political and governmental climate, the relationship of its founders to other depth psychological schools, and last but not least, the transferences of its founders to Jung. These issues have been discussed in relationship to each group and its history. Above and beyond these differences, are there general trends that we can point to? I think so.

Trend 1

In each Jungian institute across the world, there is a general change in one of two directions. On the one hand, in many major Jungian centers in Switzerland, Germany, England, and the United States, we see a movement towards *rapprochement* with newer developments in psychoanalysis. There are appropriate clinical reasons for this. The original antipathy between Freud and Jung has evolved into a cautious but positive courtship between the two disciplines. However, in some cases the courtship progressed into a love affair, and some seriously question the identity of several of these Jungian training centers. There are definitely individuals within these Jungian institutes who profess a stronger connection to Klein, Winnicott, Kohut, or Bion, than to Jung and analytical psychology. One can look at the reading lists of some of these training institutes and note that Jung is almost not read, while psychoanalysts are emphasized. While the inclusion of recent clinical and theoretical insights in psychoanalysis is generally advantageous, many Jungians remain deeply wary about over-identification with the positivistic nature of psychoanalysis.

On the other hand, some people feel that analytical psychology has been diluted by the inclusion of psychoanalysis, and that it is time to go back to the original. There is movement in the opposite direction, a return to exclusive reading of Jung and certain close followers such as Marie-Louise von Franz. Jung demonstrated, they say, through analysis of the symbolic language of the collective unconscious, all the formulations that later appeared in the personalistic language of psychoanalysis. These people fear that as his work becomes assimilated into mainstream psychoanalysis, Jung's profound original discoveries will be lost to future generations.

Extremes are developing on both ends of the spectrum, and this is troubling, because the very openness of Jung's psychology and its receptivity to unknown factors in the transpersonal dimension of the psyche has been vital. So far, the rigidity characteristic of psychoanalysis has not appeared in analytical psychology. However, as these extreme positions are articulated and polarized, the danger of ossification and stagnation increases.

Trend 2

Closely allied to the first trend is the evolution of the role of the transference in analytical psychology. Jung recognized early in his psychoanalytic career the ultimate importance of the transference. However, he did not sense the need to interpret it when the analytic relationship proceeded smoothly, but only when it caused difficulties for the treatment or if it appeared in the analysand's dream. Otherwise, he let it quietly operate in the background.

This pattern is continued by those who practice in a classical manner. However, it became evident to many analysts that the transference/

countertransference relationship required more conscious attention, as they began to notice subtle aspects of the therapeutic relationship causing difficulties for both analyst and patient. Today, there is a wide spectrum of opinion on transference/countertransference phenomena. On the one hand, in the SAP, the transference is the central feature of the analysis, while for the new Research and Training Centre in Depth Psychology in Zurich the transference is only alluded to when it comes up in a dream. The rest of the Jungians are somewhere in between. Overall the transference aspect of analysis has taken on a much greater significance for the majority of practicing analytical psychologists.

The impact of the transference relationship has affected analytical psychology in another way. Every analyst has been a patient at one time, and how analysts terminated analysis influences their practical definition of analytical psychology (Fordham 1974).

I have noted that Jung's not taking Fordham as a patient clearly swayed Fordham's later views of analytical psychology. In every Jungian institute there are different sub-groups of analysts who have been analyzed by different senior analysts in the local society. There are also those solitary analysts who have analyzed with an analyst removed from the usual power structure. This is less likely to occur where there is a separate category of "training analyst," compelling the candidate to analyze with someone from this select group of senior analysts. To the extent that the transference has been resolved, the junior analyst acts independently. However, when unresolved transferences exist, groupings based upon these unresolved transferences occur. Who has seen whom for analysis becomes an extremely important thread in the make-up of a Jungian institute. Institutional decisions can be influenced by such allegiances. As mentioned earlier, Ernst Falzeder (1998) has made a map showing who analyzed whom in psychoanalysis, and what the implications are for the development of the different kinds of psychoanalysis today. I believe that one could do the same for analytical psychology, which would help to explain some of the tensions and splits among Jungians.

Also related to the transference issue is how Jungian analytic technique has changed over the years. Jung eschewed the word "technique," but there was a general way in which he worked. He used dream analysis, active imagination, and amplification in face-to-face, relatively infrequent sessions, and fostered an active dialectic between himself and his patient. Today there is wide variation in the use of these basic analytic methods. The more developmentally oriented Jungians use a couch, require more frequent sessions, interpret the transference, and focus less on dreams, amplification and active imagination. I do not wish to imply that all Jungians who use the couch or frequent sessions are developmentally oriented. Many Jungian analysts, especially in the United States, use the couch experimentally to help induce unconscious fantasy and facilitate a state of reverie in an otherwise Jungian way. Opposite to them are analysts who adhere strictly to Jung's own method, as they understand it. Most work somewhere in between. In my experience, almost all Jungians, in addition to amplifying and interpreting dreams, recognize the primarily symbolic nature of the unconscious, the importance of working with the transference/countertransference relationship, and the necessity for maintaining strict professional boundaries.

Trend 3

In large part, Jung achieved fame during his lifetime with his theory of psychological types, his typology being based on the concept of four ego functions (thinking, feeling, sensation, and intuition), and two psychological attitudes (introversion and extraversion). He never used this concept systematically, although informally he often referred to a person's typology. Most Jungian training institutes have not focused on the study of psychological types. The single exception is the San Francisco group, where the Wheelwrights and Dr Horace Gray developed a pen-and-paper-type survey which was administered to thousands of people, and inspired the Myers–Briggs Type Test. Wayne Detloff and Kay Bradway studied the psychological types of Jungian analysts in California. Others who advanced Jung's concept of types are June Singer and Mary Loomis, who developed the Singer–Loomis inventory, and John Beebe, who has proposed a variation of type theory.

However, a whole literature of psychological type theory has developed outside of the Jungian tradition, beginning with Myers–Briggs, whose type test has been widely used in business and industry to help solve interpersonal problems, set goals for individual employees, and situate employees to their best advantage in the workplace.

SPLITS

Splitting, but not in the clinical sense of the word, is a phenomenon which has been with psychoanalysis from the very beginning (Eisold 1994). This has to do with the fact that Freud not only established himself as the founder of psychoanalysis, but also claimed ownership:

psychoanalysis is my creation . . . I consider myself justified in maintaining that even today no one can know better than I do what psychoanalysis is, how it differs from other ways of investigating the life of the mind, and precisely what should be called psychoanalysis and what would be better described by some other name.

(Freud 1914:7)

Thus, when differences in opinion occurred with Wilhelm Steckel, Alfred Adler, and Jung, Freud dismissed them. Freud was an autocratic, authoritarian figure who demanded complete personal loyalty (Eisold 1994). This pattern of authoritarianism continued when psychoanalytic institutes were established (Aguayo 1997; Eisold 1994). Differences in attitude and opinion between members evoked strong reactions, which fueled the impulse for a new and separate group.

Jung, having seen what happened to a professional organization headed by a strong leader dedicated to turning out "followers," was determined that for analytical psychology he would not play the same role as Freud. However, in spite of Jung's conscious efforts to remain in the background of analytical training, Jungian institutes have also had a problem with splits. This can be seen in what has transpired in England, Italy, Belgium, Switzerland, and Denmark in Europe; Brazil in South America; and in the Northwest and Pittsburgh in the United States. Some other institutes presently hold together only tenuously. A tension exists between the democratic use of power and authoritarianism. What begins benignly as judicious authority turns quickly into a subtle or not so subtle usurping of power.

The work of being an analyst is remarkably intense and lonely, and most of us long for like-minded colleagues with whom we can share the experience. When we perceive our colleagues promoting values which we deem alien, a rift develops. Often a feeling of woundedness accompanies this feeling of alienation. The specific issue varies from situation to situation, but this sense of woundedness and alienation is fairly constant. Otherwise reasonable and mature people become irrational when it comes to analytic institutional issues. Why this is so is only at the beginning stage of exploration.

One might explain a split on the basis of theoretical differences, but that is only partially true. Many Jungian institutes in the world, e.g., France, Germany, San Francisco, Chicago, AIPA, CIPA, ANZSJA, host a broad spectrum of theoretical and practical Jungian viewpoints under one banner, and though seismic activity has been recorded, there have been no ultimate splits. In these institutes, a mutual respect for the other's point of view exists, and differences manage to coexist.

On the other hand, we have reviewed the situations in England, Switzerland, and Belgium, where the factions within a group were so strongly opposed that only separation could relieve their tension.

If theoretical differences are not the only grounds for splits, what causes them? It is my impression that the professional analytic institute takes on the role of the family. Much of what was experienced in the family gets played out at the institutional level, in spite of everyone having been analyzed. As Alfred Adler observed, power issues are extremely difficult to resolve in analysis. When I was in a position of power as president of the IAAP, handling these delicate situations, which resembled family dynamics, required great sensitivity. In most instances, by the time they came to the attention of the IAAP, the strain was too great and a split was imminent.

Even in those circumstances where separation is based upon legitimate and genuine theoretical differences, personality conflicts usually contribute to the division. Let me give you a hypothetical scenario. Two leading figures in an institute can be vying for the "soul" of a particular training program, and they have differing views of the essential ingredients of analytical psychology. The tension between the two may go on for years, but then something happens; perhaps one analyst's candidate is not advanced to the next level of training; the reasons given for holding the candidate back may be that they are either "too archetypal," or not "symbolic enough," depending upon the prevailing attitude of the particular institute. The analyst whose candidate is not being passed takes this personally and protests the decisions of the evaluation committee. Not satisfied with the response, the analyst then decides to solicit others to join forces with him/her and form another institute where its candidates will be treated more fairly. The general issue here is how analysts deal with peers; only the peerless Freud and Jung did not have to face this problem.

Behind the scenario described above, the narcissistic and power needs of the analyst protesting, as well as the power needs of the analysts making the criticized decisions, must be questioned. In the hypothetical example cited above, was the decision really based on the fact that the candidate is either "too archetypal" or "not symbolic enough?" Or are such theoretical issues a front for personal antagonisms between analysts? When an institute fight ensues, the power needs of specific senior analysts play a large part in its outcome.

Eisold has studied this problem and states that anxiety engendered in psychoanalytic training is at its core. First, analysis and supervision are very private experiences, and they often evoke deep anxiety in the candidate. Thus, the most meaningful part of training – personal analysis

– takes place in a dyadic mode, occurring outside the physical and organizational structure of the institute (Eisold 1994). Second, a tension develops between the analyst's need to belong to the group, and his/her need to be receptive to the analysand-in-training. Third, anxiety derives from the contradiction between his membership in his institute and his affiliations to the various analytic pairs within the institute. An Institute split has often been the result of these conflicting allegiances. For example, what happens when a new analyst enters the institute, and his analyst is considered one of its outsiders? Is his/her allegiance to the analytic pair or to membership in the group? The consciousness and relatedness with which these issues are handled determine the atmosphere within an institute.

In concluding this brief discussion of splits, we must recognize that they are a common occurrence in Jungian institutes as well as Freudian institutes, and although the specific reasons given for the split within the former may differ from those given in the latter, the end result is the same. It seems to me that the powerful emotions engendered within the analytic encounter are often at odds with the individual analyst's necessary loyalty to the analytic society.

JUNGIANS TODAY

As has been mentioned several times in this book, Jung was not interested in developing a sectarian psychological "school." His interests lay in studying the unconscious as it manifested itself in comparative religion, mythology, anthropology, ethnology, psychiatry, and modern atomic physics. Although his books were widely read in England and the United States, and many words which he coined such as complex, archetype, introvert, extravert, became a part of everyday language, Freudian psychoanalysis was the predominant depth psychology during his lifetime. The lasting effects of the feud between himself and Freud, compounded by his deep interest in the non-rational aspects of the psyche, were at variance with the culture of the times. At the end of his life he had grave doubts whether he had truly been understood.

In the four decades since his death, Jung and Jungians have gained a degree of general acceptance which did not exist during his lifetime. Many of Jung's ideas have become a part of the general culture of the world, sometimes with acknowledgement and many times not. In addition, the books of many Jungian analysts have garnered wide readership, and other writers have been openly influenced by Jung. Briefly, a selected, but not exhaustive list might include: in the

United States, Jean Shinoda Bolen, Clarissa Pinkola Estés, James Hillman, Linda Leonard, June Singer, and Robert Moore; in Canada, Marion Woodman; in the German-speaking countries, Verena Kast; in Italy, Aldo Carotenuto and Umberto Galimberti; in Japan, Hayao Kawai.

Jungians have struck a chord; the culture recognizes the importance of the unconscious and desires information that does not immediately point to pathology. Professionally, to be a Jungian analyst is a legitimate occupation and, therefore, is apt to receive approbation like that earned by other schools of psychoanalysis, which means it will also have to weather similar forms of condemnation.

WHAT DOES IT MEAN TO BE A JUNGIAN ANALYST TODAY?

The issue of pluralism and diversity among Jungians has been mentioned frequently in this book. Andrew Samuels' classic study, *Jung and the Post-Jungians*, was the first publication formally to define qualities upon which a categorization could be made. He based his classification on the emphasis which different analysts placed upon the theory of archetypes, the Self, transference, and the role of developmental issues in their work. The classical analysts placed greatest attention to the emergence of archetypal themes, especially the Self, in their analysands. Transference phenomena were not emphasized and developmental issues were minimally acknowledged. The developmental group placed greatest emphasis on early developmental issues, relied heavily on transference interpretations, and paid less importance to archetypal and symbolic factors. Developmental theory also modified the use of the term "self" to include a primal self in the first half of life. A third group, following Hillman, who chose the term "archetypal psychology" to designate his particular sub-school, emphasized archetypal images and experiences and paid little attention to developmental and transference issues. When Samuels' work was published in 1985, some analysts did not like to see themselves labeled thus, while others found it valuable. He articulated trends within analytical psychology which had been obvious for over twenty years.

If we look at the picture today, we can see that the classification which Samuels described fifteen years ago has crystallized even further. Let me divide Jungians today along another series of parameters: individuation, causality, issue of the container, transference, and dreams.

Individuation

There are those Jungians, such as the classical analysts, who maintain that individuation is a process which only takes place in the second half of life. Within that group there are analysts like Edward Edinger who believe that the individuation process is closely akin to the Christian path of salvation. Other analysts like Professor Hayao Kawai, who has a Buddhist orientation, or Clarissa Pinkola Estés, who as an ethnic Latina has a legacy of *curanderismo* and the Catholic devotion to Guadalupe, have a very different orientation towards individuation and the role of the ego. Then there are the archetypal psychologists who speak about a polytheistic view of the self and individuation, questioning any mono-theistic vision of either. On the other pole, we have the "developmental school" which holds that individuation begins at birth, continuing throughout the life cycle. There are many analysts who maintain some combination of the above. Imbedded in the differences are diverse opinions regarding the role of religious experience in the analytic pro-cess. Jung's own view, and that of the classical analyst, is that everyone in the second half of life ultimately confronts spiritual questions. Other Jungian analysts do not consider the religious issues as central.

Causality

The "developmental school" ascribes psychopathology to the events of early childhood and infancy. The causes are rooted in the childhood complexes which must be analyzed in order for the adult to proceed on the path of individuation. On the other hand, there are those Jungians who see that the psyche follows an acausal pattern which needs to be understood; while not ignoring causality, they give it secondary importance.

Analytic container

As mentioned previously, Jung used alchemical symbolism in "The Psychology of the Transference" to describe the process and stages of analysis. The medieval symbolism of alchemy provides an arcane template for the intensely personal experience of analysis. Using the language of the alchemists, Jung described the various processes which take place in the analytic vessel and emphasized the need to keep the alchemical vessel hermetically sealed during certain phases of the work. As we have noted, Jungians have variably kept the container properly sealed; more often in the past than in the present the vessel badly leaked. And what is meant by "alchemical container" also has had myriad interpretations. Jung and the first generation of Jungians kept much looser boundaries than succeeding generations, often mixing social and professional relationships. Succeeding generations have been much stricter in delineating boundaries between professional and personal relationships. Self-disclosure is another issue which has undergone a shift in emphasis. While self-disclosure can be done in a conscious way that can be therapeutic, and in such a way that the container will hold, some Jungian analysts have given too literal an interpretation to Jung's belief that the analyst must be as much "in the work" as the analysand.

Transference

This issue overlaps with the role of the container in the analytic process. Although all Jungians hold to the importance of the transference, there is great variability in how and whether it is directly interpreted. The "classical" Jungian interprets the transference only when there is reference to the analyst in a dream, whereas an analyst of the "developmental" school interprets most clinical material, dream or otherwise, from a transferential viewpoint.

Dreams

For Jung and the first generation of Jungians the analysis of dreams was central to the analytic process. I know of almost no first-generation analyst who did not place dreams at the center of the analytic work, which could include bringing a typed copy for the analyst. Today that ritual is no longer prevalent. Dreams are still vitally important, but the discussion and interpretation of them often play lesser roles than they once did. Furthermore, some Jungian analysts no longer ask for dreams, and only discuss them when the patient happens to bring one in. The latter represents an enormous change in attitude, and with it a tremendous departure in how dreams are used by Jungians today.

WHAT HOLDS JUNGIANS TOGETHER?

One could cite other changes which have taken place within the Jungian community; however, I think that the above-mentioned topics show the divergent paths which analytical psychology have taken. One could ask, then, what is it that holds Jungians together today? The impetus for this book comes in part from this question.

Adolf Guggenbühl-Craig, former president of the IAAP and widely respected senior analyst in Zurich, delivered a most trenchant paper on this subject to the Swiss Society for Analytical Psychology on 2 June 1996. The first point he makes is that somehow we all come from Jung. We read something by him, were stimulated by something he said, perhaps even to the extent of choosing a career as a psychotherapist. Later on, even if many, or all, of Jung's writings might have been rejected by us, our original "historical identity" is unchanged; we are all grandchildren or great-grandchildren of Jung. Just like any extended family, we may have little in common except our ancestry. It is kinship libido that brings the extended family together. However, this is insufficient to hold us together as a professional group.

The second way in which we are all Jungians is that we share a kind of ideological identity. Guggenbühl-Craig characterizes this as a "transcendental attitude." By this he does not mean Jung's transcendent function, but rather that all Jungians believe that behind all psychological concepts and theories there exists another dimension of reality. There are few positivists among Jungians. Most Jungians have an inclination towards the twilight areas of the psyche. Some notion of individuation is important to most Jungians, which implies there are deeper aspects to the psyche.

Guggenbühl-Craig's third point is more complex. He describes three archetypal patterns which influenced Jung: the priest/theologian; the physician as natural scientist; and the shaman. One can readily see both the priest/theologian and the physician as natural scientist in Jung's writings. Shamanism, which values the ecstatic, is a path to transpersonal experience for the individual in a primitive culture. Jung was most interested in this level of experience. Personally, I do not like to hear the term "shamanism" linked to analytical psychology, because it implies a too specific and often concretizing technique to bring transpersonal reality into the awareness of a suffering individual, and is an avenue for exploitation by analysts who have not thoroughly worked through their own power complexes. However, Jungian analysis combines both the natural and the psychologically primitive with the most sophisticated use of mind and consciousness known to our Western cultural tradition and holds the tension between them so that healing can ensue from a confrontation of the patient's ego with forces greater than itself. To this extent, Jung's work may be seen as a continuation into the present of the shamanic tradition. It is Guggenbühl-Craig's view, with which I agree, that all Jungians share some sense of that value.

THE FUTURE OF ANALYTICAL PSYCHOLOGY

Analytical psychology, along with other forms of depth psychology, has been under attack in recent years. New anti-depressants have changed the way many depressions are treated and psychotherapy is no longer the first treatment of choice; health insurance, private and governmental, no longer reimburses long-term psychotherapy, threatening the economic viability of many psychotherapists, who continue to increase in number. Conditions vary from country to country, but the trend is the same the world over. Fewer people enter psychoanalysis of any sort, including Jungian analysis.

Psychoanalysis is over one hundred years old, and it is no longer the young and exciting discipline that it once was. It has failed to live up to its promises of healing the individual and of transforming society; in the 1950s it was seen by many as a panacea for the ills of the world. Although Freudian psychoanalysis bears the brunt of disillusionment, Jung and analytical psychology come in for their share of criticism. Yet, many of Jung's ideas are now part of mainstream Western culture, and much of his specialized terminology is incorporated into everyday language.

It is obviously impossible to predict what will happen to analytical psychology in the unknowable future of the new millennium. Some people think that analytical psychology will lose its separate identity, to become part of a generic psychoanalysis, following a current trend in many locations. Alternatively, in other locales, there is a return to what is essentially Jungian fundamentalism, in which the words of Jung and a few others are read and studied as sacred texts.

Clearly, there is room for a clinical discipline of Jungian analysis which does not fall into either of these camps. Jung, among others, has shown us that openness to forms of experience beyond everyday reality is historically essential to our humanness. Whether we call the level of the psyche that is in touch with that other reality the collective unconscious, the Self, the God-image, the objective psyche, or something else, it has always been, and will always be, part of us. For that reason, I believe that there will always be some psychological discipline, in addition to religion, which refers to that level of experience. The systole and diastole of life has a certain rhythm, and at present we seem to be in-between. The question is whether in the future there will be a classification of therapists called Jungians. It is what we are called now, and this book has traced the history from the beginning to the present.

Bibliography

Adler, G. (1948) *Studies in Analytical Psychology*, London: Routledge & Kegan Paul.

—— (ed.) (1959) *Current Trends in Analytical Psychology*, Proceedings of the First International Congress for Analytical Psychology, Zurich 1958, London: Tavistock Publications.

—— (1961a) *The Living Symbol*, Bollingen Series, New York: Pantheon Books.

—— (1961b) "Erich Neumann: 1905–1960," *Spring*, pp. 4–8.

Aguayo, J. (1997) "Historicizing the Origins of Kleinian Psychoanalysis," *International Journal of Psychoanalysis*, No. 78, p. 1.

Aserinsky, E.P. and Kleitman, N. (1953) "Regularly Occurring Periods of Eye Motility and Concomitant Phenomena During Sleep," *Science*, No. 118, p. 273.

Astor, J. (1995) *Michael Fordham: Innovations in Analytical Psychology*, London: Routledge.

Baudouin, C. (1943) *Psychoanalyse de Victor Hugo*, Geneva: Mont Blanc.

—— (1963) *L'Oeuvre de Jung*, Paris: Petite Bibliothèque Payot.

Baumann, Dieter (1970) "In Memory of Franz Riklin," *Spring*, pp. 1–5.

Baynes, Cary (1968) *I-Ching or Book of Changes*, third edition, Bollingen Series, Richard Wilhelm, trans. from Chinese into German, Princeton: Princeton University Press.

Baynes, H.G. (1940) *Mythology of the Soul*, London: Bailliere Tindall & Cox.

—— (1941) *Germany Possessed*, London: Jonathan Cape, also published in 1972, New York: AMS Press.

Bernhard, E. (1969) *Mitobiografia*, ed. H. Erba Tissot, Milan: Adelphi Edizioni (fourth edition, 1992).

—— (1971) "Introduzione allo studio del sogno" (Dream Interpretation), *Rivista di psicologia analitica*, Vol. II, No. 1, p. 56.

Buder, H. (1963) "Der Zeitraum von 1933 bis 1945 und die Zeit nach dem Kriege," in Michael Fordham (ed.), *Contact with Jung*, Philadelphia and Montreal: Lippincott.

Cahen, R. (1987) *L'homme à la découverte de son âme*, Paris: Albin Michel.

Carotenuto, A. (1977) *Jung e la Cultura Italiana*, Rome: Casa Editrice Astrolabio Ubaldini.

—— (1982) *A Secret Symmetry*, New York: Pantheon Books.

Casement, A. (1995) "A Brief History of Jungian Splits in the U.K.," *Journal of Analytical Psychology*, Vol. 40, No. 3, p. 331.

Cocks, Geoffrey (1997) *Psychotherapy in the Third Reich: The Goering Institute*, second edition, New Brunswick, N.J.: Transaction Publishers.

Cornford, F.M. (1957) *From Religion to Philosophy*, New York: Harper.

Davies, Robertson (1972) *The Manticore*, New York: Viking.

Edinger, E. (1972) *Ego and Archetype: Individuation and the Religious Function of the Psyche*, New York: G.P. Putnam's Sons.

—— (1990) *Goethe's Faust: Notes for a Jungian Commentary*, Toronto: Inner City Books.

—— (1994) *The Mystery of the Coniunctio: Alchemical Image of Individuation*, Toronto: Inner City Books.

—— (1995a) *The Mysterium Lectures*, Toronto: Inner City Books.

—— (1995b) *Melville's Moby-Dick: An American Nekyia*, revised edition, Toronto: Inner City Books.

—— (1996) *The Aion Lectures*, Toronto: Inner City Books.

Ehlers, H. (1985) *Here Life Goes on in a Most Peculiar Way*, Hamburg: Kellner Verlag.

Eisold, K. (1994) "The Intolerance of Diversity in Psychoanalytic Institutes," *International Journal of Psychoanalysis*, Vol. 75, pp. 785–800.

Eranos Yearbooks (1973) 6 volumes, Leiden: Brill Verlag.

Estés, Clarissa Pinkola (1992/1995) *Women Who Run With the Wolves*, New York: Ballantine/Random House.

Etkind, A. (1998) *Eros of the Impossible*, Boulder, Colo.: Westview Press.

Falzeder, E. (1998) "Family Tree Matters," Sebasco Conference Papers, *Journal of Analytical Psychology*, Vol. 43, No. 1, pp. 127–154.

Fierz-David, Linda (1950) *The Dream of Poliphilo*, Bollingen Series, New York: Pantheon.

—— (1957) *Villa of Mysteries in Pompeii*, Zurich: Psychological Club Publication.

Fordham, M. (ed.) (1944a) *Analytical Psychology Club Papers 1944*, London: Analytical Psychology Club, pp. 48–58.

—— (1944b) *The Life of Childhood: A Contribution to Analytical Psychology*, London: Kegan Paul Trench Trubner.

—— (1957) *New Developments in Analytical Psychology*, London: Routledge & Kegan Paul, pp. 117–127.

—— (1969) *Children as Individuals*, London: Hodder & Stoughton.

—— (ed.) (1974) *Technique in Jungian Analysis*, The Library of Analytical Psychology, London: William Heinemann Medical Books, Vol. 2.

—— (1976) "Discussion of T. Kirsch Article, 'The Practice of Multiple Analyses in Analytical Psychology,'" *Contemporary Psychoanalysis*, Vol. 12, No. 2.

—— (ed.) (1985) *Explorations into the Self*, The Library of Analytical Psychology, London: Academic Press, Vol. 7.

—— (1993) *The Making of an Analyst: A Memoir*, London: Free Associations Books.

Freud, S. (1914) *On the History of the Psychoanalytic Movement*, Standard Edition XIV, London: Hogarth Press.

—— (1936) *The Question of Lay Analysis*, Standard Edition xx, pp. 183–250.

—— (1953–73) References are to *The Standard Edition of the Complete Psychological Works of Sigmund Freud*, 24 vols (ed. and trans. James Strachey *et al.*), London: Hogarth Press and the Institute of Psycho-Analysis.

Gaillard, C. (1995) *Jung*, Paris: Presses Universitaires de France.

—— (1998) *Le Musée imaginaire de Carl Gustav Jung*, Paris: Editions Stock.

Gat, Geula (1980) "In Remembrance of Erich Neumann," Unpublished paper.

Goodheart, W. (1984) "C.G. Jung's First 'Patient'; on the Seminal Emergence of Jung's Thought," *Journal of Analytical Psychology*, January 1984, Vol. 29, No. 1, pp. 1–34.

Guggenbühl-Craig, A. (ed.) (1964) *Der Archetyp*, Proceedings of the Second International Congress for Analytical Psychology Zurich 1962, Basel and New York: S. Karger.

—— (1971) *Power in the Helping Professions*, New York: Spring Publications.

—— (1996) "What Makes One a Jungian?," Paper presented at the Annual Meeting of the SGfAP, 2 June.

Hannah, Barbara (1976) *Jung, His Life & Work*, New York: G.P. Putnam's Sons.

Harding, E. (1963) *Psychic Energy*, New York: Pantheon Books, Bollingen Foundation.

—— (1965) *The Parental Image*, New York: C.G. Jung Foundation and G.P. Putnam's Sons.

—— (1970a) *The I and the Not I*, Princeton: Princeton University Press.

—— (1970b) *The Way of all Women*, New York: C.G. Jung Foundation and G.P. Putnam's Sons.

—— (1972) *Woman's Mysteries*, New York: C.G. Jung Foundation and G.P. Putnam's Sons.

Henderson, J. (1964) "Ancient Myths and Modern Man," in C.G. Jung (ed.), *Man and his Symbols*, New York: Doubleday and London: Anchor Books.

—— (1967) *Thresholds of Initiation*, Middletown, Conn.: Wesleyan.

—— (1982) *Jungian Analysis*, ed. Murray Stein, La Salle, Ill.: Open Court Publisher.

—— (1984) *Cultural Attitudes in Psychological Perspective*, Toronto: Inner City Books.

—— (1990) *Shadow and Self*, Wilmette, Ill.: Chiron.

—— (1996) Panel Discussion on "Seminal Women," 24 November, Unpublished paper, San Francisco: C.G. Jung Institute.

Henderson, J. and Oakes, M. (1963) *The Wisdom of the Serpent*, New York: George Braziller.

Heyer, G.R. (1934) *The Organism of the Mind; An Introduction to Analytical Psychotherapy* (Der Organismus der Seele), New York: Harcourt, Brace.

—— (1941) "Review of C.G. Jung's 'Psychology and Religion'" (Terry Lectures), *Psychiatrische–Neurologische Wochenschrift*, August, p. 16.

Higuchi, Kazuhiko (1996) "News from Japan," *IAAP Newsletter*, Vol. 16, p. 99.

Hillman, James (1960) *Emotion*, London: Routledge & Kegan Paul.

Humbert, Elie (1988) *Jung*, Wilmette, Ill.: Chiron (originally published in French, 1983).

Jacobi, Jolande (1943) *The Psychology of C.G. Jung*, New Haven, Conn.: Yale University Press.

—— (1959) *Complex/Archetype/Symbol*, Princeton: Princeton University Press and Bollingen Foundation.

Jacoby, Mario (1974) "In Memory of Jolande Jacobi," *Journal of Analytical Psychology*, January, Vol. 19, No. 1, pp. 94–96.

Jaffé, A. (1964) "Symbolism in the Visual Arts," in C.G. Jung (ed.), *Man and His Symbols*, London: Aldus Books Limited.

—— (1970) *The Myth of Meaning*, London: Hodder & Stoughton.

—— (1979) *C.G. Jung, Word and Image*, Princeton: Princeton University Press.

Jones, E. (1953) *Life and Work of Sigmund Freud*, 3 vols, New York: Basic Books.

Jung, C.G (1904) *Studies in Word Association* (*CW* Vol. 2), London: Routledge & Kegan Paul (reissued 1969).

—— (1913) "The Theory of Psychoanalysis" (*CW* Vol. 4).

—— (1929) "The Secret of the Golden Flower" (*CW* Vol. 13).

—— (1933a) "A Study in the Process of Individuation" (*CW* Vol. 9, paras 525–626, pp. 290–354).

—— (1933b) *Modern Man in Search of a Soul*, trans. W.S. Dell and Cary F. Baynes, New York: Harcourt, Brace.

—— (1934) "The State of Psychotherapy Today" (*CW* Vol. 10).

—— (1935) "Tavistock Lectures" (*CW* Vol. 18, pp. 151–152, 168).

—— (1936) "Wotan" (*CW* Vol. 10, para 381, p. 185).

—— (1939) Foreword to D.T. Suzuki's "Introduction to Zen Buddhism" (*CW* Vol. 11, pp. 538–557).

—— (1940) "Psychology and Religion" (Terry Lectures: *CW* Vol. 11).

—— (1946) "The Psychology of the Transference" (*CW* Vol. 16).

—— (1948) "Symbolic Life," Address on the Occasion of the Founding of the C.G. Jung Institute in Zurich, 24 April (*CW* Vol. 18, pp. 475–476, paras 1137–1141).

—— (1953) "Psychology and Alchemy" (*CW* Vol. 12).

—— (1953–1977) *Collected Works*, 20 vols. Except where indicated, references are by volume and paragraph number (eds Herbert Read, Michael Fordham and Gerhard Adler; trans. R.F.C. Hull), London: Routledge & Kegan Paul and Princeton, N.J.: Princeton University Press.

—— (1958) "A Psychological View of Conscience" (*CW* Vol. 10).

—— (1963) *Memories, Dreams, Reflections*, ed. Aniela Jaffé, New York: Pantheon Books.

—— (1973–1974) *C.G. Jung Letters*, eds Gerhard Adler and Aniela Jaffé, London: Routledge & Kegan Paul.

—— (1990) *Analytical Psychology: Notes of the Seminar given in 1925*, ed. W. McGuire, Princeton: Princeton University Press.

—— (1991) *Psychology of the Unconscious, CW* Supplementary volume B, rev. and trans. by Beatrice Hinkle of *Wandlungen und Symbole der Libido*, originally published in 1916.

Jung, C.G., von Franz, M.L., Henderson, J., Jacobi, J., and Jaffé, A. (joint authors) (1964) *Man and His Symbols*, London: Aldus Books.

Jung, Emma and von Franz, Marie-Louise (1971) *The Grail Legend*, London: Hodder & Stoughton.

Kalsched, D. (1996) *The Inner World of Trauma*, London: Routledge.

Kerr, John (1993) *A Most Dangerous Method*, New York: Alfred Knopf.

Kirsch, James (1965) *Shakespeare's Royal Self*, New York: C.G. Jung Foundation.

—— (1973) *The Reluctant Prophet*, Los Angeles: Sherbourne Press.

Kirsch, Thomas (1976) "The Practice of Multiple Analyses in Analytical Psychology," *Contemporary Psychoanalysis*, Vol. 12, No. 2, pp. 159–167.

—— (1995) "IAAP and Jungian Identity: A President's Reflections," *Journal of Analytical Psychology*, April, Vol. 40. No. 5, pp. 235–248.

Kluger, Rivkah (1991) *The Archetypal Significance of Gilgamesh*, ed. Yechezkel Kluger, Einsiedeln: Daimon Verlag.

Knickerbocker, H.R. (1939) "Diagnosing the Dictators," *Cosmopolitan Magazine*, January (quoted in *C.G. Jung Speaking*, eds W. McGuire and R.F.C. Hull, London: Thames and Hudson 1978).

Kohut, Heinz (1977) *The Restoration of the Self*, New York: International Universities Press.

Lee, Doreen B. (1983) "The C.G. Jung Foundation – The first 21 years," *Quadrant*, Fall 1983, Vol. 16, No. 2, pp. 57–73.

Ljunggren, Magnus (1994) *The Russian Mephisto: A Study of the Life and Work of Emilii Medtner*, Stockholm: Almqvist & Wiksell International.

Lockot, Regine (1985) *Erinnern und Durcharbeiten: Zur Geschichte der Psychoanalyse und Psychotherapie im Nationalsozialismus*, Frankfurt: Fischer Taschenbuch Verlag.

—— (1994) *Die Reinigung der Psychoanalyse*, Tübingen: Edition Diskord.

López-Pedraza, Rafael (1989) *Hermes and His Children*, revised edition, Einsiedeln: Daimon.

—— (1990) *Cultural Anxiety*, Einsiedeln: Daimon.

Lyard, Denise (1998) *Les analyses d'enfants*, Paris: Albin Michel.

McGuire, W. (ed.) (1978) *C.G. Jung Speaking* (by C.G. Jung), London: Thames & Hudson.

—— (1995) "Firm Affinities: Jung's Relations with Britain and the United States," *Journal of Analytical Psychology*, Vol. 40, No. 3, pp. 301–326.

Maidenbaum, A. and Martin, S. (eds) (1991) *Lingering Shadows*, Boston: Shambala.

Mattoon, M.A. (ed.) (1990) "Personal and Archetypal Dynamics in the Analytical Relationship," *Proceedings* of the XIth International Congress for Analytical Psychology in Paris, 1989, Einsiedeln: Daimon, pp. 461–499.

—— (ed.) (1996) "Open Questions in Analytical Psychology," *Proceedings* of the XIIIth International Congress for Analytical Psychology in Zurich, 1995, Einsiedeln: Daimon, p. 714.

Medtner, E. (ed.) (1935) *Die Kulturelle Bedeutung der Komplexen Psychologie*, Festschrift zum 60. Geburtstag von C.G. Jung, Berlin: Julius Springer.

Meier, C.A. (1967) *Antique Incubation and Modern Psychotherapy*, Evanston, Ill.: Northwestern University Press.

Mitchell, R. and Friedman, H. (1994) *Sandplay, Past, Present, and Future*, New York and London: Routledge.

Muser, F.E. (1984) "Zur Geschichte des Psychologischen Clubs Zürich von den Anfängen bis 1928," *Sonderdruck aus dem Jahresbericht des Psychologischen Clubs Zurich*, Zurich: Analytical Psychology Club.

Neumann, Erich (1954a) "On the Moon and Matriarchal Consciousness," *Spring*, pp. 83–100.

—— (1954b) *The Origins and History of Consciousness*, trans. R.F.C. Hull, New York: Pantheon Books, Bollingen Foundation.

—— (1955) *The Great Mother*, trans. Ralph Manheim, New York: Pantheon Books, Bollingen Foundation.

—— (1956a) "The Psyche and the Transformation of the Reality Planes," *Spring*, pp. 81–111.

—— (1956b) *Amor and Psyche: The Psychic Development of the Feminine*, trans. Ralph Manheim, New York: Pantheon Books, Bollingen Foundation.

—— (1958) "Creative Man," *Spring*, pp. 1–32.

—— (1959a) "The Genetic Aspect for Analytical Psychology," in G. Adler (ed.), *Current Trends in Analytical Psychology*, London: Tavistock.

—— (1959b) *Art and the Creative Unconscious*, trans. Ralph Manheim, New York: Pantheon Books.

—— (1959c) *The Archetypal World of Henry Moore*, trans. R.F.C. Hull, New York: Pantheon Books.

—— (1968) "Mystical Man," *Eranos Yearbooks*, Vol. 6, New York: Bollingen Foundation, pp. 375–415.

—— (1969) *Depth Psychology and a New Ethic*, trans. Eugene Rolfe, London: Hodder & Stoughton.

—— (1973) *The Child*, trans. Ralph Manheim, New York: G.P. Putnam's Sons.

Neumann, Micha (1991) *Lingering Shadows*, eds A. Maidenbaum and S. Martin, Boston: Shambala, pp. 273–289.

Nolan, Mary (1997) "The C.G. Jung Institute of Chicago," *Round Table Review*, Vol. IV, No. 4, pp. 24–23.

Noll, Richard (1994) *The Jung Cult*, Princeton: Princeton University Press.

—— (1997) *The Aryan Christ*, New York: Random House.

Osterman, E. (1996) Panel Discussion on "Seminal Women," Unpublished papers, C.G. Jung Institute of San Francisco, 24 November.

Papadopoulos, R. (1996) "Report on New Center," *IAAP Newsletter*, No. 16, pp. 94–97.

Pattis, Eva (1997) *Abortion*, trans. Henry Martin, London and New York: Routledge.

Perry, John (1953) *The Self in Psychotic Process*, Berkeley: University of California Press.

Riklin, Franz (ed.) (1955) "Studien zur analytischen Psychologie," *Festschrift* zum 80, Geburtstag von C.G. Jung, Zurich: Rascher.

Roazen, Paul (1974) *Freud and His Followers*, New York: New American Library.

Roloff, Lee (1999) "In Memory of Vera Bührmann," *Journal of Analytical Psychology*, January, Vol. 44, pp. 139–140.

Rosen, Marion (1995) *Bone, Breath, and Gesture*, ed. Don Hanlon Johnson, Berkeley: North Atlantic Books.

Roudinesco, Elisabeth (1988) "Jung, de l'archétype au Nazisme," *L'Infini*, automne, pp. 73–94.

—— (1997) *Jacques Lacan*, New York: Columbia University Press.

Samuels, A. (1985) *Jung and the Post-Jungians*, London: Routledge & Kegan Paul.

—— (1994) "A Jung Club Is Not Enough. The Professionalization of Analytical Psychology, 1913–1957," *Harvest*, Vol. 40, pp. 155–167.

Samuels, A., Shorter, B., and Plaut, F. (1986) *Critical Dictionary of Jungian Analysis*, London: Routledge & Kegan Paul.

Schaerf, Rivkah (1948) "The Figure of Satan in the Old Testament," in C.G. Jung (ed.), *Symbolik des Geistes*, Zurich: Rascher Verlag, pp. 153–307.

Shamdasani, Sonu (1998a) *Cult Fictions*, London: Routledge.

—— (1998b) "The Anatomy of an Error," *Round Table Review*, March, Vol. 5, No. 4, pp. 12–15.

—— (1998c) "From Geneva to Zurich: Jung and French Switzerland," *Journal of Analytical Psychology*, Sebasco Conference Papers, Vol. 43, No. 1, p. 115.

Singer, June (1972) *Boundaries of the Soul*, New York: Doubleday.

Spiegelman, M. (1963) *In Contact with Jung*, ed. M. Fordham, Philadelphia: J.B. Lippincott Co.

Spier, Julius (1955) *The Hands of Children*, second edition, trans. Victor Gove, London: Routledge & Kegan Paul.

Stein, M. (1983) *In Midlife*, Dallas, Tex.: Spring Publications.

—— (1985) *Jung's Treatment of Christianity*, Wilmette, Ill.: Chiron.

—— (1993) *Solar Conscience, Lunar Conscience*, Wilmette, Ill.: Chiron.

—— (1996) *Practicing Wholeness*, New York: Continuum Publishing.

—— (1998a) *Jung's Map of the Soul*, La Salle, Ill.: Open Court.

—— (1998b) *Transformation: Emergence of the Self*, College Station, Tex.: University of Texas A&M.

Süle, Ferenc (1992) *Valla Vagy Pszichotherapia?* (Jungian Psychology Nowadays), Budapest.

Taylor, E. (1998) "Jung before Freud, not Freud before Jung: The Reception of Jung's work in American Psychoanalytic Circles between 1904–1909,"

Journal of Analytical Psychology, Sebasco Conference Papers, Vol. 43, No. 1, p. 97.

Time Magazine, 25 August 1958, Report on First International Congress for Analytical Psychology, p. 35.

von Franz, Marie-Louise (1970) *The Problem of the Puer Aeternus*, Toronto: Inner City Books (reissued 2000).

—— (1980) *Alchemy – An Introduction into the Symbolism and the Psychology*, Toronto: Inner City Books.

—— (1993) *The Feminine in Fairy Tales*, revised edition, Boston: Shambala.

Walker, William (1980) "History of the IRS," Unpublished paper.

Wallerstein, R. (1988) "One Psychoanalysis or Many?," *International Journal of Psychoanalysis*, Vol. 69, part 1, pp. 5–21.

Weaver, Rix (1991) *The Wise Old Woman*, Boston: Shambala.

Wells, H.G. (1912) *Floor Games*, Boston, Mass.: Small, Maynard.

Wheelwright, J. (1974) "Jung and Freud Speak to Each Other," *Psychological Perspectives*, Vol. 5, No. 2. pp. 171–176.

Wickes, Frances (1927) *The Inner World of Childhood*, New York: Appleton–Century.

—— (1938) *The Inner World of Man*, London: Methuen (second edition 1988, Boston: Sigo Press).

—— (1963) *The Inner World of Choice*, New York: Harper Row.

Wolff, Toni (1995) "Structural Forms of the Feminine Psyche," privately printed for the Student Association, Zurich: C.G. Jung Institute; trans. Paul Watziliwak of "Strukturformen der Weiblichen Psyche," *Der Psychologie*, Heft 7/8, Band III, 1951, pp. 303–315.

Woodman, Marion (1982) *Addiction to Perfection*, Toronto: Inner City Books.

Zacharias, G. (ed.) (1968) *Dialog über den Menschen. Eine Festschrift für Wilhelm Bitter zum 75. Geburtstag*, Stuttgart: Klett.

Zoja, Luigi (1988) *Drugs, Addiction and Initiation*, Boston: Sigo.

—— (1995) *Growth and Guilt*, London and New York: Routledge.

Index

Boldface page numbers indicate substantial treatment of a topic